MODERN LANGUAGES IN PRACTICE 16
Series Editor: Michael Grenfell

Language Learners as Ethnographers

Celia Roberts, Michael Byram,
Ana Barro, Shirley Jordan and Brian Street

MULTILINGUAL MATTERS LTD
Clevedon • Buffalo • Toronto • Sydney

Library of Congress Cataloging in Publication Data

A catalog record for this book is available from the Library of Congress.

British Library Cataloguing in Publication Data

A catalogue entry for this book is available from the British Library.

ISBN 1-85359-503-9 (hbk)
ISBN 1-85359-502-0 (pbk)

Multilingual Matters Ltd

UK: Frankfurt Lodge, Clevedon Hall, Victoria Road, Clevedon BS21 7HH.
USA: UTP, 2250 Military Road, Tonawanda, NY 14150, USA.
Canada: UTP, 5201 Dufferin Street, North York, Ontario M3H 5T8, Canada.
Australia: P.O. Box 586, Artarmon, NSW, Australia.

Typeset by Florence Production Ltd.
Printed and bound in Great Britain by the Cromwell Press Ltd.

Contents

Part I
Language Learning and Ethnography: Theory and Practice

Chapter 1
New Goals

Language Learners

In recent years, language learners have come to be described in terms of 'cultural mediators', 'border-crossers', 'negotiators of meaning', 'intercultural speakers' and such like. Language learning is becoming increasingly defined in cultural terms and these new names and targets for language learners imply a reconceptualisation of the language learning endeavour. In this book, drawing on the developing frameworks for cultural studies in language learning, we add a further name to the list: language learners as ethnographers.

Ethnography can be broadly described as the study of a group's social and cultural practices from an insider's perspective. It is both a method involving the detailed observation and description of particular forms of behaviour and a written (and sometimes audio-visual) account based on social and cultural theories. So, it combines both an experiential element in which ethnographers participate in the life of a community, and an intellectual element, in which theoretical concepts are used and then developed, in order to 'write culture' (Clifford & Marcus, 1986).

The attraction of ethnographic principles and practice for language learning lies in this combination of the experiential and intellectual which are so often presented as dichotomous in language programmes. As Kramsch (1993) suggests, language learning has not been helped by dichotomies such as content versus skills, teacher versus learner centredness, and indeed, language versus culture. She advocates, instead, multiple options and, along with the recent literature on cultural studies in foreign language learning, a multidisciplinary approach.

An ethnographic approach to language learning is multi-disciplinary in that it draws on social and linguistic anthropology and aspects of sociolinguistics. Conceptual frameworks are developed for observing and understanding daily life in an environment where the language in question is spoken by native (and other) speakers. This approach also implies training in methods of observation, analysis and writing which engage

3

learners in a process of encountering 'otherness' and representing that
experience not as a set of facts but as one interpretation mediated through
their own cultural understandings.

The ethnographer goes out into 'the field' – a cluster of huts on a
small atoll or the kitchens of a neighbouring housing estate – in order
to participate in the lives of a specific group and learn about their
everyday affairs and what gives meaning to them. Given that language
learners will often visit a country or countries where the language they
are learning is widely used, they too have a 'field' in which to participate and observe. The opportunities for some period abroad as a visitor,
on a school exchange or as part of a university course are increasing
(Freed, 1995). This is not only evident in Europe, with European Union
student mobility schemes, but in many other parts of the world including
the USA, Japan, Latin America and Australia.

The idea of using such periods abroad as an opportunity to develop
cultural learning by undertaking an ethnographic project is the theme
of this book. The programme developed at Thames Valley University,
Ealing, in London, as part of a modern languages degree, is used as a
case study to illuminate the notion of the language learner as ethnographer and to illustrate how this idea can be realised within the
constraints and opportunities of an undergraduate degree course. A
somewhat similar approach has also been developed at university level
(Jurasek, 1996), for upper secondary school level (Byram & Morgan
et al., 1994; Baumgratz-Gangl, 1990), for teacher education purposes
(Kane, 1991; Zarate, 1991), for lower secondary school students (Snow
& Byram, 1997; Dark *et al.*, 1997), and for younger learners in a bilingual setting (Heller, 1994). There are also interesting connections with
the general idea of the student as ethnographer in a range of educational settings, not specifically concerned with second or foreign language
learning (Heath, 1983; Egan-Robertson & Bloome, 1998).

The case study is focused on advanced language learners – under-
graduates who spend a compulsory year abroad as part of an applied
languages degree. Both the intellectual demands of the ethnography
course and the level of linguistic and communicative competence
required to undertake and write an extended ethnographic study in the
foreign language pre-suppose a certain level of linguistic and educational sophistication. However, the experience of the project suggests it
is clearly possible to adapt aspects of the ethnographic approach to upper
secondary school level and to other levels, and we hope that this book
will act as a stimulus for further creative adaptations. We leave the
notion of 'advanced level' deliberately vague since there is no particular

stage language learners must reach before they are ready to take on the ethnographic approach. Our experience and those of others (Jurasek, 1996) is that those students with the most advanced language skills do not necessarily undertake the most interesting ethnographic projects or produce the best ethnographic assignments.

Nonetheless, although there is no self-evident relationship between level of language skill and cultural learning, the central message of this book is that language and cultural learning are not separate areas of learning: cultural learning *is* language learning, and vice versa. Moreover, it is no accident that the cultural component of language learning should have begun to receive some attention at a time when issues of language and culture and their relation to notions of identity are being radically re-thought. At a practical level, the evidence of the case study presented in this book suggests that introducing an ethnographic approach can contribute to enhanced language learning.

Although the approach in this book focuses on modern language students and the period of residence abroad, we live in complex and turbulent times when cultural learning is an experience for everyone. The multilingual, multicultural environments which are typical of urban sites in late modernity provide a continuing source of intercultural contact and learning.

New Times

A group of writers within the tradition of cultural studies coined the expression 'new times' in their analysis of the dispersal, fragmentation and conflict experienced in the political, economic and cultural life at the end of the twentieth century and the beginning of the twenty-first. In the 'new times' in which we live, the old certainties around particular social class, ethnic, national and other groupings and identities have fallen apart. In their place are new alliances and the formation of new identities. As boundaries are crossed and new maps of social and cultural life are drawn and redrawn, so there is more turbulence, more ambivalence and more negotiation is needed.

This cultural analysis of change and difference in late modernity can be added to the widely reported changes in the economy, in communications and in the linguistic and cultural elements of urban societies (cf. Kress, 1985). The 'global village' and the internet superhighway have created networks of communication throughout the technological world. The market economy and the enterprise culture lead business to sell to ever more varied markets. And most fundamental of all, the increasingly multiethnic, multilingual urban communities which are a commonplace of the late twentieth century world create rich resources for encountering and learning about otherness (Hallam & Street, 2000). But they also produce conditions for marked social stratification and inequality. Issues of diversity and difference within power relations, of contested identities and of the need for tolerance and mutual understanding are the stuff of both everyday and academic discourse.

The quest for tolerance and an understanding of diversity are, of course, part of a general liberal ethic of harmony and equality. This is reflected in many recent language curricular statements and is seen, increasingly, as a necessary goal of language learning. The 'new times' studies add an intellectual analysis to the understanding of difference and otherness. In particular, the studies on 'race' and ethnicity (Bhabha, 1990; Hall, 1992) critique the stereotyping of national groups and the commonly held assumptions that national groups speak one language and have one culture. The idea of groups having fixed and essential characteristics are challenged as new solidarities within multilingual societies are formed (Street, 1993). The experience of living with difference as part of everyday life, of using ethnicity as a means of highlighting or down-playing a particular aspect of social identity, is a significant part of youth culture in most urban settings (Hewitt, 1986; Rampton, 1995).

One purpose of this book is to claim the experience of difference and dispersal as a central element in the process of learning for advanced language learners. Many language learners already speak several languages or are growing up in multilingual societies where language and ethnic differences are a part of youth culture. They can draw on these experiences in developing a foreign language, and as they interact more in the foreign language and with speakers and writers of it, so their own identities and sense of self may be further challenged. The traditional binary divide between 'them' and 'us', which may already be put in question by the multilingual society in which they live, comes under further pressure as they move towards bilingual competence.

The idea of new solidarities and of living with difference can, therefore, be extended to the experience of using the foreign language and interacting with those who speak it. Language-and-culture learning involves a repositioning of the self both intellectually and at the level of 'felt reality', the apprehension of relationships and material reality and their impact on us as thinking, feeling beings (Althusser, 1971). In this way, becoming part of another group's way of looking at the world, by learning some of their language varieties, combines more traditional priorities of cultural harmony with a more recent cultural and critical analysis of changing boundaries and identities in the 1990s and the beginning of the twenty-first century.

The global economy and the rapid pace of change in international and intranational communications have raised many questions about the use of a lingua franca. Many language students will be learning a new language in order to communicate with others who may be native speakers of it or who are also using it as a second or foreign language (Pennycook, 1994; Clyne, 1995). In contexts where a second language is used as a local lingua franca, for example in certain domains in Francophone Africa or the use of English in Southern India, there is a strong case for curricular content and textbooks which reflect styles of speaking and sociocultural knowledge appropriate to such contexts. But other learners are developing the foreign language in order to communicate internationally. Tying language to culture, it has been argued, is irrelevant in these contexts. The argument is that what learners need is a 'culture-free' language which can be used as a neutral tool with speakers from a wide range of cultural and linguistic backgrounds. We argue, here, that there is no such thing as a neutral culture-free language and that what students need is more cultural sensitivity and understanding, not less. In other words, for many language learners, one of the main goals is *intercultural* communicative competence.

The idea of 'interculturality' acknowledges that communication is always a cultural process and that communicating in a foreign (and in some contexts a second) language involves mediating and establishing relationships between one's own and other cultures. Byram (1997a) suggests that such mediation means that learners need a point of reference outside their own local practices in order to compare and contrast their own ways of interacting and signifying meaning with those outside their own social group. The issue is what points of reference should be chosen? In developing language learners as ethnographers, a range of different cultural contexts are used, selected on the basis of how well they illustrate the key concepts and methods of the course. For example, students may learn about the housewives in a small village in the Valloire region of France, about the system of patronage in southern Spain, or about the structure of meal times in a British working-class community. The goal is to develop 'critical cultural awareness' (Byram, 1997a) through a process of comparing and contrasting so that when learners come to use the foreign or second language as a lingua franca, they can acknowledge, and have some measure of understanding, that a common language does not iron out differences and may, indeed, cause further misunderstandings that do not come to light in a supposedly neutral code. Speakers bring their social identities and their learned ways of using the lingua franca to any intercultural encounter; they do not bring a neutral tool. For this reason, whatever the purpose of language learning may be, the cultural and social dimensions are an essential part.

To sum up, the conditions of late modernity require new qualities of the language learner and so a new curriculum, one in which intercultural communication and understanding are given priority and students develop intellectual tools to understand the 'cultural diaspora' (Hall, 1990) of which many are themselves a part. Not surprisingly, this is reflected in recent policy statements. The notion of 'cultural learning', 'cultural studies', 'sociocultural competence' and 'intercultural communication' are included in policy initiatives on language learning in the UK, in France and Germany and a number of other European countries, the USA, Canada and Australia, and in the documents of international bodies such as the Council of Europe, and UNESCO (for example, Delors, 1996; _Standards for Foreign Language Learning_, 1996; Stern, 1992; van Ek & Trim, 1991). Important though these statements are, realising them as practical action has only just begun. This book is a contribution towards that goal.

Language Learning as Social Practice

The increasing interest in the social and cultural aspects of language learning marks a new turn in theory and research on second language learning and second language acquisition (SLA). Language within the SLA research tradition has tended to mean grammar, and acquisition has been defined in cognitive and psycholinguistic terms (Ellis, 1994; Klein, 1984). Although there has been research on language use in social interaction, it is largely seen as a means of understanding aspects of the learners' linguistic code (Gass & Varonis, 1985; Hatch, 1983; Long, 1983). Recently, there has been more interest in pragmatic and sociocultural theories in SLA (Kasper, 1994; Lantolf & Pavlenko, 1995; Lantolf, 1999) and it may be that at least one strand of SLA will conceptualise the language learning process as a social practice. If this interest continues to develop, then the kind of theories of language learning which underpin this book will connect more closely to at least some approaches within SLA.

Some aspects of SLA have drawn on the social psychology literature. But the issues of social identity and 'acculturation' from this literature tend to deal either with the motivation of individual learners to acculturate or with generalisations about groups divorced from any 'insider' perspective on their social relations and interactions (Gardner, 1985; Giles & Byrne, 1982; Schumann, 1978). The central concern, therefore, with cognitive models of SLA and psychological models of integration has tended, until recently, to sideline language as social and cultural practice.

The assumption has been that what is important is what is going on in people's heads, as if language development was a private and individual achievement. Yet recent studies of language and literacy learning show it is a social endeavour, often most effective when it is the result of activities in actual situations. This 'situated learning' (Lave & Wenger, 1991) can be contrasted with much foreign language learning. Although survival skills are taught at basic and intermediate levels, at more advanced levels, the foreign language experience becomes increasingly cognitive. Students know a lot *about* French, German, English or Japanese but the learning no longer connects with the social practices of their everyday life in their first or dominant language. An obvious exception to this is communicative language teaching at advanced levels, to which we shall return in a later chapter. However, communicative approaches tend to take a sociolinguistic rather than a sociocultural perspective, focusing on language behaviour without considering the practices and knowledge which give meaning to this behaviour. So whether language learners are studying grammar, appropriate language use, translation, political institutions, the economy or the literature of the 'target' language and culture, there is little opportunity to relate these activities to their habits of thinking, feeling, interacting or valuing associated with their own everyday language(s) and communities. Using a foreign language is not experienced as a social practice until students find themselves in an environment where the language is all around them, usually in a foreign country.

This book argues that foreign language learning can be a social practice, and so more meaningful and motivating, if it is based on a model of *language socialisation*. The concept of language socialisation describes the process whereby a child becomes an emergent member of the community in which they are growing up (Ochs and Schieffelin, 1979). It involves both the socialisation required to use language and the process of socialisation through language. The former is concerned with how to use language in specific interactional sequences – how to become communicatively competent – and the latter with the indirect means of developing sociocultural knowledge (Ochs & Schieffelin, 1979; Schieffelin & Ochs, 1986). This is a central aspect of primary socialisation. Once at school, children are expected to learn the institutional practices of schooling and schooled ways of knowing things. This is widely known as secondary socialisation (Berger & Luckmann, 1966). It can also describe the process whereby a young person or adult gradually develops the capacity to use language in ways which make them acceptable members within a new community which they have joined.

Although the foreign language learner may not be joining a new community in any permanent way, their goal is to understand the social practices of that community and to behave in ways which will allow some continuing relationship with it. These are the goals which have led to the policy initiatives on 'sociocultural competence' and 'intercultural communication' mentioned above. The process of entering into the social practices of the foreign language community we call *tertiary socialisation*. This includes both the ability to communicate in a wide variety of situations in a foreign country, and to learn about and come to some understanding of what is different and unfamiliar in the social worlds encountered abroad (Byram, 1997a; Doyé, 1992). In other words, it is the process of language socialisation, taken beyond narrow functional competencies, which requires learners to reconsider the taken-for-granted 'natural' realities constructed in primary and secondary socialisation.

Language Learning and Ethnography

Schieffelin and Ochs' (1986) notion of language socialisation, as well as assuming the capacity to interact in socially appropriate ways within a specific community, also involves the indirect means of developing sociocultural knowledge. As children learn, for example, how to behave at meal times, so they are taught implicitly the social rules of interacting and the values associated with them. This process of language socialisation describes well what 'doing ethnography' means. Ethnographers, by participating in the everyday lives of a group, gradually acquire an understanding of how interactions get done, but they also develop an understanding of what meanings are associated with the ways of talking and behaving that they both observe and are involved in.

The system of meanings that the ethnographer begins to learn about, will include an understanding of roles and relationships and the social values of messages and how these relate to and serve to maintain wider social structures. Children learn this sociocultural knowledge indirectly as part of their primary and secondary socialisation, but ethnographers have to use a mix of indirect and direct methods, constantly moving between participation, questioning and analysis. They 'hang around' with a purpose, as 'lurkers and soakers' (Werner & Schoepfler, 1989). The many different interactions which they observe or participate in, some going on around them, some purposefully orchestrated for their study, continually create new opportunities for language development and cultural understanding.

This mix of learning to communicate appropriately and developing an analytic understanding of another group's system of meanings is the goal of language learners as ethnographers. An example from one student's ethnographic project illustrates this mix (Barro & Jordan, 1995). She was interested in the *pétanque* (a game played with bowls) circles in Aubervilliers in France. Her research involved her in gaining access to a very male-dominated local club, participating in many games, observing larger competitions, and doing many interviews. She learnt how to perform the ritual communicative practices of the game, to understand the social relations around it and how to use (or where necessary avoid using) the nicknames habitually given to players.

She also began to learn what these rituals and the nicknames meant to the players and to situate these meanings within the local politics of the club and its functioning within the community. An important understanding for her was the role of the club in reflecting and maintaining some of the social changes in the area, with players from the *troisième âge* (third age) category playing alongside but in competition with, in several senses of the word, unemployed youngsters. In gradually developing these understandings, she was involved in the process of language socialisation, learning the specific ways of speaking used by the group to carry out their everyday business and construct their social identities.

This student project is typical of what a languages student can achieve during their period of residence abroad. There is no intention that students of modern languages should be turned into anthropologists or even professional ethnographers. The idea is that they can acquire some theoretical concepts and ethnographic skills so that they are able to understand the local cultural practices sufficiently to write an ethnographic project, rather than undertake a full-scale ethnography.

It is useful to distinguish at this point between the discipline of anthropology, and ethnography as method. While any discipline is concerned with particular ways of seeing the world, based upon particular epistemologies and associated concepts, ethnography is a method for doing fieldwork and writing up the results. It is used in disciplines other than anthropology, such as sociolinguistics, sociology and education studies although its foundations are in anthropology, and it is largely from this discipline that the Ealing ethnography case study is drawn.

We can make a further distinction between methods and purposes. Whereas the professional anthropologist or sociologist will use ethnography for the purpose of researching and writing a monograph on a particular group or set of practices, we argue in this book that language teachers and students can use ethnography to develop their cultural learning in general, and their capacity to mediate between different cultural groups in particular. Thus, the purpose of ethnography in this context is to integrate language and cultural processes as will be seen in later chapters. In some respects, the idea of language learners as ethnographers turns the anthropologist's concern on its head. Anthropologists (usually) learn a new language in order to understand the cultural practices of the group they are studying. (Many never succeed in becoming communicatively competent and many rely on local interpreters.) Language learners, on the other hand, who are already able to communicate, at least to some extent, in the local language, immerse themselves in the culture of another group in order to become better communicators and mediators in intercultural encounters and so better language users.

Connecting language learning to the disciplines of social and linguistic anthropology and sociolinguistics provides an opportunity to translate general programmatic statements about intercultural learning and cultural awareness and so on, into practical and coherent provision for cultural and linguistic learning. Just as second language acquisition studies have demonstrated what a long and complex endeavour learning a language is, so policy and curriculum developers need to argue the same case for language-and-culture learning. Short programmes of cultural awareness or an assumption that intercultural understanding can simply be 'caught' rather than taught are not so different from the message in the advertisements for language learning books and tapes which suggest that it is possible to learn to speak a language in three weeks.

The Ealing Ethnography Research Project

The general principles outlined above and developed in later chapters in detail will be exemplified, here, through the Ealing ethnography research project. The project began as an experiment and was funded as such, but with the intention that it should become part of the normal curriculum.[1] There were a number of components to the project, at different levels. At the core of the project was what we will call throughout the book the ethnography programme. This consists of :

(1) A taught course in the second year of a four-year languages degree. This is a module of 45 classroom hours in which the teaching of basic anthropological and sociolinguistic concepts is combined with an introduction to ethnographic method.

(2) An ethnographic study while abroad. Students are sent to two different countries, each for a period of four to five months. They are required to carry out an ethnographic study in one of these countries, usually their first placement, and this may influence how they set about their second project which need not be ethnographic.

(3) Writing up the ethnographic project on return from abroad and integrating these projects into the curriculum. This includes assessment of the ethnographic project as part of the final degree award. (See Figure 1.)

We will refer to the taught element as the ethnography course and the students' write-up of their fieldwork as student ethnographic projects. An umbrella to the development aspects of the project was the research element in which the whole process was monitored and research interviews were conducted with staff and students. To sum up, therefore, the objectives of the experiment were the following:

• the development of new approaches and methods in structuring the learning experience of the year abroad and its integration into the undergraduate course as a whole;
• the training of lecturers in the use of these approaches and methods;
• the evaluation of the approaches and their feasibility on languages programmes.

Specifically, the research questions we asked were:

(1) Can modern language lecturers learn to teach an ethnographic programme?
(2) Can students learn to use ethnographic approaches to develop their cultural learning and make the period abroad an active learning experience?

Purposes and Audiences for this Book

As we have already suggested, although the period of residence abroad built into modern languages degree programmes in Britain makes such an approach particularly relevant, the idea of language learners as ethnographers can be transferred to many other contexts. In many countries in Europe, America, Australia and elsewhere, there are students on

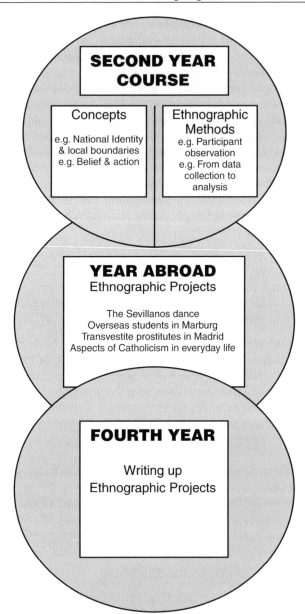

SECOND YEAR COURSE

Concepts

e.g. National Identity & local boundaries
e.g. Belief & action

Ethnographic Methods

e.g. Participant observation
e.g. From data collection to analysis

YEAR ABROAD
Ethnographic Projects

The Sevillanos dance
Overseas students in Marburg
Transvestite prostitutes in Madrid
Aspects of Catholicism in everyday life

FOURTH YEAR

Writing up
Ethnographic Projects

Figure 1   Ethnography programme

European Studies courses, Business and Language Studies courses, and a range of combined language and science, law and arts courses, who will have an opportunity of working in some capacity abroad or who study as international students in a foreign university and need to develop their linguistic and cultural competence for the new learning environment. Similarly, there are a large number of school exchange programmes where an element of the ethnographic approach can be included both in the preparation for and activities during the stay abroad (Dark *et al.*, 1997; Snow & Byram, 1997). Finally, there are the thousands of school and college programmes throughout the world where there is no immediate possibility of visiting the country or countries where the foreign language is the dominant language but where an ethnographic component can be integrated into the language curriculum.

This book is thus designed for a number of different audiences. First, there are the Modern/Foreign Languages lecturers, both those in language departments and others in Language Centres, Business Studies Departments and others. Secondly, there are lecturers in European Studies, Latin American Studies and other programmes where students need to be prepared for a period of residence abroad. Thirdly, there are teachers of upper secondary school pupils (both student teachers and those on in-service programmes). A wider audience still includes trainers in intercultural communication and language for professional purposes, lecturers in anthropology interested in teaching aspects of the discipline to non-anthropologists and in new developments in research methods and in the applications of anthropology and, more generally, all those in departments of education and in other areas involved in innovations in teaching and learning in Higher Education. Finally, this book may also be illuminating to a number of postgraduate students, particularly students of anthropology.

Implied in the argument throughout this book is the case for interdisciplinarity in language learning. Linking language learning to ethnography involved us in putting together an interdisciplinary team including: a language educationist, a sociolinguist, an anthropologist and language specialists from the French, German and Spanish departments with an interest in the social sciences. It must, however, be stressed that this is not a manual on how to train language learners as ethnographers, but more a theoretical book which uses extensive illustration from the Ealing Ethnography course and student projects as a case study of innovative approaches. For readers interested in obtaining the materials used on the course and suggestions on how to use them, a contact address is given in Note 1 at the end of this chapter.

The book is the product of working together as a team over several years. It reflects our varied perspectives and backgrounds and although we have learnt a great deal from each other, there is no single voice with which we all speak. As a result, the book speaks with several voices and we have, purposefully, kept it this way. Just as this project was about both conceptual and experiential learning, so the different chapters and sections of chapters are written, sometimes, from a relatively more conceptual perspective, and sometimes, a relatively more experiential, depending on the author(s) and their focus. A consistent voice may be a more comforting and comfortable read but learning about otherness from the inside, so to speak, is often uncomfortable. And since this book charts that experience for students (and staff), the voices which narrate their story should chime with the mix of discomfort and exhilaration that they have so often reported.

The book is divided into two parts. The first part, Chapters 1 to 5, provides some theoretical background on the relationship between language, cultural processes and ethnography. The second part, Chapters 6 to 10, is a case study of the Ealing Ethnography Project. A final chapter links an evaluation of the project with some thoughts about language and cultural studies to take us into the twenty-first century.

Part I: Language Learning and Ethnography

(1) A discussion of the problematic relationship between language, culture and language pedagogy. Here, some of the theoretical frameworks from anthropology and sociology set the context for an overview of the language and culture relationship and its relevance for language learning. [First drafts and the main voice of Chapters 1 to 4 were from Celia Roberts.]
(2) The development of the concept of ethnography as one possible solution (Chapter 5). [First draft and the main voice of Chapter 5 was from Brian Street.]

Part II: The Ealing Ethnography Project: A Case Study

(3) Introduction to the Ealing Ethnography Project, focusing on ethnography as staff development. [First draft and the main voices of Chapter 6 were from Ana Barro, Shirley Jordan and Brian Street.]
(4) Chapter 7 uses examples from the project to illustrate the development of principles for an ethnography course. [First draft and the main voices from Ana Barro and Celia Roberts.]

(5) The next three chapters (Chapters 8, 9 and 10) are a 'thick' description of the project itself. Chapter 8 describes in depth how a particular unit was taught, and Chapter 9 looks at the students' ethnographic projects and how they were assessed. Chapter 10 focuses on the students' experience, particularly the process of doing an ethnography while abroad. [First draft of Chapter 8 and the main voices were from Shirley Jordan and Celia Roberts. First draft of Chapter 9 and the main voices were from Ana Barro, Michael Byram and Celia Roberts. First draft of Chapter 10 and main voice was from Michael Byram.]

(6) An evaluation of the project and its wider implications (Chapter 11). This chapter reviews the whole project and looks ahead to the ways in which language and cultural processes will be more firmly embedded in the language curricula of the future. [First draft of Chapter 11 and the main voice was from Michael Byram.]

Note

1. This book is based on a two-and-a-half year project funded by the Economic and Social Research Council (R232716): Cultural Studies in Advanced Language Learning. The original project team was: Celia Roberts and Michael Byram (co-directors), Ana Barro and Hanns Grimm, teacher/researchers, and Brian Street (anthropological consultant). During the course of the project and as a result of some additional funding from the Enterprise in Higher Education Initiative, Shirley Jordan and Marc Bergman joined the team as teacher/researchers. The programme was developed and taught at Thames Valley University by Ana Barro, Marc Bergman, Hanns Grimm, Shirley Jordan and Celia Roberts. This book is not intended as a 'how to' manual. Rather, it relates some of the current thinking about language and intercultural communication to a specific set of practices designed at Ealing. For those interested in running a similar type of programme, guidance and a complete set of materials for the 'Introduction to Ethnography' course is available from: Language and Residence Abroad (LARA) project, School of Languages, Oxford Brookes University, Oxford OX3 0BP.

Chapter 2
Introducing Cultural Learning into the Language Curriculum

The increased interest in cultural aspects of language learning in the last decade has led to discussions of what cultural learning might consist of. In this chapter we look briefly at some of the influences that have led to new notions of cultural and intercultural learning in the language curriculum and we start with the problem of what notion of 'culture' language teachers might work with.

Cultural Work

'Culture' is a notoriously slippery word and like many slippery concepts it is subject to over-definition on the one hand and misunderstandings and over-simplifications on the other. It is not surprising that no single definition of culture has ever been arrived at (Kroeber & Kluckhohn, 1952; Geertz, 1973; Williams, 1981; Featherstone, 1992). Recently, there has been a shift away from the noun 'culture' with its connotations of abstraction and reification towards a more active, verb-like notion of cultural practices and processes. It is not so much what culture is but what it does (Street, 1993). And part of 'doing culture' includes the discussions and struggles over what counts as 'culture'. So what does 'doing culture' look like? An example from an Ealing student project gives a number of insights into the concept of cultural processes and how involvement in them can develop cultural learning.

Antonia's project in Seville

Antonia spent five months studying in Seville as part of her year abroad. She also worked as an 'au pair' looking after a five-year-old called Quino. Her project examined the influence of Catholicism in everyday life in Seville and in particular how the rituals of food and eating were connected to religious practices.

The first extract introduces a chapter on how people in the family with whom she lived explained the rituals of food, eating and cleanliness inside and outside the home both to her as a foreign outsider and to the child of the family, Quino.

Decidí que quizás existiera una fuerte conexión entre la religión y la comida después de una conversación con Maribel en la cual me explicó varios aspectos de las fiestas religiosas en las que participa la familia y mencionó varias veces la comida. Me comentó por ejemplo que una parte integral de la peregrinación al Rocío es la comida y el hecho de que todos beben y comen juntos. Dijo que 'en Sevilla lo celebramos todo con las copas y la comida, cualquier acto social, desde las bodas, los bautizos, ir a misa el domingo, después lo normal es tomarse una cerveza, reunirse, hablar, contarse cosas'. Pero curiosamente, y lo que me llevó a escribir esta sección del proyecto, cuando quise indagar más en esta cuestión, ella insistió en que 'no había ninguna relación entre la comida y la religión en sí: eso no tiene que ver con la Iglesia, ni con la religión ni con nada'. Esto lo matizó con el siguiente comentario: 'Aquí en Andalucía nos gusta celebrarlo todo . . . hablando de las hermandades . . . cualquier motivo que haya es normal que terminen en una copa, suele haber un pequeno bar'. Otro comentario, acerca del hecho de que, según se dice, 'alrededor de una mesa se firman los mejores contratos', me hizo preguntarme por qué se separaban tan claramente los aspectos sociales de ir a misa o a una boda o reunion de hermandad, de sus aspectos 'religiosos' cuando para alguien de fuera como yo, parecían casi inseparables en la práctica aunque quizás no en sus significados, por lo que decían continuamente mis informantes.

Translation
I decided that there could be a strong link between religious practices and eating following a conversation with Maribel when she explained how her family participates in religious celebrations and mentioned food several times in this context. She explained that an integral part of the pilgrimage to Rocio is the food and the fact that everybody eats and drinks together. She said several times that 'In Seville we celebrate everything with food, any social event, from weddings and christenings, to going to mass on Sundays, you normally go for a beer afterwards, to meet friends, chat etc'. But what led me to this section of the project was her insistence that there was no relation whatsoever between religion and eating. 'It has nothing to do with the Church, or religion or anything'. She

then added: 'Here in Andalucia we like to celebrate everything . . . speaking of hermandades (meetings of religious fraternities) or for whatever reason, you always end up with a few drinks, there is usually a small bar there'. Another comment, referring to what is often said to the effect that 'the best contracts are signed around a dinner table', raised a question for me about the clear separation between the social aspects of going to a wedding, to church or to an hermandades meeting, from what I considered to be 'religious' aspects. To an outsider such as myself, they seemed inseparable in practice if not in the meanings attributed by my informants.

The Andalucians are represented here as a fun-loving, eating and drinking community, maintaining a strict separation between religion and pleasure. This is the kind of easy stereotype which gives 'culture' a bad name but appears all the more authentic because spoken by a native of the place. But as Cohen (1983) suggests, a community speaks with many voices and the voice used to represent a group to those outside it is not the same as that used to represent that group to itself. In other words, the ways in which a group talks about its own practices within the group may contrast with how they talk about themselves to strangers, even if, in Agar's term, their ethnographic stance makes them 'professional strangers' (Agar, 1980).

This extract also raises questions about the relationship between surface practice or behaviour and the meanings associated with it. The connection between religious practice and eating and drinking is problematised by Antonia, suggesting a number of culturally taken-for-granted relationships which became the focus of the study.

In the second extract, Antonia pursues this theme, turning to Quino for help:

Sin embargo, a mí me pareció ser un tema digno de investigación. Al fin y al cabo, la relación entre comida y religión nos rodea en imágenes de la Pasión de Jesús que empezó con una cena con sus discípulos, y el primer milagro lo realizaron en un banquete de boda. Quería saber, hasta qué punto se pueden relacionar en la práctica, y por eso me pareció que si los mayores no me lo podían explicar que quizás fuera mejor observar cómo se explicaba al niño de la familia. Las referencias de Quino a significados que a mí me parecían 'religiosos' se expresaban en comentarios como el que me ofreció un día cuando le pregunté por qué comía tanto pan, y me contestó 'porque en la Biblia dice nuestro pan de cada día'. En Navidad aumentaron los comentarios explíctos de la familia dirigidos a Quino que relacionaban valores cristianos como la caridad por ejemplo, con la comida. En un caso Quino me contó que le habían explicado que en Navidad hay que dar dinero a los pobres ya que 'sin dinero cómo van a comprar turrón?'.

Así las preguntas que elaboré para ayudarme en esta parte de la investigación fueron las siguientes:

– Cuál es el papel de las copas y las comidas en las actividades que son claramente religiosas para la familia como ir a misa, o celebrar las Navidades ?
– Qué clase de explicaciones le ofrecen al niño que tiene que aprender estas normas sociales de pequeño ?
– En qué términos se lo explican a alguien de fuera, y que se puede deducir sobre los valores culturales tanto en términos propios como en términos de lo que pueden querer dar a entender a la gente que quiera aprender algo sobre la cultura sevillana ?

Estas preguntas resultaron ser bastante difíciles porque siempre me decían cosas que describían lo típico, lo atractivo de las costumbres y no sabían explicarme ni cómo lo habían aprendido ni lo que signifi-caba mas allá de que era una costumbre. La segunda pregunta también creó problemas porque por un lado, como ya he dicho, solían negar cualquiera relación que yo sugiriera, aunque por otro lado, yo veía que al nino le explicaban muchas cosas dentro de un marco religioso, y normativo, aunque fuera en el sentido más amplio de la palabra. Eso me pareció interesante y al final conseguí mucha información observando y hablando con el nino.

Translation
Nonetheless to me it warranted further investigation. After all, the links between religion and food can be seen in images of the Last Supper and Christ's first miracles were performed at a wedding banquet. If my friends couldn't explain these things perhaps I could look at how these matters were explained to the child. One day for instance he explained to me that the reason he ate so much bread was 'Because it says in the Bible . . . our daily bread'. At Christmas I heard more explicit comments directed at Quino relating for example Christian charity to the need to give money to the poor. So in Quino's words: 'without money how can they buy turron?' (a nougat-type sweet traditionally eaten at Christmas).

So the questions I used to guide my research for this section were the following:

- What is the role of eating and drinking in activities that are clearly religious in nature for the family? (such as going to mass or Christmas)
- What kind of explanations are offered to children as part of their socialisation into these practices?
- In what terms are these aspects explained to an outsider such as myself? Here I was interested in finding out about their cultural values not just in their own terms but also as they show themselves to outsiders who are interested in finding out more about their culture.

These questions proved to be quite difficult because my informants tended to only talk about things that were typical, attractive customs. They did not know how to explain how they had learned them, or what they meant to them in any other terms. The second question also raised problems; on the one hand, they denied any links I suggested and, on the other hand, I could see that explanations to the child were often framed in broadly religious, normative terms. This situation seemed interesting to me and in the end I got a lot of information from observing and talking to the child directly.

In this extract, the child's use of religious discourse and the rituals surrounding food come into focus. Furthermore, the links are made between a child's socialisation into understanding the implicit links between food and religion and the explicit discourses presented to the child and to the outsider. The student reflects on her own role and is analytic about the different versions of cultural values that may be proffered.

For the student ethnographer, therefore, cultural learning involved both specific cultural knowledge about religious practices, about family dinner-table behaviour and conversation, and a more implicit cultural awareness of a general kind. This included the process of relating and comparing her own English Catholicism with Sevillano Catholicism, becoming sensitive to the discourses of religion and family life in partic-ular local contexts and analysing the way members of a community will represent themselves to outsiders.

If we link together the two student projects that we have considered so far, the local *pétanque* club in France and the Sevillano project, we can draw out some features of cultural learning. It is perhaps easier to start with what cultural learning is not.

It is not simply a question of acquiring facts about another country, although such facts are indeed useful. Nor is it about 'reading off' from

particular events generalised beliefs, values and attitudes in an unproblematic way. This can only foster the misconception that there is some
essential set of national characteristics which add up to French, Japanese,
or Spanish culture and which are waiting prone to be 'discovered' by
students on their arrival. Rather, cultural learning involves understandings, developed over time, of a number of inter-related cultural processes
which include:

- communication – ways of speaking and interacting and means of
  self-presentation, such as the linguistic rituals of the *pétanque* game
  or the child's language socialisation at the dinner table;
- the structuring of social relations around what is meaningful to the
  group; for example the hierarchies, privileges and reputations of
  the *pétanque* club members, the negotiation of both social and business relations over a good meal or eating and drinking as both
  celebratory and an affirmation of order;
- the ways of representing one's own group both to different
  members of the group and to those outside and the discourses used
  to do this; for example the ways in which the Sevillanos represent
  themselves as fun-loving;
- the connection of local meanings and relations to a larger system
  of meanings associated with wider social, political and economic
  relations; for example youth unemployment and its impact on
  the *pétanque* club, and the religious institutions which support
  Catholicism in Seville.

Analysing and understanding these cultural processes implies a certain
way of knowing about the world which is based in anthropology
and sociolinguistics. In particular, the idea of language learners as
ethnographers draws on social and linguistic anthropology and interactional sociolinguistics. Cultural and social anthropology are concerned
with the belief systems, values and behaviours of a community. But
whereas cultural anthropology tends to focus on beliefs and values
as cultural systems in their own right, social anthropology ties this
'cultural' dimension to the institutional structure of social relationships. Beliefs and values are learnt and used within these relationships,
although not necessarily determined by them (Hannerz, 1992), as is illustrated in the two ethnographic projects above. For example, Quino's
understanding of the power of the Church and its Christian values
are learnt through family interaction and participation in the community's religious rituals.

Linguistic anthropology has been defined as 'the study of language as a cultural resource and speaking as a cultural practice'. (Duranti, 1997: 2). The interest here is not just in language use but in language as a symbolic resource and means of representation. Linguistic anthropologists have a particular interest in language as performance and in the ways in which the structure and vocabulary of a language signal cultural and social relationships. In very many respects linguistic anthropology cannot be easily differentiated from interactional sociolinguistics. The differences may be only a matter of degree. So an interactional perspective on sociolinguistics (Gumperz, 1982a and see Chapter 3) links together the fine-grained detail of face-to-face interactional processes with an understanding of how social knowledge enters into these processes. There is relatively more focus here on the detailed ways in which people, as they talk, create contexts for each other and so create and sustain social relations through talk. Whereas, in linguistic anthropology there is relatively more interest in how both spoken and written language represent aspects of cultural and social knowledge (see Chapter 4). For the purposes of this book, interactional sociolinguistics and linguistic anthropology will be treated as overlapping multi-disciplinary areas which students can draw from when relating wider ethnographic studies to specific language practices.

Both social and linguistic anthropology and interactional sociolinguistics link local action and meanings with wider social and cultural concepts and institutions. This means that the strength of a study on a particular group or event lies not only in its sense of 'felt reality' – the dusty thud of the *pétanque* balls or the social frisson which meets the young player who flouts the game's ritual – but also in its contribution to concepts which both frame and deepen our understanding of this particular group or event, and of other contexts and activities and wider social processes.

Cultural Learning and Communicative Language Teaching

The first of the list of cultural processes mentioned above, and a central aspect of language socialisation, is 'communication'. Given that some anthropologists define culture as communication (Hall, 1959) and that the notion of 'communicative competence', on which communicative language teaching is based, originated in anthropology (Hymes, 1972), it could be argued that language learning through its emphasis on communicative language teaching already has a significant sociocultural dimension (van Ek, 1986).

Hymes' notion of communicative competence stresses the cultural in the development of communicative competence. Just as children acquire grammatical competence so they acquire competence for use:

> From a finite experience of speech acts and their interdependence with sociocultural features, they develop a general theory of speaking appropriate in their community, which they employ, like other forms of tacit cultural knowledge in conducting and interpreting social life. (Hymes, 1972: 279)

And later, when discussing the notion of appropriacy he argues:

> From a communicative standpoint judgements of appropriateness may not be assigned to different spheres, as between the linguistic and the cultural; certainly the spheres of the two will intersect. (Hymes, 1972: 286)

Hymes' notion of communicative competence, therefore, implies the native speaker's intuitive grasp of social and cultural rules and meanings that are present in their ways of speaking. For example, as we discussed in Chapter 1, the student in Aubervilliers gradually became more communicatively competent as she learned the specific ways of speaking used by the players in the *pétanque* club to construct their social identities both as bowls players and as 'players' in the wider social game that served to construct their community.

However, despite its roots in Hymes' work, it is probably fair to say that, in the 1970s, communicative language teaching (CLT) has drawn more from speech act theory in developing notional and functional approaches (Candlin, 1981; van Ek, 1975; Trim, 1983; Richterich & Chancerel, 1978; Widdowson, 1978; Wilkins, 1976) and, in the 1980s and 1990s, on discourse analysis and notions of social variety (Canale & Swain, 1980; McCarthy & Carter, 1994; Richards & Schmidt, 1983; Widdowson, 1990) and, with a more cognitive turn, on task-based learning (Legutke & Thomas, 1991; Prabhu, 1987; Skehan, 1999), than on cultural dimensions of language.

This is not the place to go into a wide-ranging discussion of CLT. It has done a great deal to define the social contexts of language use, to introduce and debate authenticity in language learning materials and to provide a rich environment for relatively unself-conscious language use. However, the recent interest in cultural studies in language learning and the idea of mediating between languages and cultures can be viewed as something of a critique of CLT. To be specific, the focus on communicative language *behaviour* informed by 'functional' approaches and traditional sociolinguistics has tended to eclipse the conceptual and methodological tools of anthropology and more interpretive and inter-actional sociolinguistics:

> As a generalization one can say that language teaching theory is fast acquiring a sociolinguistic component but still lacks a well-defined sociocultural emphasis. (Stern, 1983: 246)

It is ironical that despite being originally anchored in anthropological notions of communicative competence, so much CLT floats free from its theoretical moorings. Communicative competence has come to be interpreted somewhat narrowly and prescriptively, as appropriate language use rather than competence in the social and cultural prac-tices of a community of which language is a large part (Dubin, 1989; Fairclough, 1992).

The concentration on appropriate language use does not mean that the cultural dimension is ignored. Most CLT textbooks include a cultural element and recent developments in content-based and genre-based materials in English language teaching (Mohan, 1986; Cope & Kalantzis, 1993, 2000) are concerned with the sociocultural dimensions of academic literacies. Nonetheless, the difference between the majority of CLT texts and the approach suggested here is that we are suggesting a way of looking at cultural learning which is more explicit, systematic and more demanding of learners than the communicative approach has often implied. We have already indicated, when discussing the Sevillano project, what this cultural learning looks like and the ways in which it links understanding everyday interaction and organisation of the local environment to wider social systems and cultural processes. In the next section, we examine some of the recent studies which demonstrate how CLT is developing what Stern calls: 'a well-defined sociocultural emphasis'.

Cultural Studies and Language Learning

Stern's wide-ranging and in many respects prescient survey of theories in language teaching makes a strong case for a clearer sociocultural dimension based on anthropology and sociolinguistics. He argues that despite attempts to assert the inter-relationship of language and culture in the 1970s and 1980s (Rivers, 1983; Seelye, 1984, 1988) and produce what he calls a 'cultural syllabus' (Stern, 1992): 'the anthropological concept of culture has been much more difficult to incorporate into language teaching than most of the writings have admitted so far' (Stern, 1983).

He suggests several reasons for this including the slipperiness of 'culture' as a concept, the lack of ethnographic descriptions and the confusion over the various kinds of cultural teaching. Ethnographic descriptions of modern urban life could, he asserts, form the basis for pedagogical guides for teaching the sociocultural component of the syllabus. But given, he argues, the dearth of such studies (at the time of writing):

> Teachers who generally are untrained in the methods of social science are obliged to rely on their personal experience, background knowledge and intuitions as a basis for their teaching of culture. There is a real danger, therefore, that such teaching has similar defects as the teaching of *Kulturkunde* in Germany of the twenties and thirties: stereotyping and prejudice. (Stern, 1983: 253)

Stern's is perhaps one of the first clear statements linking the sociocultural dimension of language learning to ethnography. However, the link relates to studies to inform teaching rather than to the idea of language learners as themselves ethnographers. He also asserts that: 'Culture teaching must not be confused with a formal course in social and cultural anthropology and needs to be more informal and personal' (Stern, 1992: 222).

Over the last 10 years, several different strands of cultural studies in language learning have developed:

- the reworking of literary and textual approaches using discourse and textual analysis (Brøgger, 1993; Carter & Long, 1991; Kramer, 1990; Kramsch, 1993, 1996; Kramsch & McConnell-Ginet, 1992; Murphy, 1988; Wallace, 1992; Widdowson, 1988, 1990), in aspects of British Studies (Basnett, 1997; Kramer, 1997; Montgomery, 1993), and in the notion of a discourse syllabus (McCarthy & Carter, 1994);
- the specification of content areas such as work, life and study and the social structures and relations in which they are embedded (Andersen & Risager, 1979; Sercu, 1995; van Ek & Trim, 1991) and, particularly in the German tradition, with a focus on social problems and human rights (Buttjes & Byram, 1991; Kramer, 1997);
- the combination of communicative language teaching with cultural awareness (Baumgratz, 1985; Baumgratz-Gangl, 1993; Candlin, 1987; Meyer, 1991; Valdes, 1986), and with a critical perspective, linking critical thinking to moral development (Melde, 1987);
- an anthropological/ethnographic strand focusing on the practices of daily life (Barro & Grimm, 1993; Barro & Jordan, 1995; Buttjes

& Kane, 1978; Byram & Fleming, 1998; Byram *et al.*, 1994; Roberts, 1993, 1995; Zarate, 1986, 1991, 1993);
• preparation for the year abroad (Barro *et al.*, 1998; Jurasek, 1996; Parker & Rouxeville, 1995; Roberts, 1995, 1997); and understanding the language practices in students' bilingual community (Heller, 1994). While drawing on a number of other strands, the language learners as ethnographers project described in this book belongs with this last area of work.

What is clear from the growing literature on cultural studies and language learning is the gradual shift from literature and background studies towards a cultural studies paradigm (Buttjes, 1991: 11). This includes elements of the more traditional aspects of language courses in terms of content areas but adds a cultural theory and ethnographic dimension. The most influential of the studies of culture, combining cultural theory and ethnography, is that originally associated with the Centre for Contemporary Cultural Studies in Birmingham and now a major multidisciplinary movement. The origins of this movement lie in the reaction against cultural elitism and the reworking of the tools of literary criticism for the analysis of everyday cultural practices (Hoggart, 1957; Thompson, 1968; Williams, 1958, 1976, 1981). For the theme of this book, the most significant element of Cultural Studies, in the Birmingham mode, is the focus on everyday life and popular culture experienced both within relations of domination and as resistance to them. The sociologist's and the anthropologist's cultural lens is turned on the everyday practices of modern urban living: the soap opera, the street market or the classroom. These practices are analysed in terms of the values, meanings and beliefs which constitute them in particular local contexts – what Willis calls 'the bricks and mortar of [their own] most commonplace understandings (Willis *et al.*, 1977: 185). Yet these local and everyday meanings are also analysed in terms of the wider power relations and economic conditions within society. So, for example, aspects of contemporary fashion or new forms of family life are studied both for the meanings they have to those involved and as markers of accommodation or resistance to the dominant view of what 'fashion', 'art' or 'family' is.

The influence of Cultural Studies in language learning programmes is most typically found in the analysis of texts (as in the first strand in the list above). Here discourse analysis plays a central role, drawing on literary traditions of textual analysis and applying them to media and a range of other popular cultural texts which may be print-based, film, visual images and so on, to develop our understanding of social patterns.

The aim is to bring the more general social analysis of cultural themes down to a level where there can be an active engagement with the text. Brøgger, for example, drawing on Bakhtin's work on the socially charged nature of language ('Each word tastes of the text and contexts in which it has lived its socially charged life') argues for a cultural semantics in the teaching of American Studies. He gives as an example a study of the discourses used by Reagan in his 1984 State of the Union address. In a close textual analysis, he argues that Reagan's talk holds in tension three positions: the ideology of the new, an ambivalent, middle position and the ideology of the restoration of the old. Brøgger argues that this tension helps to make Reagan's conservatism appear dynamic and appeals to the ambivalence in the USA between a nostalgic, laissez-faire position and a belief in progress and social change. This example is fairly typical of a critical, textual approach to cultural studies in undergraduate language learning, linking the analysis of specific texts to wider social and cultural themes. The texts are at the centre of the cultural learning and are used to bring out the ideological resonances of such topics as gender, popular culture, life-style, and national and community politics.

We cannot attempt here to discuss the major themes and impact of Cultural Studies (see Fiske, 1989; Grossberg *et al.*, 1992; Hall, 1992) but there is no doubt that Cultural Studies has developed a rich set of interpretive tools for the analysis and critiquing of texts that cultural learning within a modern languages framework has much to learn from (see Basnett, 1997). However, Cultural Studies has tended increasingly to deal with texts and their semiotic analysis rather than with social and cultural practices in an ethnographic way. It is also dauntingly theoretical. Culture is presented as text for theoretical analysis, rather than as processes to be engaged with from which students forge their own text. Cultural learning, therefore, if it depends solely on a Cultural Studies approach, can remain at the level of learning *about* rather than *in* and *through*.

Ethnography and the Intercultural Speaker

The notion of language learners as ethnographers is a new departure in that it retains the cultural as it is used in Cultural Studies but draws much more explicitly on anthropology and sociolinguistics. This has two main advantages. First, it shifts the emphasis away from written and audio-visual texts and towards the fashioning of texts out of participant observation. Secondly, in doing this, it builds a bridge between communication skills, as generally presented in CLT, and conceptual understandings of cultural processes. In this way, it can connect texts and practices, the cognitive and the palpable, learning about and living/doing culture.

An ethnographic view of cultural studies in language learning subordinates the daunting cultural theory of Cultural Studies to what Geertz calls 'thick description' (Geertz, 1973) (and see Chapter 3). This involves extended participation in the everyday lives of a group; a detailed description of some aspects of these lives and an analysis and interpretation of them through the eyes and ears of the 'outsider'. Ethnographers are both participant and observer, both part of and separate from the community they are studying. This experience of closeness and distance, of being oneself and yet part of another group, defines the new identity of the language learner – liberated (or condemned) to be forever in-between. But language learners are not just in-between, they are also go-betweens, as the recent literature on mediating between languages and cultures suggests (Buttjes & Byram, 1991; Byram, 1997b; Kramsch, 1993). For language learners to be mediators, the notion of communicative competence as understood by language educators is too limiting.

The recent literature mentioned above assumes that language learners also need to have cultural competence. But just as the notion of communicative competence assumes bilingual competence as the ultimate goal so cultural competence suggests that bicultural competence is the ultimate goal. Hymes' original notion was based on a native speaker model but its incorporation into FL/SL learning has not brought with it a discussion of how such a model could possibly be attainable. Similarly, the goal of biculturalism is in virtually all cases an impossible one (Paulston, 1992).

A more realistic suggestion and one that is more in tune with the idea of multiple identities and blurred boundaries of the 'new times' mentioned in Chapter 1, is that of an 'intercultural speaker' (Byram & Zarate, 1994; Byram, 1997a; Kramsch, 1998; Doyé, 1992). An intercultural speaker is aware of both their own and others' culturally constructed selves. Rather than assuming that they know in some straightforward factual way either their own or the other's cultural worlds, they are aware of a constant process of formation and transformation. Culture is not a given but constituted in the everyday practices of groups and individuals. So, an intercultural speaker is always alert to what is both patterned and predictable in these practices and what is changing and contested: they are always in process.

Such a speaker operates in what Kramsch calls a 'sphere of interculturality' (Kramsch, 1993: 205). The great strength of an intercultural speaker is that they understand that meaning is relational. No one can say that a word or utterance has an absolute meaning, but intercultural speakers can come to what Gee (1996) calls a 'consensual meaning'. The example he gives is from a law case in which the definition of 'sausage' was in dispute. What ingredients could or could not be included for a sausage still to be a sausage? It is a matter of discussion and negotiation as the differences between a 'saucisson' and a 'sausage' amply demonstrates. The great strength of the *notion* of the intercultural speaker is that the learners are not expected to become native or near-native speakers but to become intermediaries, mediating between potentially conflicting behaviours and belief systems in their own and others' social lives (Byram & Zarate, 1994). The old dichotomy of native and non-native speaker breaks down as the intercultural speaker is someone, who in a comparative and relative way, is learning about their own and others' cultural practices in a mutually reinforcing relationship. As well as a comparative perspective, the intercultural speaker takes a critical perspective both on their own cultural practices and that of others (Byram, 1997a; Doyé, 1992; Kramsch, 1996; Melde, 1987; Singerman, 1996 and the final chapter of this book).

So, both functionally and symbolically, the intercultural speaker can replace the old 'non-native' speaker label with its deficit connotations and uni-directional assumptions about learning to communicate in a second language. Instead, language learners and language users more generally are learning from each other and working out together the grounds for mutual understanding.

The Intercultural Speaker and Cross-cultural Communication

Given the slippery nature of 'culture', it is not surprising that the notion of 'intercultural' should be claimed by a number of discipline areas which tag it with different assumptions and meanings. Fields other than anthropology and sociolinguistics have employed the term 'intercultural' but, we would argue, in different ways from those suggested here. For instance, 'cross-cultural' and 'intercultural' are used in the social-psychological literature and in cross-cultural training programmes in more functional and reductionist ways than in this book.

The work on intercultural and cross-cultural communication (Brislin, 1993; Gudykunst, 1989; Kim, 1998; Kim & Gudykunst, 1988; Ting-Toomey, 1988) draws on a general communication theory and is concerned with comparing cultural differences across such broad dimensions as individual/collective, personal/positional or even more generally as high versus low context cultures (Hofstede, 1984, 1994). In this tradition, attitude surveys are used to construct general statements about a national group. For example, Japan is said to have a high context culture (dependence on implicit assumptions and shared values) whereas America is said to be a low context culture (one in which roles and relationships are more explicitly negotiated). Similarly, the cross-cultural training approach (Bennett, 1986; Brislin, 1994; Gudykunst & Hammer, 1983) although it combines experiential and reflective components, concentrates on developing a rather general cultural awareness through decontextualised exercises or imaginary and role play games.

By contrast with these models of culture, the approach taken here focuses on the lived experiences of everyday life in a local and holistic way. Instead of broad brush statements about a 'culture', difference and otherness is studied in all its local particularity. Differences are not turned into inventories of facts and used to explain history or communication problems, as in the cross-cultural communication studies. Instead, behaviour and meanings are analysed to *understand* differences (Thornton, 1988) and 'thick descriptions' are written to develop particular cultural knowledge as well as general cultural awareness.

Within the disciplines of anthropology and its use of ethnography, cultural awareness and cultural knowledge cannot be separated. For example, in Sophie's project on the *Carnaval*, she was learning about the myths and historical events which are part of a group's memory but she was also becoming aware of the ways in which the *carnavaliers* were constructing their identity and how they positioned themselves in relation to the women who also worked for the *Carnaval.*

The Integration of Language and Cultural Studies in Higher Education

We turn now to the implications of this discussion for teaching and learning languages in Higher Education. The idea of integrating language learning with other approaches and subjects is not a new one, nor is an interdisciplinary language programme a new development. Language and literature or language and a range of social science subjects is the norm in many countries. However, both the extent and the nature of the integration of these different subject areas is often not clear, nor is the link between language skills work and Area Studies, Civilisation or Landeskunde. The difficulty with traditional literature degrees and with more recent applied languages programmes has been to integrate knowledge-based, intellectual fields of enquiry with what are generally seen as skills-based, performance models of language learning. There is also the issue of how more 'objective' information-based background studies in politics, history, economics and so on can be related to Cultural Studies. Even where cultural, media and communication studies are part of the modern languages curriculum, the connection between these and language learning is far from fully developed. Furthermore, as we have suggested above, Cultural Studies with its focus on cultural theory and the analysis of text as object can provide only a partial solution.

An ethnographic approach, as well as linking language and cultural processes, puts the period of residence abroad, with careful preparation beforehand and debriefing and integration into the mainstream curriculum afterwards, centre stage as a means to integrate linguistic and cultural learning, and the classroom and field experiences.

Language Learning for Mobility

There is a good case for linking cultural learning systematically to any direct experience of staying in the foreign country. 'Language learning for mobility' (Byram *et al.*, 1992: 7) prepares students for any period of residence abroad and also for any contact with similarly mobile students who visit their country.

In many parts of the world:

> The possibility of including the experience of a foreign country as part of language learning is developing very quickly; language learning is becoming a 'practical' subject 'in the field', just as the natural sciences changed from demonstrations by the teacher to proper experimental work by the learners with trips into the field to investigate the phenomena in their eco-systems. (Byram, 1994: 7)

We are not suggesting here that ethnographic learning is a question of collecting samples or simply giving practical experience, as a science or geography field trip is designed to do, but the idea of being 'in the field' participating in and observing new practices gives a new dimension to the language curriculum. An immediate issue arising from this increase in student mobility is the quality of experience and learning which the students achieve. However, simply spending a period abroad may not create significant changes in competence, understanding or ways of thinking. An intellectually rigorous and personally challenging set of goals is needed for this period of learning away from the home institution.

Recognising the learning opportunities of an exchange visit or stay abroad, there is now some literature on the 'pedagogy of exchange' (Zarate, 1986; Alix & Bertrand, 1994; Byram, 1997c). The experience of the stay and how it involves the whole social person (Baumgratz-Gangl, 1990; Byram & Alred, 1993) creates an environment for systematic cultural learning (for example, see Zarate on the observational diary (Zarate, 1991) and Keller in relation to stereotypes (Keller, 1991).

For university students, the Erasmus and Socrates programmes in Europe and the year abroad for modern language students, compulsory in virtually all British universities, provides an opportunity for a relatively extended period abroad. This is not quite the one or two years that an apprentice anthropologist might spend (although even PhD students may only spend nine months or so actually in the field) but certainly long enough to engage intensively with a community over many months and to make an ethnographic project a valid and productive learning experience.

Renewed interest in Britain and the USA in assessing the value of the Year Abroad has led to a number of recent discussions on how best to use it and how effective it is (Coleman, 1996; Freed, 1995; Parker & Rouxeville, 1995). Coleman estimates that, annually, some 12,000 UK students spend a year abroad but that the effectiveness of what is perceived as a costly operation is not clearly established. The great majority of studies either try to assess the student's linguistic competence (Coleman, 1995; Dyson, 1988; Freed, 1995; Meara, 1994; Towell & Hawkins, 1994) or the effect of the year on their attitudes and stereotypes towards the foreign nationals they encounter (Coleman, 1996; Willis *et al.*, 1977).

While the great majority of findings confirm the value of the period abroad in terms of language proficiency, quite what aspects of linguistic competence do improve is less clear (Coleman, 1996). The research on the affective aspects of the year abroad are more controversial although it must be emphasised that assessing attitude is itself highly problematic. Coleman's study suggests that one in six students return with more negative stereotypes of foreign nationals than when they went. However, neither set of studies addresses the sociocultural dimensions of learning and the relationship of communicative competence, cultural awareness, cultural knowledge and empathy. These issues may be raised in the preparation for the year abroad (Byram, 1988) but have not been systematically carried through into course development, structured learning while abroad and assessment on return.

The discourse of 'mobility' assumes a period of time 'in the field' where students, borrowing concepts and methods from anthropology, can undertake ethnographic projects. If language learners are to develop an ethnographic frame of mind and a set of methods for this field work, then their teachers will also need to become ethnographers.

Language *Lecturers* as Ethnographers

The social science components which make up the Area Studies, Civilisation or Landeskunde element of modern languages degrees are usually taught by those with discipline specialisms in politics, history, economics and so on. It is relatively rare for anthropologists to teach on these courses. Few British universities have departments of anthropology and even fewer teach courses in social anthropology relevant to language students (but see Delamont, 1995).This situation is similar in other countries too. However, even if there were anthropologists available for every modern languages course, the argument of this book is that language specialists, with some additional ethnographic training, are best placed to develop the language learner as ethnographer.

First of all, they have an inside view on the students' linguistic competence and on the opportunities that might be available for ethnographic studies during a period abroad. On most courses in Britain, for example, it is staff from language departments who visit students while abroad and can provide essential supervision in the early stages of the ethnographic project.

Secondly, language staff are in a unique position to integrate language and cultural studies. The theories underpinning communicative language teaching make available to language teachers some of the inter-connectedness of language and cultural practice, as we suggested earlier. This is evident, for example, in norms of appropriacy, the sociocultural knowledge required to undertake activities such as managing conversation or a bureaucratic encounter, and the misunderstandings that can arise in intercultural encounters. These are precisely some of the issues which students meet during their residence abroad.

The final reason why languages staff, with appropriate training in this area, are well placed to develop language learners as ethnographers focuses on the difficulty and apparent irrelevance of much anthropological literature to non-anthropology students. Language teachers, provided they have the appropriate guidance and materials to start them off, can select what is accessible and relevant to students both in terms of key introductory texts (see Delamont, 1995; Spradley & McCurdy, 1988) and ethnographic studies of the areas students will be visiting. Since the aim of the ethnography programme is to *integrate* language and cultural experience, it is important for language staff to develop *themselves* as ethnographers so that they can teach an integrated course rather than bolting on what would be seen as an 'outsider' course given by someone from a different discipline. As we detail below, in Chapters 5 and 6, such an approach entails an explicit staff development component for languages lecturers.

Intercultural Competence and Ethnographic Fieldwork

The task of the lecturer is to develop the student into an 'intercultural speaker', as we have defined it above; in other words to help them develop their intercultural competence by linking the cultural knowledge, processes and methods learnt on the ethnography course to the experience of living abroad. The comparative and conceptual are allied to the communicative. Students draw on sociopolitical and historical knowledge but use it in a practical way to observe and grapple with how meanings are produced in everyday practices. In this sense, the experiential aspect of the year abroad is also a conceptual and intellectual process.

If we look at the idea of family, we can see how ethnographic fieldwork can add an intercultural dimension to this well-worn topic which is generally covered only at the linguistic and communicative levels. At the *linguistic* level, this topic includes the vocabulary of familial relationships and, in more formal settings, the language of bureaucratic categories. The family setting may also be used to present and practise certain syntactic structures. At the *communicative* level, students may be taught a range of functions for communicating with a foreign family. For example, they may learn how to greet, offer a present or thank the parents of the family with whom they have had an exchange. At a more advanced level, they may develop an appropriate register that will facilitate the communicative competence involved in participating in a family dinner.

At the level of *intercultural competence*, the theme of family involves understanding the discourses attached to the word 'family' as it is used interactionally within a particular community. This goes beyond textbook knowledge of the family, to a dynamic understanding of what 'family' means to a particular group, how those meanings are lived out in the routine practices of everyday life, and how they relate to institutional constructions of the term. For example, Rachel in her study of the blind students in Marburg, Germany, found that many of them distanced themselves from their families in unexpected ways and had to manage a tension between recognising the support the family gave them, on the one hand, and resisting it, on the other. Given that this understanding is local and dynamic, it is difficult to see how someone could be considered as interculturally competent without direct experience in the everyday life of the community with whom they are, at least temporarily, resident and without a reflective stance that enables them to locate that experience in its broader theoretical and ideological context.

Added to this dynamic understanding of 'otherness' is the capacity to mediate between one's own cultural practices and those of others. By developing social relations with the group to be studied, the student ethnographer, in effect, learns from her own mistakes. Every time she uses her own conventions and assumptions to get things done or make a comment, she discovers how her ways of doing or thinking differ from those of her informants:

> (The ethnographer) ... can take advantage of a performative inadequacy not by trying to accomplish the impossible task of becoming a member, but by systematically exploiting the fact that s/he is not a member and acting on the basis of his or her cultural rules to find out to what extent they differ from those of the actors. Ellen, 1984: 32

So, a comparative perspective develops in which the social construction of family in one community can be explicitly discussed in relation to that of another community and both can be used to critique the other. By raising family practices to an analytic level, an explicit discourse level, and using these discourses in intercultural encounters, potential misunderstandings can be tackled and stereotypes challenged.

The interconnectedness of the experiential, the analytic and the intellectual creates the conditions for intercultural understanding and critical cultural awareness. Language lecturers and learners become immersed in a process of cultural *and* language learning. So, as we suggested in Chapter 1, the notion of 'intercultural competence' assumes that cultural learning *is* language learning and vice versa.

Implied in this discussion of intercultural competence is the issue of methods. As we have suggested above, going out into the field gives students the opportunity to participate in the lives of others and collect data which can then be subjected to a cultural analysis. The raw material of ethnography is the daily lives of, usually, ordinary people (Sheridan *et al.*, 1999). It cannot be stressed enough that doing ethnography involves studying the ordinariness and dailiness of people's lives. This may mean looking at 'kitchen table society' (Gullestad, 1984), at how friends and family weave together the fabric of their social lives around the kitchen table; or how employers and passengers manage interactions at the Gare du Nord (one of the main railway stations in Paris) (Lacoste & Levy, 1994); or the way in which an ice hockey team in Eastern Germany constructs itself as a group (student project). The wider sociopolitical and historical contexts feed in, of course, to this everyday living but it is the texture of these lives, material, social and symbolic which an ethnographer studies.

Up until the 1960s, anthropology students went out into the field with little more advice than to take a notebook and pencil with them. Precisely how an ethnographic study was to be conducted and then written remained a mysterious process. The methods of participant observation, interviewing and analysis are now the subject of numerous methods books and it is increasingly evident that doing ethnography is an enormously skilful task, involving the whole social person. The central chapters of this book illustrate both its complexity and yet its relative accessibility to those from other disciplines.

This account of the engagement of the whole social being in a highly skilled activity presents the work of the period abroad in a rather different light from usual. It is often regarded by universities and students as 'time out' from their regular studies. Precisely how students can best use this period and what the outcomes are meant to be is often vague. Developing the language learner as ethnographer and requiring an ethnographic study to be made while abroad provides clear learning and cultural objectives within a framework of student autonomy.

Learning Theories and Outcomes

Before considering learning outcomes in more detail, it is useful to discuss the learning theories which have some relevance to a programme of cultural and linguistic learning. Ethnography involves 'putting oneself in someone else's shoes'. In other words, to take the metaphor further, it involves finding out about and adapting to the shapes and contours of the other's shoes. Being in someone else's shoes does not make you that other person, but it is a constant reminder to you that the experience, however temporary and unlike you, has become a part of you.

In the developmental psychological literature this capacity is described as *empathy* (see Byram & Morgan, 1994: 25–30). Unlike sympathy, it does not imply a compassion for others' plight, but it does indicate the ability to understand the other, to apprehend their point of view and their felt experiences. This ability to understand others implies a process of social interaction and dialogue. In the literature within sociology and social psychology, the capacity to develop understanding in and through interaction is called 'intersubjectivity' (Schutz, 1964; Henriques *et al.*, 1984).

This empathy or intersubjectivity can be related to the stages of moral development that children and adolescents go through (Piaget & Weil, 1951; Kohlberg *et al.*, 1983). Although this model has been criticised for being too inflexible, the later stages of development are relevant in considering how the period abroad can affect attitudes and stereotypes. These stages involve the process of decentring and reciprocity in which young people learn that there are other ways of looking at the world apart from their own; to understand the perspective of others, reflect on their own perspectives and start appreciating how they are seen by others. Melde (1987) citing Habermas, adds to this the educational aim of developing a critical awareness and capacity to argue through the differences between one's own and others' values and belief systems.

It is possible to sum up the 'understanding' which leads to empathy as consisting of three interlocking dimensions: (1) the local, immediate, palpable: the capacity to feel in ways which approximate to others; (2) 'making sense', apprehending and seeing the meaning of concrete, everyday behaviour (this is the element that sociologists would call intersubjectivity); (3) the comparative, discursive and critical: the ability to argue through another's point of view.

Although 'emotion' has generally been viewed as too awkward a concept to deal with in the sociological and anthropological literature (but see Besnier, 1990; Lutz & Abu-Lughod, 1990) and at Higher Education (HE) level, moral and attitudinal development of students is not usually seen as a suitable subject for discussion, the notion of an intercultural speaker implies a mix of the affective, the reflective and the intellectual suggested in the three dimensions above. A purely conceptual and analytical interpretation of empathy is inadequate.

However, within the constraints of HE, it is the more reflective and intellectual dimensions of empathy which can be explicitly taught and assessed, and so, inevitably, there is more emphasis on these aspects in this book.

In addition to empathy, the theories of 'experiential learning' (particularly Kolb's learning cycle, 1984) are relevant for the language learner as ethnographer. Although Kolb's theory was not applied to ethnography, it is possible to relate it to the ethnographic learning while abroad which we propose in this book. His learning cycle suggests a recurring circularity in which experience (the time spent in the field), reflection (data analysis and the writing of the ethnographic project) and learning (integration of the experience and the reflection into the curriculum after the return from abroad) reinforce each other. The three elements of experience, reflection and learning may also be integrated in any one component of the Ealing ethnography programme. Direct experience is central to this cycle and the shock of immersion in a new way of living, and how that 'culture shock' can be managed, has been documented (Furnham & Bochner, 1986).

Although the connection between theories of empathy, experiential learning, culture shock theory and cultural learning are only speculative, such theories are broadly relevant to those aspects of cultural learning concerned with attitude change, ethnocentrism, challenging stereotypes and intercultural competence. In addition to these elements, the intercultural learner has to enter into the conceptual worlds of others, to experience the knowledge structures necessary to get things done and make sense of the information that surrounds them.

In language learning theory, the notions of 'schema' (Bartlett, 1932) or script theory (Schank & Ableson, 1977), widely used in social psychology and aspects of discourse analysis, have become important and we draw on them here for cultural learning purposes. Everyday practices such as using public transport, going to a restaurant or playing a sport rely on 'scripts' that are internalised as part of our socialisation (and see Chapter 3 on the ethnography of communication). Similarly, to make sense of advertisements, newspaper copy or a TV documentary requires networks of cultural references organised in schemata which can be readily accessed. Part of the process of cultural learning is to acquire these schemata first in one's own and then in the second and subsequent languages as part of primary, secondary and tertiary socialisation. They feed into the discourses of everyday life and provide cognitive maps for both routine and not so familiar social practices.

Schema development involves learning the significance of particular concepts in context. Agar (1991) illustrates this well in his attempt to find out the significance of the Viennese German word 'Schmäh' (Agar's rough gloss on this would be that things are not what they seem to be but are, ironically, much worse). He collected data on this word through anecdotes and interviews, chipping away at the surface meaning of the concept which he saw as 'heavily puttied' with associative meanings.

Work on schemata and semantics in cognitive linguistics and linguistic anthropology has considerably enhanced our understanding of how knowledge is stored in script – like forms and of the processes of classification of concepts relative to particular cultural groups. But as with the psychological theories, direct use of these themes in developing cultural learning is, at best, suggestive. Schema theory has been criticised for its implications that scripts are fixed structures of knowledge whereas work on 'connectionism' in psychology (Churchland, 1995; Gee, 1992) and on interaction in sociolinguistics (Gumperz, 1982a and b), suggests that such knowledge is negotiated in interaction and is variable depending on the context. This reinforces the point that cultural knowledge is not separate from language use but that the two are interdependent.

Finally, the work on language learner autonomy (Holec, 1981; Little, 1994) is of some relevance. Autonomous learners are those who set their own learning goals, decide the means whereby they can achieve them, how they can evaluate them and how long they need in order to achieve them. Much of the practical work arising from the studies of language learner autonomy (particularly at the Centre de Recherches et d'Applications en Langues [CRAPEL]) has been concerned with either learning to learn strategies (Wenden & Rubin, 1987) or the development of self-access centres (for example, Sheerin, 1989). However, any period of residence abroad is, in many respects, a more complete experience of autonomy. Language learners as ethnographers have to set their own goals, choosing an ethnographic topic to research; decide on the means to produce an ethnographic project, how to gain access, what methods to use and so on; evaluate their own data and be reflective about the process of writing up. They also have to choose how much time to put into the ethnographic project in order to meet their goals.

The learning theories briefly discussed here are drawn from psychology and linguistics. Another obvious source for descriptions and theories of cultural learning are ethnographers themselves. There has been, however, surprisingly little in the monographs and diaries of ethnographers about their own language and cultural learning. James Clifford in the introduction to what is now a classic text on ethnographic writing (Clifford & Marcus, 1986) suggests that anthropology has had to reposition itself by challenging some of the old assumptions about the discipline and its methods. These old assumptions account for the lack of interest in the ethnographers' role and in the processes of learning which they must, inevitably, have gone through. Until recently, ethnographers saw themselves as standing outside the objects of their study, writing with authority about people who it was assumed could not speak for themselves. There was no hint of their own culturally constructed selves in the relatively stylised descriptions of actual field experience.

The recent interest in ethnographic writing is part of the more general repositioning of anthropology which has also included reflections on participant observation (Stocking, 1983) and field notes (Sanjek, 1992) as well as more wide-ranging fieldwork accounts (Beaujour, 1981; Crapanzano, 1986). It is in these reflections on fieldwork and writing up, that the ethnographer as learner emerges, particularly in their discussions of how to 'translate' from one cultural experience to another (Agar, 1985; Asad & Dixon, 1985, and see Chapters 3 and 4).

This brief overview of some sources of learning theories sets the scene for looking at the type of *learning outcomes* planned in the project. We are anticipating Chapters 10 and 11 here in order to provide a framework for the next few chapters. It will be obvious from the discussion so far that a major learning outcome will not be knowledge about *a* 'culture' or *the* 'other' of an encyclopedic or positivist kind. For example, information about political structures, regional or economic policy or the history of changing national boundaries might be useful background knowledge but it is essentially book-based information, usually presented as facts in an unproblematic way and abstracted from the everydayness of people's ordinary lives. By contrast, the learning envisaged here is more personal and reflexive. It falls into four broad categories:

(1) *Local social and cultural knowledge*
    This involves developing an understanding of one's own and others' particular cultural practices in local contexts. It includes ways of communicating and developing an understanding of how social relations are structured around what is meaningful to a group. The particular and local is set within a wider conceptual framework. So, local meanings are connected to larger systems of meaning. For example, the general notion of 'exchange' or 'reciprocity' could be used to understand how a group of neighbours managed their social relationships or youth unemployment is considered in terms of its impact on the pétanque club in France.

(2) *Processes of interrogation and relativisation*
    This involves developing in students the habit of constantly interrogating the source of their knowledge and so questioning their own assumptions about how they construct meanings, values and attitudes. This, in turn, leads to developing the habit of relativising, of seeing one's own and others' worlds as socially constructed and not natural, normative or universal. Allied to this is learning how a group represents itself to itself and to those outside.

(3) *Observation, social interaction and analytic skills*
This involves developing a number of skills out of ethnographic methodology and the opportunities for interaction created by the demands of an ethnographic project. Students gradually acquire a palpable sense of being with a group, of rubbing shoulders with those in it as cultural beings. For example, they learn how to establish field relations in the foreign language, how to observe systematically and how to draw on conceptual categories to analyse data. The group a student chooses to work with may involve them in learning to interact with people with very different social identities from their own and who use varieties of the target language far removed from the language of the foreign language classroom and written texts.

(4) *Personal development*
This involves developing initiative, autonomy, self-confidence and flexibility. These personal skills and orientations are, as we have suggested above, rarely described in ethnographies although the more recent reflexive fieldwork accounts are suggestive of the learning that ethnographers have experienced. Language students need to develop these general personal skills for the specific intercultural contexts they are likely to be working in. For many students, this type of personal development was one of the most important aspects of the ethnography programme (see Chapter 10) .

The planned learning, therefore, is a blend of intellectual inquiry, conceptual development and affective change. It can be summed up as the development of 'an ethnographic imagination' (Atkinson, 1990) – a new way of seeing social life based on an intense engagement with it. There is no intention, perhaps it is worth repeating, of turning students into anthropologists or even ethnographers in any full sense of the term. The aim is to help students develop enough of an ethnographic imagination so that, as 'language people' (Evans, 1988), they can come to understand better and so mediate between different language and cultural practices and, like all good ethnographers, in doing so, understand themselves and their own cultural contexts.

Chapter 3
Theoretical Issues in Language and Cultural Practices

Why Bother with Theory?

We argued in the previous chapter that a model for the language learner is the speaker with intercultural competence. This chapter and Chapter 4 explore some of the theoretical issues around the idea of an 'intercultural speaker'. Inevitably they draw on theories from studies of both culture and language but there is no neat portmanteau term for looking at the two together. Agar in his book *Language Shock* (1994) uses the notion of *languaculture* and others have used a variety of hyphen-ated terms such as language-in-culture. This lack of an easy term makes it difficult to explore the theories which bring language and culture together, but the aim of this chapter, and indeed the whole book, is to do just that. There are several reasons why it is worth discussing the theoretical background in more detail. Much language teaching is conceived as practical action and any theories tend to be discussed in terms of *learning* theory despite the fact that theories about language and culture drive the teaching and learning process, albeit implicitly. An obvious instance of this is the assumption that language and culture are separate and that culture, therefore, has to be 'tacked on so to speak to the teaching of speaking, listening, reading and writing' (Kramsch, 1993: 1). Similarly, it can be very difficult to help language students recognise their own theories about other cultural groups and, indeed, more gener-ally, their implicit theories about social reality which influence their views on learning and on experiencing otherness. As students, for example, of French or German, they tend to discuss 'the French' or 'the Germans' in terms of facts about them as national groups. Unlearning these assumptions, and that involves seeing them for what they are – theories not facts – is a major part of the ethnography programme.

As we have already indicated in the previous chapters, the theories drawn on in the notion of language learners as ethnographers come

mainly from social and linguistic anthropology and that branch of sociolinguistics closest to anthropology called 'interactional sociolinguistics'.
There is an analogy between the social anthropologist going out into the
field, living and studying in a particular community and the foreign
language student using their time abroad to learn about a new set of
social, cultural and communicative experiences. The metaphor of the
'field' is a useful one but it can be misleading if it is assumed that
the field is somewhere out there rather than part of one's everyday life:

> Social anthropology is concerned with the whole of life, and not just
> something you do until six o'clock. The study of social anthropology
> encourages you to have a new kind of consciousness of life; it is a
> way of looking at the world, and in that sense it is a way of living.
> (Pocock, 1975: 1)

So before language students go out into the foreign field, they need to
start looking at their own worlds in an anthropological way. Many of
the tasks on the ethnography course, and what we call the 'home ethnography', are designed for this purpose. The aim here is to bring to the
surface, so to speak, the implicit knowledge and ways of acting which
make us part of a particular community. We experience these from the
inside and they need to be 'made strange', if we are to understand our
own process of socialisation generally, and language socialisation, in
particular. Foreign-language learners, even if they spend some time
in the target language country, rarely experience the gradual accretion
of ideas, values and ways of doing interactions which we experience
with our dominant and, in some cases, second languages.

Incorporating some aspects of social anthropology into the modern
languages degree gives students concepts and methods which help them
to reflect on their own sociocultural knowledge and use this reflection
to compare their lives with those of the group they study while abroad.
Interactional sociolinguistics puts a magnifying glass on interactions
themselves and examines the processes of language use and socialisation of different groups. As we have already suggested, it forms a bridge
between communicative language teaching and anthropology, drawing
on the anthropological theories of the ethnography of communication
and the fine-grained detail analysis of conversation developed within
one branch of sociology. In Chapter 4, some of the theories of language
which are particularly relevant for developing the language learner as
ethnographer will be discussed but a more general framing will be
given first. We describe two different analytic perspectives on the social
world, three views of culture arising from them and the interactional

sociolinguistic perspective which combines cultural practices and detailed analysis of interaction.

Functional and Constructivist Perspectives of Culture and Language

The foundation of much thinking in anthropology and linguistics in the last 70 years or so has been within a *functional* paradigm. A society's activities and ways of thinking are seen as matters of responding to needs and demands. So, for example, people gossip because they need to affirm social relations, or interviews are run the way they are because that is an effective way of eliciting information from people. Beliefs and values are described in terms of behaviour; for example, the French bourgeois families Le Wita (1988) studied taught their children not to interrupt their parents in the drawing room. The functional message was that children should not be disruptive. Similarly, language is seen as action – words are deeds – in a functional view of the world. This functional view of language, based on speech act theory, informs most communicative language teaching in which language functions and the situations in which they occur are interconnected. For example, language students will all be familiar with course books that teach how to give instructions for cooking a local delicacy, how to make requests in workplace settings or how to describe your weekend to friends.

Functionalism has been an important influence in understanding 'culture' since Malinowski's early work (see Chapter 5) and remains a significant element in ethnography. After all, we eat because we are hungry and gas leaks are repaired because otherwise we might die. Most informants when talking about their lives to ethnographers will describe it in functional terms. So, an important part of an ethnographic project is to describe what people do and to understand, in their terms, why they do it. As Malinowski asserted, understanding what meanings an activity might have or indeed what a particular word means requires the ethnographer to be involved in practical action:

> Meaning does not come . . . from the contemplation of things, or analysis of occurrences, but in practical and active acquaintance with relevant situations. The real knowledge of a word comes through the practice of appropriately using it within a certain situation. (Malinowski, 1923: 325)

Functionalism also connects to *realism* and to the idea that it is possible to see and describe the world as it is – that there is a reality out there waiting prone to be discovered. Until quite recently, ethnographers would see their task, unproblematically, as one of getting close to the social reality of the new community. The idea of 'being there', it was considered, gave them the authority to describe another culture as 'real'. This assumption is still, of course, a defining aspect of ethnography (see Chapter 5) and underlies the arguments for a period abroad. It is assumed that by 'being there', seeing how society goes about its business, language students will learn what that society and culture 'is'. But this functional realism, if the dominant or only view can, as we have already suggested, lead to generalisations and negative stereotypes of other cultures. This is what anthropologists and sociologists have critiqued as 'essentialism' – a view of national and ethnic groups as having certain essential characteristics which define them as if every member of that group thought and behaved in the same way. So a functional, realist approach has to be critiqued by drawing on a different way of seeing and knowing the world.

An alternative paradigm, but one that is not incommensurable with functionalism, is *constructivism*. In this perspective social life is seen as constructed or constituted out of interactive behaviour and texts. So language is not simply a tool for expressing some prior reality; it actively helps to create that reality. The 'real world', it is argued, does not exist out there as a set of concrete, objective facts; it is constructed by us as social beings in our everyday lives and language is the chief instrument for doing this. If we return to Le Wita's study of upper middle-class Parisian families, mentioned above, (a part of which is read, either in French or English, by students in Unit 5 of the ethnography course on *Families*) we can see the active construction of the notion of 'family' within dominant class relations. Children are taught not to interrupt so that parents and their friends can converse in peace, but such socialisation is also, de Wita suggests, part of a large symbolic order in which this class is perpetuating notions of self-control as a means of reproducing their class power. She also discusses such routines as everyday lunches and dinners, learning how to negotiate the drawing room as a social space or the summons to sit down for dinner (passer à table).

> Deuxième épreuve: le moment de passer à table. On assiste alors à une curieuse scène: le groupe est arrivé dans la salle à manger et reste en arrêt à quelques pas de la table. Il ne saurait être question d'y prendre place en ordre dispersé et avant l'arriveé de la maîtresse de la maison [. . .]
> Chaque élément du groupe participe ainsi à la vacuité du moment. On pourrait comparer cette scène à une longue règle de politesse où

chaque partie s'excuserait de faire attendre le tout. Évoluant discrète-
ment autour de la table chacun patiente donc sans chercher à faire
quoi que ce soit. (Le Wita, 1988: 88)

Another ordeal is the moment of sitting down to eat. The summons
to do so gives rise to a curious scene. Having entered the dining
room the group will come to a halt a little way from the table. There
can be no question of just sitting anywhere and taking their places
before the hostess arrives . . .
     Every member of the group shares in the emptiness of the moment.
The scene might be compared to one prolonged rule of politeness
in which every party apologises for holding everyone else up.
Circling the table discreetly, everybody waits without attempting to
do anything. (trans. Le Wita, 1994: 76–7)

These are part of a set of ritualised practices which teach self-control,
one of the crucial characteristics, Le Wita argues, of Bourgeois person-
hood:

L'ascetisme bourgeois est une méthode de conduite visant à
surmonter 'le status naturae', à soustraire l'homme à la puissance
des instincts, à le libérer de sa dépendance à l'égard du monde et
de la nature. (Le Wita, 1988: 83)

Bourgeois asceticism is a mode of conduct aimed at overcoming the
status naturae, removing man from the power of instinct; and freeing
him from his dependence upon the world and nature. (trans. de
Wita, 1994: 72)

The mode of conduct which has everyone circling the table actively
constructs an element of self-control. The ritual of seating becomes
as, if not more, significant than the act of eating. A functional perspective would say that everyone is simply waiting to be told where to
sit. But from a constructivist point of view, the dinner guests are
performing a ritual which helps to build up the notion of what it
means to be a bourgeois family in Paris in the 1980s. The fact that
everyone does not just sit down and enjoy the meal both reflects
and constructs the notion of self-control as an aspect of 'bourgeois
asceticism'.
     Constructivism is also a defining element of ethnography, especially
in more recent ethnography, in that 'facts', 'reality' are not taken
for granted but are seen as constitutive and representative of some
version of reality. So, for example, the Spanish student who did his

home ethnography on 'Reyes', the Twelfth Night celebrations in Spain, began to see these celebrations in more than simple functional terms or as some fixed or natural 'reality' – 'we give presents because it is the custom'. He began to analyse the practice as a constructed reality based on a cultural system of obligations and reciprocity which help to maintain the idea of family.

Language is the fundamental means of constructing social reality because it classifies and 'fixes' the flow of experience so that we can think , talk, know and write about it in ways which make it accessible to others (Berger & Berger, 1972; Berger & Luckmann, 1966; Schutz, 1964). It is through language that we are socialised and it is language itself which makes social life 'real':

> First of all, of course, it is the child's micro-world itself that is structured by language. Language *objectifies* reality – that is, the incessant flux of experience is firmed up, stabilized into discrete identifiable objects. Language also structures, by objectification and by establishing meaningful relations, the human environment of the child. It populates reality with distinct beings, ranging from Mummy . . . To the bad-little-boy who throws tantrums next door. And it is by means of language that the fact becomes established that Mummy knows best, but that bad-little-boys will be punished: and, incidentally, it is only through the power of language that such propositions can retain their established plausibility even if experience offers little or no proof. (Berger & Berger, 1972: 69)

The idea that reality is socially constructed and that language not only reflects and expresses reality but constitutes it, is an entirely new way of looking at things for many language students. It requires a shift in perspective from a positivist view – from seeing social reality as a positive fact whose origin is not questioned – to a constructivist. one where social reality is made out of the interactions and discourses of a particular time in history. A constructivist take on the experience of living and learning abroad would be a cautious and relative one. Conversations overheard, rituals observed and informants' comments would all be treated as *versions* of reality constructed by speakers as they interacted, as representations of 'reality'. People would be observed getting things done, making things work – functioning within certain contexts – but as well as describing these activities in functional terms, the constructivist pauses to question how these activities have come about, what makes them significant and how participants work at making them into 'reality'.

Both the functional and the constructivist paradigms have informed the three models of 'culture' which are now presented: the cognitive, the symbolic and the critical.

A Cognitive View of 'Culture'

In the cognitive view, culture is seen as knowledge. This is a mentalist perspective in which culture is abstracted from actual behaviour and practice and instead consists of knowledge structures. These can then be analysed as interlinked components. For example, in cognitive and linguistic anthropology, language is used to draw up taxonomies such as names for family relationships, plants and animals. These linguistic components are then related to cultural concepts within a particular society or group. For example, kinship terms are traditionally studied to understand the ways in which 'family' is constituted. A well-known example is the way in which different languages categorise uncles, aunts, cousins, etc. In some languages, a distinction is made between relations on the husband's and on the wife's side – such as 'aunt on the husband's side' and so on, whereas in others there is no such distinction. The anthropologist most closely associated with this approach is Ward Goodenough and his definition of culture represents the classic one within this school:

> A society's culture consists of whatever it is one has to know or believe in order to operate in a manner acceptable to its members ... Culture is a not a material phenomenon; it does not consist of things, peoples, behaviour, or emotions. It is rather an organization of these things. It is the form of things that people have in their mind, their models for perceiving, reacting and otherwise inter-preting them. (Goodenough, 1964: 36)

So people organise the way they do things in their heads and these mental representations or models are what cognitive and linguistic anthropologists deem is culture. In an interesting collection of essays on cultural models (Holland & Quinn, 1987), the model of an American marriage draws on the metaphors commonly used: 'broken marriages', 'working hard on your marriage', 'trying to mend the relationship' and so on. These build up a cultural model of marriage as a fragile thing which can be easily broken. There are links here with the cognitive models, such as schema, scripts and frames, of artificial intelligence (see Chapter 2) and both cognitive anthropology and schema and script theory are concerned with *learned* behaviour – that is behaviour based on cultural knowledge.

A Symbolic View of 'Culture'

The symbolic or semiotic take on culture sees it as a system of *public* meanings. Cultural meanings do not reside in people's heads but are shared and acted out publicly among those who could be said to have the same culture. These cultural meanings are realised in symbols and in behaviour which itself is seen as symbolic action. We eat certain kinds of food, live in certain kinds of households not just because it is functional to do so but because it has symbolic significance. For example, our notion of who we are is linked to what food we classify as edible or not (as we discuss in Unit 16 of the ethnography course on Belief and Action). Similarly, we greet others the way we do, present ourselves in certain routinised ways and manage issues of embarrassment or imposition in particular ways, not because we need to do so in this specific form but because as members of a community, it is the way we act out our identity and sense of communality and our relation to others. These actions have symbolic meanings.

This approach is closely associated with Clifford Geertz and his notion of culture as 'socially established structures of meaning':

> Believing, with Max Weber, that man (*sic*) is an animal suspended in webs of significance that he himself has spun, I take culture to be those webs, the analysis of it to be, therefore, not an experimental science in search of law but an interpretive one in search of meaning. (Geertz, 1973: 5)

So, whereas Goodenough would see 'culture' as knowledge in, so to speak, the spider's head, Geertz sees it as public behaviour – the web – which has symbolic significance to those who can bring meaning to it. So, he is asking the question: How do people come to make meanings out of their lives? What are the structures and layers of meaning in which people are enmeshed? Each interpretation of meaning is itself embedded in another so that cultural analysis is 'intrinsically incomplete – worse than that, the more deeply it goes the less complete it is'. So the cultural learner has to 'pick his (*sic*) way' through 'piled up structures of influence and implication' (1973: 7).

Geertz uses the philosopher Gilbert Ryle's notion of 'thick description' to illustrate the interpretive complexities in trying to understand behaviour and the value systems embedded in it. Ryle illustrates the notion by comparing the difference between a blink and a wink. A 'thin description' might be a rapid contraction of the eyelid. But a 'thick description' must not only describe and account for the context in which

the wink/blink occurs but also explain whether it was a wink or not. In other words, did it have *symbolic* significance? Was it a conspiratorial sign or a reflex action? Or was it a fake wink because the winker wanted the others to think there was a conspiracy going on? And so on.

For the language student, resident abroad, every piece of observation raises questions such as these, whether it is learning about the symbolic significance of the Sevillano dance or understanding the routines and use of social space in the kitchens of the student hostels at Marburg University. What meanings do these behaviours have? How is their action symbolic of wider themes and assumptions? This approach to culture with its emphasis on systems of meaning and symbolic action, on complex and unresolvable interpretations and on context as something both brought in and brought about in interaction may be quite daunting. But it encourages the habits of observation, interrogation and reflection which characterise the intercultural speaker. These issues are tackled in the ethnography course in different ways. Students are first introduced to the idea of shared cultural knowledge and 'thick description' in Unit 4 where they use observations from their daily lives to distinguish between description and interpretation. Later in the course, they are introduced to the symbolic significance of gift giving (used by the Spanish student in the 'Reyes' project mentioned above) and how symbolic signs and classification shape our notions of what is acceptable, appropriate and so on (see Chapter 6 for detailed examples).

A Critical View of 'Culture'

More recently, the symbolic and cognitive views of culture have been criticised for presenting a relatively unproblematic, static and ahistorical image of 'culture'. A critical perspective has been added to the descriptive and interpretive in anthropology, linguistics, applied linguistics and ethnography and other discipline areas. Issues of power and political responsibility are at the centre of this debate. A critical perspective goes beyond description to ask critical questions about how such things came to be, how did the dominant view come to prevail? (Asad, 1973, 1980; Grillo *et al.*, 1987):

> The verification and naturalisation of 'culture' hides the kinds of questions about power and social change that are currently in the forefront of anthropological enquiry. (Street, 1993)

Current anthropology has been particularly sensitive to the colonial associations of its earlier days and so its critical turn has been significant in redefining itself. In particular, a critical view of 'culture' challenges the essentialist notion of a group having a culture – some essential set of meanings that define them. So just as ethnographers writing today would not talk about a group they had studied as, for example, *The Nuer*, as the Oxford anthropologist, Evans-Pritchard described the tribe he studied, so language students need to resist the temptation to talk of 'The Germans', 'Parisians', 'Eastenders' and so on. There is a danger in taking dominant cultural practices as the 'givens' of a culture. In any community there are varieties and struggles over meaning which are observable in the actions of small groups.

This perspective assumes that we are all interpreting the world from:

within particular discursive practices, entailing particular interests, commitments, inclusions, exclusions and so forth [and that] aspects of these discursive practices may serve to sustain relations of domination and may hence be ideological. (Fairclough, 1996: 4–5)

(and see Gee, 1999 and the section on discourse in Chapter 4). In other words, any analysis of a text or piece of interaction must be understood as coming from a particular set of values and beliefs and can be interpreted in different ways according to the values and beliefs of the analyst. We have all had the experience of presenting our 'case' as if it were the facts, whether we are defending our country's foreign policy, the value of a university education or an accusation that we are racist. We talk from particular positions and with *our* interests in mind. Critical anthropologists and linguists argue that these positions and interests need to be recognised and unpacked so that we can see the ideology working away and can identify, in particular, how dominant groups come to establish their view as the normal and natural one.

This ideological view can be contrasted with an 'autonomous' model (Street, 1984) in which language and culture are separated off from their historical and social contexts and are treated as neutral knowledge systems and tools. A critical position would not, for example, just accept the assumptions about what constitutes knowledge or appropriate academic language in a particular school system, but would ask how this knowledge and these values come to be the dominant ones. In a similar vein, Chris, the student who undertook an ethnographic study of transvestite prostitutes in Cadiz, had to try to understand not only the symbolic meanings around why they dressed the way they did or approach potential clients in particular ways – in other words develop a 'thick description' – he also had to ask how this group comes to resist dominant values and social relationships. So, he attempted a critical

interpretation of how this state of affairs was constituted and reproduced. In constantly interrogating how texts and practices come to be
produced, this critical view owes much to social constructivism and
symbolic anthropology. But it goes further, in questioning categories
which are apparently presented as natural, value-free and shared and
asks about the relationships of power which have caused these categories and ways of thinking to be seen as the 'real' or the 'right' ones.
As Kramsch argues, culture is arbitrary but is 'cloaked in rightness' to
justify itself (Kramsch, 1995).

Culture is a Verb

All three views of culture are drawn on, in developing the notion of
the language learner as ethnographer but in different measure. The cognitive view is useful in helping students focus on the cultural models
implied in language, but its static, mentalist assumptions can lead the
student ethnographer to revert to a folk view of people having 'cultures'
which can be caught like butterflies in a net. The critical view is important, similarly, in challenging essentialist notions and in pushing students
beyond interpretation to explanations of cultural practice which include
the dimension of power. And this critical appreciation is something to
be developed in both the foreign 'culture' and in the learners' own culture
(Melde, 1987). It is also useful in helping them to be reflexive about their
own ethnographic writing – about their own interests and commitments
– and see their own writing as ideological. But since ethnography is a
new method for the great majority of students, it is difficult to teach
them to adopt a strongly critical approach when they are still in the
early stages of learning about the more traditional one. So, the critical
perspective acts as a lens, focusing students on the habits of interrogation – questioning the categories and ways of thinking that are presented
as natural and universal and asking how texts and interactions come to
be produced. It is in this more general sense of 'critical' that this perspective is used in the language learners as ethnographers project.

It is the symbolic/semiotic view of culture which is drawn on most
heavily – the focus on meanings and the interpretation of meanings. But
Geertz's notion of culture as action is taken further here. As we
mentioned, at the beginning of Chapter 2, even using the word culture
suggests something too noun-like, as if it were an entity, something that
can be readily named. Instead a more active verb-like notion is needed
(Street, 1993) or as Ochs says 'members of society are *agents* of culture,
not merely *bearers* of culture (our italics) (Ochs, 1997: 416). Culture is

'doing' rather than 'being'. We can get somewhat closer to this active, dynamic view of culture if we talk about cultural processes or practices (and see the section on 'practice' in the next chapter).

So far, we have suggested two general ways of looking at the world, the functional and the constructivist, and three views of culture which draw to varying degrees on these two views. In the final part of this chapter, we will look at one aspect of cultural practice – styles of communicating and self-presentation – as part of a wider ethnographic approach.

Language-and-Cultural Practices

The following conversation was overheard in a small restaurant in a relatively affluent suburb of West London. Two women with young children were discussing their 'au pairs'. One was telling the other how the week before she had had to have a serious talk with her 'au pair'. The young woman had invited a male friend into her bedroom without introducing him first to the family. Her employer had admonished her for this lapse and told her 'In England, if you are staying in someone else's house, you introduce any visitor to the head of the household.' The woman went on to tell her friend that her 'au pair' had explained that this was not the custom where she came from.

A number of issues arise out of this bit of eavesdropping which link back to the points made in Chapter 2 based on the student ethnographies of the pétanque game and the family's religious practices in Seville. They also provide a connecting link to the theories of language- and-cultural practice described below:

* Communication – the presentation of self through styles of speaking, what are accepted topics (here the grumbles about the 'au pair') and how these styles of speaking express and construct a particular social identity. For example, here cultural misunderstandings are dealt with explicitly by a rule-giving approach to social etiquette.
* The everydayness and smallness of things: the ways in which passing interactions build up patterns of behaviour and values – how gossip and chat have values embedded in them.
* The structuring of social relations and the formation of boundaries between different groups – here the distinction made between family and visitor.
* Representations of one's own group and others. Here the concept of 'the head of the household' indexes a particular model of family.

Part of this representation is the 'native's' stereotyping of her own customs to present a single voice to the outsider: 'In England you behave like this'.

- The connections of the local to larger systems of meaning associated with social, political and economic relations. For example, 'the grumbles about servants' topic is part of a cultural theme, historically, of the dominant class and the 'head of the household' notion is one, fundamentally contested, way of structuring family relationships.

Of course, it is not possible to simply read off from this one small instance the cultural practices of a group. But keeping an ethnographic eye and ear open might over time lead to the identification of some interesting patterns among this group of women in this West London suburb. To draw these kinds of points out of a little piece of observation requires the observer to have some background in the theory and methodology of some aspects of anthropology and sociolinguistics and we now turn to these. We shall look at five themes – the first one in this chapter and the remaining four in the next:

- Interactional sociolinguistics – the ways in which styles of communicating index social identity and the need for a method which examines the fine-grained detail of interaction.
- Issues of ethnicity and nationality – how language is used to represent ethnic and national identity.
- Linguistic relativity – the idea that language influences our view of the world.
- Discourse, text and practice – the relationship between 'lived experiences' and the discourses and practices which represent it and the way these are written up as text.
- Non-verbal communication and the use of social space – the significance of the human body in language-and-cultural practices.

Interactional Sociolinguistics

Taking a social constructivist view, interactional sociolinguistics draws on the literature in the *ethnography of communication* and *conversation analysis* and is most closely associated with the work of John Gumperz. His work draws together detailed studies of interactional life, social identity and cultural practices to answer the question: 'How do people come to make sense of, and to, each other and how do these interpretive processes feed into the structuring of social groups and identities?'

Another way of putting this is Sack's definition of culture as 'an inference-making machine' (Sacks, 1994). If we examine the ways in which people make inferences about what they see and hear and we trace these inferences through innumerable interactions, we begin to see the patterns of social life which sustain us as groups and individual social beings. Similarly, misunderstandings – when the inference-making machine breaks down – can act as a magnifying glass to show us the different language-and-cultural practices across different groups.

Misunderstandings are central to this approach because they bring to the surface the styles of communicating which have caused the misunderstandings in the first place (Tannen, 1984). What was judged as rude or incompetent behaviour, for instance, turns out to be based on culturally communicative styles. For example, Beale's work (1990) on the contrast between Australian English speakers and French English speakers suggests that the two groups manage aspects of social relations in the workplace quite differently. Whereas the Australian English speakers will chat briefly about how they spent their weekends to any colleague in the workplace, the French English speakers manage the Monday morning contacts in different ways. If their colleagues are friends, they tend to talk at some length about their weekends while with colleagues with whom they only have a distant relationship, greetings would be minimal and no weekend chat is embarked on. Beale reports that both sides found this difference uncomfortable. The context created by the Australian English speakers by such exchanges as: 'Did you have a good weekend?' 'Yes, fine thanks' spoken with a falling tone, gives off a message that contact has been made but that no real interest in the other's weekend has been conveyed or is, indeed, necessary. For the French English speakers in Beale's study 'Did you have a good weekend?' creates a context in which, at the least, several exchanges are expected. As McDermott and Gospidinoff (1979) put it, people make environments for each other which are not always ones they are comfortable living in. Not surprisingly misunderstandings were reported on both sides and negative judgements were made of the other group.

This study illustrates some of the points made above about the West London women: the smallness and everydayness of passing comments and specific styles of self-presentation (Goffman, 1959), the boundary making between 'them' and 'us' and how these feed into wider social structures, including national stereotyping. In doing so, Beale's study also illustrates two central concerns of interactional sociolinguistics: how ways of interacting index, or signal, ethnic identity and how this is done, dynamically, in and through everyday interactions by the ways in which speakers create contexts for each other. This *contextualisation* work, as Gumperz (1982a) calls it, helps speakers to track each other's meaning and at the same time signals to the other that they share the same way of doing things, that in this respect they are part of the same community. Because the French and English speakers in the Australian workplaces studied give different *contextualisaton cues* (Gumperz, 1982a, 1992a and b) they are unintentionally giving off two messages simultaneously: that they do not share the same way of making social contact through talking about the weekend and because of this lack of sharedness, they are confirming and perhaps reinforcing the differences between them: that they are not part of the same community.

Gumperz and his associates in their studies of intercultural communication linked to both ethnicity and gender (Gumperz, 1982; Tannen, 1990, 1993) have charted the misunderstandings which occur when people bring different presuppositions and style of talking to the encounter – in other words when they create different contexts together and draw different inferences from the interaction. The potential for misunderstanding is at the heart of a conflict model of intercultural communication (Kramsch, 1993) in which diversity becomes problematic in face-to-face interaction. Not only do speakers come across to each other as not conforming to their own norms of how to be and get things done, but they do not have the shared means for repairing misunderstandings. For example, a very indirect way of communicating may cause a problem and when the speaker tries to repair it, they use the very same indirect style which caused the problem in the first place. So, cultural differences in communicating are not simply about not understanding the meaning of an utterance but are to do with sharing (or not) the conditions for negotiating meaning together. These are the seeds from which negative ethnic stereotyping grows or from which confirmation of old stereotypes is made. Language students, negotiating their ethnographic projects in the target country, can, in contrast, be reflective about the misunderstandings that they may well encounter and can use these critical moments as part of the experience of cultural learning.

The important point here is that cultural learning cannot happen in the abstract, in a classroom, with relatively decontextualised examples of communication breakdown from which learners tend to draw generalised conclusions. But it can happen in the actual contexts of communication in which all the features of the local environment affect interpretation and where students are part of the context and can use it for on the spot or later learning through discussion with participant or other locals. For example, Sophie studied the 'Carnaval' and the *carnava-*

liers in Nice. She found that women were excluded from becoming carnavaliers. When she tried to talk to the older men about this exclusion she met with little response and experienced a number of uncomfortable encounters. Later, she made contact with some women who were active in the carnival but were not allowed to be carnaval-ières. From them she learnt about the gender contestations around the carnival tradition and could link them to wider issues of gender and inequality.

The connection between language and wider social systems, which has informed the studies of misunderstandings, has been the particular concern of the *ethnography of communication* (Bauman & Sherzer, 1974). Until Dell Hymes' ground-breaking work in this area (Hymes, 1966a, 1972, 1974) ethnography had used language as evidence of patterns of behaviour but language had not been seen as creating activities in its own right. These language created activities or 'speech events' are, in a sense, microcosms of the larger community. The detailed ways in which people assemble an event – a religious ceremony, a formal story-telling or even asking for a drink (Frake, 1964) – shows that speaking, like the linguistic code, is patterned and functions as part of our cultural system:

> People who enact different cultures do to some extent experience dis-
> tinct communicative systems, not merely the same natural commu-
> nicative condition with different customs affixed. (Hymes, 1966b: 116)

Hymes' influence on communicative language teaching, and the rather limited way in which CLT has interpreted his work, has been briefly discussed in Chapter 2. For the student who is resident abroad, partic-ipation in and analysis of speech events such as formal celebrations, ceremonies or even sporting fixtures soon reveals that they are made up of much more than socially appropriate language. The whole physical and social event as well as the bodily movements, pacing and rhythm of speakers' turns and so on have to be apprehended and then (tenta-tive) links made to wider social knowledge and practices. It is this level – the speech event – that Gumperz argues should be the unit of analysis rather than the level of sentence or speech act, and the student abroad is well positioned to analyse events at this level.

Saville-Troike (1982), in her introduction to the ethnography of commu-nication suggests that to be communicatively competent speakers need:

- knowledge of the social structure;
- an understanding of the values and attitudes related to language;
- a network of conceptual categories resulting from shared experience;
- an understanding of the way knowledge and skills are transmitted.

These are, of course, broad areas and students can bring with them from their home environment only some general frameworks to guide their experiential learning. For example, knowledge of the social structure includes some understanding of how social categories are ranked and the ethnography course includes a unit looking at how language is a marker of social categorisation in female/male encounters (Unit 6). Language related values and attitudes include assumptions about what counts as 'good' or 'appropriate' language and how language functions in the formation of social identity (see below and Unit 14 of the course). Conceptual categories include the type of models and metaphors discussed above in the section on cognitive anthropology and referred to again in the section below on linguistic and cultural relativity. Students are encouraged to develop their understanding of these categories through analysis of ethnographic interviews (Units 9, 10, 11 and 12). Finally, an understanding of the way knowledge and skills are trans-mitted is the theme of Unit 7 of the course on education and socialisation in which students use classroom interaction data to examine educational processes as cultural reproduction.

More recently, the ethnography of communication has moved away from an exclusive analysis of formal, ritual events in faraway settings and towards the more informal routines of everyday life usually in complex urban environments. Interactional sociolinguistics studies these everyday encounters, combining ethnography of communication with *Conversation Analysis* which looks at the fine-grained detail of conversation.

Conversation Analysis (CA) is the study of the mechanisms of everyday talk in order to account for how social organisation is accom-plished through interaction. Just as many theories in anthropology challenge the notion that culture is something separate from daily activity, including talk, so CA sets out to show that society is organised not 'out there' but in the details of routine conversations and talk more generally (Atkinson & Heritage, 1984). In this respect, like much recent anthropology, it owes a great deal to a social constructivist perspective. Its concerns include how people take turns in talk (Sacks *et al.*, 1974), repair moments of trouble, start and finish conversations, especially on the telephone, and manage their institutional identity through the way they orientate to clients, customers, patients and so on (Drew & Heritage, 1992). CA does not take categories such as 'counselling', 'selling' or 'doctor–patient consultations' for granted. Instead, it asks how does the talk and non-verbal features associated with it show that, counselling work, for example, is being done. This problematising of routine categories is a useful method for language learners as they encounter otherness (Hallam & Street, 1999) and focuses them on the detail of conversational mechanisms as a means to understanding wider social formations. For example, Lacoste describes the 'work' that patients have to do in consultations with doctors. One of the pieces of data shows how uncomfortable an interaction can become if the patient's work challenges the doctor's position as the authoritative one:

(The patient, an engineer who is a diabetic, has produced a table showing his symptoms and treatment)

M: (the doctor) Je ne sais pas comment vous faîtes – pourtant vous avez l'habitude des plans et tout
I don't know how you are going about it, and yet you are used to making plans and all that
(. . .)
Ah vous faîtes comme ça, vous, ah c'est vraiment l'ancienne méthode
Aha you're doing it like that, are you? er it's really the old fashioned way of going about it
Je suis désolé hein c'est pas normal hein vous qui êtes ingénieur
I'm sorry but it's a bit odd, I'd have thought that as an engineer . . .

P: Mais c'est parfaitment logique
But it's perfectly logical
(. . .)

M: Mais je vous avais déjà dit que c'était ridicule d'augmenter d'une unité
But I'd already told you that it was ridiculous to increase the dose by a unit
(. . .)

M: Asseyez vous Monsieur c'est pas la peine // vous avez fini votre croissance
Sit down, Mr X, standing up won't make you feel any taller!
(Lacoste, 1993: 96 [our translation])

This is a very difficult consultation because the doctor treats the patient as a child since he has overstepped the mark of what constitutes a proper patient. The fact that the doctor responds to the patient's initiative by taking the floor and commenting on the patient's action shows that he is orientating to his role as the one with the medical knowledge who can take charge. The tape recording of such interactions allows for the detailed analysis of talk and indicates both how events are constructed in the interaction and how the mechanisms of talk maintain speakers in role.

In addition to the type of institutional encounters that this patient interview represents and the more informal contacts of day-to-day living, language learners who undertake ethnographic projects are constantly putting themselves into intercultural encounters. They are both participant observers of new cultural practices and are involved in negotiating the complex business of transforming strangers into informants. Any of these encounters may provide the data for their project but if they are to study them as *interactions* they need the methodological frameworks provided by interactional sociolinguistics. The methods used draw on the ethnography of communication and CA. Detailed ethnographic observations and audio and video recordings are made and transcribed. These transcriptions are then analysed both for content, attitude and the CA features of turn taking, etc. in order to build up a picture of communicative style and to trace the phases of understanding and possible misunderstanding which throw light on assumed cultural practices. In the ethnography course students are encouraged to tape record, transcribe and do a preliminary analysis of naturally occurring interactions although there is not time to give students more than the rudiments of CA.

The aim of the course, at this point, is for students to learn to combine more general ethnographic methods with a sensitivity to actual language use and the mechanisms of interaction. This combination of ethnographic and CA methods is well illustrated in Michael Moerman's suggestively titled book *Talking Culture*. As Gumperz and Hymes have also shown, these methods illuminate the ways in which social and cultural knowledge enter into talk at all points:

> In all conversation, people are living their lives, performing their roles, enacting their culture. The motives and meanings of all talk are thick with culture. (Moerman, 1988: 22)

In a number of detailed transcripts based on ethnographic work in a Thai-Lue village, Moerman shows how talk is interactionally managed but also how it takes on special significance because of local cultural knowledge the participants bring to it. In one transcript, the villagers are talking about Lue folksongs. The visiting District Officer (DO) asks about a particular performer, the pipe player, who is known in the village as 'the leper' (Moerman, 1988: 20–2). However, S, the main speaker, is anxious that the DO be kept ignorant of this information since if the pipe player was suspected of having leprosy he would be taken away to a leper colony. One of the villagers starts to name the pipe player as 'the leper' but S immediately overlaps this speech with his own description of the pipe player as a 'sick person'. In conversation analytic terms this overlap is carefully designed to blot out the other speaker's talk although the DO has been asking for clarification about who the pipe player is. The detailed analysis of talk shows how accurately, S starts his turn to hide the 'leper' information – in other words, S's overlap shows his social knowledge in managing the interaction. But without the ethnographic information about the different villagers and how important it is for S to keep the DO ignorant of the name 'leper' given to the pipe player, the overlap does not have much cultural significance.

This example illustrates the way in which social and cultural knowledge enter into talk and how talk enters into and helps to create and sustain cultural knowledge and practice. So language students, as intercultural speakers, in contact with other linguistic and cultural groups do not need to look for culture elsewhere – outside or beyond the talk. They can find it in the talk itself in the assumptions that speakers make about what is known, in their rhetorical strategies and in the way they manage their conversations. Any simple categorising of the other as 'polite', 'too direct' or 'over excited' needs to give way to an analysis of difference in which, for instance, 'politeness strategies' (Brown & Levinson, 1987) or 'conversational involvement' within a particular group's speaking practices are detailed. These in turn can be linked to a developing understanding of broader cultural themes to do with 'face' needs and wants. For example, Maria's ethnographic project was on the compliment system in Majorca. She looked at how different types of compliments indexed particular relationships. This project combined analysis of conversations and ethnography in that Maria was not simply collecting or eliciting lists of compliments but was observing how they were used to manage the 'face' needs of people in different social relationships.

This chapter has focused on 'talking culture' – on the inference-making machine – using interactional sociolinguistic theory and method. It has looked at the detailed ways in which cultural and social knowledge feed into interaction and how in turn interactions contribute to wider social and cultural themes and forms. The next chapter shifts to a consideration of language-and-cultural practice as representation, discourse and practice.

Chapter 4
Representations, Discourses and Practices

Issues of Ethnicity and Nationality

The relationship between language, ethnicity and nationality is a critical issue for language students during their period abroad. Most foreign language learning is underpinned by the assumption that these three are one: French speakers, say, are French and so have a French culture and relate to France as a nation. This is a caricature but not such an extreme one since this is how other linguistic groups are so frequently represented. Students' preparation for their residence abroad can reinforce this assumption when guidance is given about what to expect of, for example, the German or Spanish way of doing things. When students first get to know local people, they tend to either see them as individuals or think of them as representatives of a national group with that 'culture'. An ethnographic approach, by contrast, orientates students towards understanding people's identities – their roles as students, mothers, landlords and so on and their regional, ethnic and class identity. In other words, their identities as members of a particular group or community rather than as individuals or nationals.

Linguistic and cultural theories that are most relevant here are drawn from the disciplines of sociolinguistics, anthropology, discourse analysis within a social psychological tradition, and the multidisciplinary area of cultural studies. Only some aspects of these theories can be touched on in an ethnography course for language students, although some students have taken their own studies further by attending courses in these disciplines in the foreign university. In their different ways, these theories all conceive of language as a symbolic and political resource (Grillo, 1989) which constructs and reflects difference, and this sense of difference is used to assert solidarity and power. The role of language in the construction of nationality and ethnicity works in two inter-related ways: as a means of representation – to represent the community to itself and to talk about others outside it – and in interaction as a way of claiming membership of a particular social and ethnic group. In both senses language is used to categorise difference and define (and sometimes defend) boundaries.

For language students to have the intellectual tools to challenge national stereotyping when they go abroad they need to have some understanding of 'ethnicity' and its relationship to discourses of 'nation'. The sense of being different, of there being a group boundary that encloses you and excludes others is a rough definition of ethnicity (Barth, 1969; Edwards, 1985; Wallman, 1979):

> Ethnic identity is allegiance to a group . . . with which one has ancestral links. There is no necessity for a continuation over generations, of the same socialisation or cultural patterns, but some sense of a group boundary must persist. (Edwards, 1985: 10)

Traditionally, ethnicity has involved a sense of belonging, of shared social networks, of being part of a group. More recently, ethnicity has come to mean more than similarity or sharedness. It has become a much more conscious notion used to assert political and social rights and access to resources. Markers of ethnic identity have been developed or revived as 'ethnic weapons' within the larger nation-state. Since boundary marking is done through the symbolic order, language has a central role in boundary maintenance. For example, Creole-based London Black English or the language of working-class Paris suburbs function as symbolic weapons to assert difference in the face of the dominant, centralising language practices of the nation-state. Joshua Fishman, in a recent book on language maintenance among ethnic minorities, discusses the significance of boundary maintenance among groups 'forced to spend almost all of one's cultural resources on damage control, that is, on merely staying alive within a cultural reality that is not of one's own making'. (Fishman, 1991: 411).

One of the major sources of stereotyping arises because it is widely assumed that nation and ethnicity are one and the same thing. Hobsbawm (1992) quotes Massimo d'Azeglio who said, after Italy had been politically unified: 'We have made Italy, now we have to make Italians'. In other words, we have made a political unit, now we have to make a cultural one. (Just as today Europe is a political unit and there is much discussion about becoming 'European'.) The more recent forms of ethnic awareness have asserted minority rights within the nation represented by the majority but, paradoxically, the rise in new forms of nationalism based on ethnicity make it more difficult to unpick the national from the ethnic in certain geographical regions. Students who go to such a region may be inevitably immersed in issues of ethnicity. For other students, where these issues are not part of everyday discourses, some background to these concepts will make them more sensitive to what constitutes national and ethnic identity for their informants and will alert them to the hidden or more indirect ways in which ethnicity and ideas of nationhood are asserted.

Just as language has a central role in indexing ethnicity, so it is a powerful way in which the concept of national identity is maintained. The nation is represented through language (and other symbols, most obviously the flag). Language is not just a way of talking about the nation through its power to represent, it actively constructs the nation. It is, in Anderson's (1983) terms, 'an imagined community'. The process of creating this community is a mythical, symbolic and ideological process created through discourse and other representations – a construction of commonality out of difference. In other words, although nations may feel very real to us, there is nothing natural about them, as recent history in the Balkans, for example, has shown.

Michael Billig (1995) in his study of what he calls 'banal nationalism' examines how the homeland is 'flagged' on a daily basis in the media, weather reports and so on. So, every time 'Britain' or 'British' is used a statement is made about Britain as a united political, economic and *cultural* entity. Thus:

> . . . the reproduction of a nation does not occur magically. Banal practices rather than conscious choice or collective acts of imagination are required. Just as language will die for want of regular users, so a nation must be put to daily use. (Billig, 1995: 95)

When the political and cultural units are bonded together in this way, ethnic and national identities are conflated and the process of simplifying and stereotyping other groups, usually negatively, is in place. It is this essentialising of groups which much critical theory in anthropology and cultural studies has challenged, as we mentioned above. Paul Gilroy, who has been a key figure in this ongoing critique, argues that the construction of race is endemic to the process of nationalism. *In There Ain't No Black in the Union Jack* (1987) he suggests that tradition, history and culture become, in effect, codes for 'race'. So British culture is represented implicitly as white culture. Those not identified as part of this white culture are at best marginal, at worst, 'outsiders', as much racist discourse attests. Similar processes are, of course, at work in other countries where regional and ethnic differences are marginalised. In Unit 13 of the ethnography course, students are given a reading by Forsythe (1989) in which the racist discourses about the Gastabeiter in Germany are articulated in terms of cleanliness and pollution. The negative outsider images of pollution are based on the assumption that there is one German nation – 'a people'. But if Germany is represented and understood as a political unit made up of many cultural groups, then the question of being an insider or an outsider cannot be so easily resolved.

Notions of marginalisation, pollution, the swamping of 'us' by 'them' and so on, paint a much more negative picture of ethnicity than the idea of allegiance and sharedness. Hobsbawm talks of ethnicity as a way of defending 'our' territories, against . . . 'the unknown, the darkness into which we may fall when the landmarks which seem to provide an objective, a permanent, a positive delimitation of our belonging together disappear' (1992: 4). To counteract the negative ethnic stereotyping which such fear engenders, a group of researchers within cultural studies has argued for a cultural politics of difference in which we talk of multiple identities and not one identity (Hall, 1990, 1992). In this way, any individual is not simply French or British or Cameroonian but has an ethnic and regional and class and age identity as well, which is more 'real' than their national identity because it is locally realised in day-to-day living. The 'new times' in which we live (see Chapter 1) provide the social and historical conditions in which such multiple identities can be lived out.

In his book on small rural communities on the periphery of Britain, *Belonging* (1983), Anthony Cohen explores what identity means from an insider's perspective as it is lived from day to day. These studies are concerned with how people experience difference, how this difference informs the social organisation of the community and how they represent this sense of difference. People perceive themselves as different when they come into contact with another group and the sense of difference reinforces their perception of belonging to a particular group (an experience that students are bound to have in the early stages of being abroad). Although the settings Cohen describes are very different from the complex urban environments that most students will experience or which are researched within a cultural studies tradition, he makes the important point that the differences perceived by a group could be called 'culture' by outsiders. But if you are in the group you are not aware of it as culture but as identity. You think of yourself as Sevillanos, a student, a Catholic or a crofter – as belonging to that group, rather than having that culture. It is only when you come into contact with another group that your cultural and linguistic practices come into focus.

As well as language representing ethnic and national differences, the routine interactions of daily life serve to construct your sense of identity. As we saw in the previous chapter, language establishes and maintains identity. An individual's communicative style is a resource which is used to claim membership of a particular group or groups – a particular speech community (Gumperz, 1968). It may index ethnicity or as Heller (1994), Hewitt (1986) and Rampton (1995) have shown, switching between styles and codes may be used to show either that speakers want to assert their membership of an ethnically *diverse* community or, on the other hand, that issues around their particular race/ethnicity are particularly salient at that moment. For example, Hewitt showed that the black teenagers he studied used a non-ethnically marked London English most of the time but switched into Creole for strategic purposes when issues of race and racism were explicit. So language acts symbolically to give off messages about group membership and the maintenance of multiple identities. One of the students, Rebecca, explored some of these issues in her study of code-switching between Castellano (the Spanish of the majority in Spain) and Catalan spoken by the natives of Catalonia, the north-east region of Spain. She was interested in the ways in which code-switching between the two symbolised the relationship between the Castellano-speaking groups from southern Spain and the Catalan speakers (see also Woolard, 1989).

Language as a symbolic and political resource, therefore, both repre-sents and constructs what a nation is, what it is to be an ethnic minority and also signals membership of particular groups, ties to certain iden-tities. This knowledge circulates more widely in the media, in everyday gossip and comments and in institutional behaviour. Language learners as ethnographers have the dual task both of becoming aware of the discourses of nation and ethnicity and of reaching beyond them to an understanding of their own informants' sense of identity.

In attempting to do the latter, Cohen offers a helpful methodological insight. There is always the danger, he argues, of hearing the voice that a particular community uses to the wider world – for example to explain or define itself – as the voice used to its own members. A beginner ethnographer could easily assume that what they read or are told, as an outsider, is the way that community sees itself from within (see below and Chapter 5 on Bourdieu's notion of informants' data as constructed). It is all too beguiling to listen to a community's self-stereotyping to those outside. But the chances are these messages are greatly simplified and condensed. For example, as we discussed in Chapter 2, Antonia was told that, in Seville, religion and food were seen quite separately but, after a lot of participant observation and ethnographic conversations, she began to see how complex the relationship between these two was. Of course, this is not to say that an informant's self-stereotyping should be dismissed. It is, in many ways, as interesting to learn how a community presents itself to the outside world as it is to find out how they represent themselves to themselves. However, for students it is important to enter the field aware of their own and of the participants' own stereotyping of the inhabitants of this field and aware of the complex processes that bind people together, on the one hand, but keep them apart, on the other.

Students who go into the field with some background on notions of identity and some awareness of how discourse is used to represent national and ethnic identity will have some tools to help them become intercultural speakers. They should be aware of the ideologies that are used to construct national stereotypes and be critical of their own and others' identity formation as they interact together and relate to the discourses on 'nation' and 'ethnicity' which circulate.

Linguistic Relativity

So far, we have looked at language-and-cultural practices as communicative and symbolic resources in creating social and cultural identity, their potential for creating misunderstanding and stereotyping and the danger of essentialising ethnic groups, or what Hall (1992) calls 'ethnic absolutism'. This section, on relativity, draws on a more cognitive view of language-and-cultural practice to pursue the same argument and looks, specifically, at how language, symbolically, represents the world we experience.

Even a short period abroad can produce feelings of anomie – a sense of disequilibrium – but it is much more difficult for the foreign language speaker to gauge to what extent people see the world differently in terms of beliefs, values and interpretations. Does a family meal, a trip on the metro or a seminar *feel* different to a local student from the way it feels to a student from the UK when they are at home? And how is it possible to find out? Do we share universal ways of thinking and acting or do our 'distinct communicative systems' mean that we always see things differently if we speak another language?

The notion of linguistic relativity has obvious connections with the idea of socially constructed reality discussed above. It is most closely associated with Benjamin Lee Whorf and his work on the unconscious influence of language on habitual thought. Whorf himself had been influenced by Edward Sapir and his ideas that if language constructs reality, then different languages will construct reality differently:

> Human beings do not live in the objective world alone, nor alone in the world of social activity as ordinarily understood, but are very much at the mercy of the particular language which has become the medium of expression for their society. It is quite an illusion to imagine that one adjusts to reality essentially without the use of language and that language is merely an incidental means of solving specific problems of communication or reflection. The fact of the matter is that the 'real world' is to a large extent unconsciously built up on the language habits of the group. No two languages are ever sufficiently similar to be considered as representing the same social reality. The worlds in which different societies live are distinct worlds, not merely the same world with different labels attached. ... We see and hear and otherwise experience very largely as we do because the language habits of our community predispose certain choices of interpretation. (Sapir, 1949 [1929]: 162)

Whorf, drawing in part on Sapir, argued that the way in which language categorises the world for us affects our notions of time, of whether we see something as a state or a process or how we attend to a particular entity because of the name we give it (the infamous example here is the different names for snow used by Inuits):

> We dissect nature along lines laid down by our native languages. The categories and types that we isolate from the world of phenomena we do not find there because they stare every observer in the face: on the contrary, the world is presented in a kaleido-scopic flux of impressions which has to be organised by our minds – and this means largely by the linguistic system of our minds. (Whorf, 1956: 213)

Whorf was concerned with large-scale linguistic patterns in the grammar and lexis of a language. These 'fashions of speaking', as Whorf described them, influence concepts which in turn are used to interpret experience. Whorf stressed that he was concerned with the everyday concepts of what he called habitual thought rather than with abstract concepts. In turn, habitual thought influences the cultural patterns of belief and behaviour which form the social institutions of a particular community. Contrary to the over-simplified interpretations of his work that stated that there were simple and general correlations between individual features of language and cultures, that in Sapir's terms we are 'at the mercy of language', he asserted:

> a looser, more indirect connection wherein language influences culture in some cases via its effect on the habitual thought world of speakers. Specific configurations in the grammar influence thought, which then in turn influences the development over time of particular cultural institutions. (Lucy, 1992: 63)

Whorf makes the connection between immediate subjective experience and linguistically conditioned habitual thought, using the principle of *linguistic analogy*. Words and grammatical structures have a specific local meaning but people also relate to them in a more abstract, habitual sense. He gives the example of the 'empty' gasoline drums which were dangerous if workers smoked near them because they still contained explosive vapour. He suggested the word 'empty' is being used in two senses: first, a direct physical one – that the drums had no gas in them – and secondly, in a more abstract, general but *habitual* sense – as a synonym for null and void. Speakers apply the first more physical sense and then interpret it in the second more abstract sense. Since both senses are linked by the same word 'empty', speakers make an analogy between the meaning of the word in its immediate physical context and the more general meaning of the word and its wider associations. In this way, a particular word in a given language has an immediate, local meaning and also calls up wider social meanings which link speakers together into a community. To put it another way, words typify experiences.

This principle of linguistic analogy was used by Whorf in his contrastive studies of Hopi (an American Indian language) and English. For example, he contrasted English and Hopi concepts of time. He showed that in English, and other European languages, concepts of time are expressed through nouns which are treated in the same way as nouns used to refer to physical objects. This aspect of grammar joins with other patterns in English to construct a view of time as a linear presentation of discrete units. This in turn, influences the view that the past is a series of discrete happenings, separated from the present and from the acts of recording and remembering the past. In Hopi, by contrast, past events are there still in the present and it is also possible for activities in the immediate present to be happening with presumed future effect (Lucy, 1992: 61). So time is not a ribbon of activities with a clear past and future but a cluster of past, present and future.

In this and many other examples, Whorf claimed connections between language and broad cultural patterns, but not in any obvious or simple causal way. Linguistic categories, by analogy, group experiences and conceptual thinking together to form complex structures of meaning which in turn lead to related patterns of behaviour. The individual's habitual thinking, Whorf sees as the mediator between linguistic patterns and cultural practice. The ways of thinking of individuals, collectively, create dispositional tendencies towards general concepts, for example, of time, which contribute to cultural activity and organisation. For example, the home ethnography of one of the students, Chris, on despatch riders, showed that most of his informants talked of 'freedom' when asked about their work and why they did it. Collectively, the idea of going to different places each day, riding fast and often dangerously and being alone on a motorbike had led them to develop the concept of 'freedom'. Yet in many respects they were not free but were controlled by the companies who sent them on their numerous daily rides.

In the same way, Whorf does not argue that the absence of a lexical item means that the speaker cannot think about or categorise this concept, object and so on. For example, in French 'La belle mère' is used for both stepmother and mother-in-law. In English the roles and associated myths around these two kinship terms require the distinction between them to be lexically marked. But of course this does not mean that French speakers do not make a distinction between stepmother and mother-in-law. It is just that in English it is easier to use the two different terms out of context and build up mythologising stories around them such as the wicked stepmother and the 'mother-in-law' jokes so that the categorical differences between them are more attended to than in French.

More recent work on the imaginative aspects of language has looked at the cultural and linguistic relativity of metaphor (Lakoff & Johnson, 1980; Fernandez, 1991). In *Metaphors We Live By*, Lakoff and Johnson (1980) argue that 'our ordinary conceptual system is fundamentally metaphoric in nature'. For example, to look at the concept of time again, 'time' as a valuable commodity structures our lives and is expressed in many metaphors such as: save, waste, cost, invest, spare, running out of Time. Similarly, as we mentioned above, the metaphors used to produce an American cultural knowledge of marriage represent it as a fragile thing. Of all types of metaphors the ones that play the most basic role in structuring experience are what Lakoff and Johnson call the ontological metaphors – that is, metaphors about entities and substances. For example, the mind is expressed as a machine in such metaphors as 'running out of steam', 'breakdown' , 'going to pieces'. In relation to language and cultural learning, no dictionaries can explain the metaphorical structuring of language and no dictionary takes account of the fact that most of our understanding is metaphorical rather than objective. Similarly, both the capacity to use metaphor and its profoundly cultural nature is central to a language-and-cultural learning approach. And this is not only a cognitive learning but also an affective one since 'metaphorical imagination is a crucial skill in creating rapport'. Understanding how a speaker is using a metaphor – the webs of meaning entangled in it – is a way of sharing and perhaps empathising with that speaker.

For language students, Whorfian notions of relativity present an intriguing challenge. Not only, it could be argued, do they need to learn the lexico-grammatical system and pragmatic skills but also they need to be aware of the ways in which language influences habitual thought. In other words, the dispositions and habits of thinking of 'the French' for example can be understood by looking at the large-scale patterns of the linguistic code and the ways they may influence this habitual thought. This sounds both a daunting task and, indeed, an essentialising one. Luckily, recent rethinking of Whorfian notions of relativity, while still claiming its importance, have reconceptualised it to counteract its apparent essentialising tendencies and to ground it in the local and everyday uses of language where language learners as ethnographers can work with it to develop their intercultural competence.

In *Rethinking Linguistic Relativity,* Gumperz and Levinson (1996b) argue that relativity remains a significant concept in our understanding of the relationship between thinking, language and cultural practice. Despite the many criticisms of Whorfian theory and his analysis of Hopi, particularly from those working in the cognitive sciences, linguistic relativity, according to Gumperz and Levinson, is a notion which, if extended, helps us to see how people make sense to each other and how such meaning making is linked to wider social processes. Researchers in cognition argue that there is a universal language of thought which underpins all language and any relative differences between languages is insignificant compared with these universal constraints on cognition. The re-examination of relativity in Gumperz and Levinson's volume eschews the either/or position on universals versus relativity. Instead, they take a middle way, acknowledging that there are universals but also arguing that there are different meaning systems which reflect cultural variety: 'Universal constraints (act) as filters leaving open indefinite possible cultural variation within outer limits' (Levinson, 1996, 196).

The shortcomings in Whorfian notions of relativity are based on the assumptions that Whorf was making a relationship between a whole language and a particular world view: Hopi thinking is like this . . . etc. Although this is not tenable as a position, there is increasing evidence

that lexical and grammatical systems, in certain respects, direct our attention to ways of constructing reality. As Slobin says: 'There is a special
kind of thinking that is intimately tied to language – namely, the thinking
that is carried out, on-line, in the process of speaking' (Slobin, 1996: 75).
In his cross-linguistic studies with young children, he found that English,
German, Hebrew, Spanish, Russian and Turkish differed in the ways in
which, for example definiteness, progressiveness, aspect, spatiality and
so on were encoded. Sometimes, for instance, English and Spanish were
similar, as in their use of aspect, but in other areas, for example, German
and English were more similar in the attention given to trajectory rather
than location and so on. These differences affect the way in which particular language speakers experience the world because events and states
are categorised differently in their use of grammar. But it is not possible
to say that a German speaker categorises the world differently from, say
a Turkish speaker, but rather that particular linguistic domains will be
similar or not to linguistic domains in other languages.

Similarly, since categorisation has an imaginative aspect, certain lexical
items and concepts will have associations in one language which they
will not have in another. Lakoff gives the example of the category of
'mother'. In many Western societies this category includes women who
have given birth to children, women whose eggs have developed into
children, women who are given the legal right to raise children and
women married to a father. This category will be different in other societies and indeed groups within societies and will, as social constructivists
assert, construct reality along somewhat different lines:

> Cultural categories are real and they are made real by human action.
> Governments are real. They exist. But they exist only because human
> beings conceived of them and have acted according to that concep-
> tualisation. In short, the imaginative products of the human mind
> play an enormous role in the creation of reality. (Lakoff, 1987: 208)

Another limitation of Whorfian relativity is that it is confined to lexis
and grammar and appears abstracted from actual local language use,
despite his assertions that it is not. Once relativity is extended to
discourse and context, then it connects to networks of people interacting
and not to abstractions, such as 'language' and 'culture':

> If meaning resides in interpretive practices, and these are located in
> the social networks one is socialised in, then the 'culture' and
> 'language' bearing units are not nations, ethnic groups or the like –
> they are not units at all, but rather networks of interacting individ-
> uals . . . (Gumperz & Levinson, 1996a: 11)

If we look at what people actually do when they communicate, in the way that interactional sociolinguistics suggests (discussed above) then we can see that meaning is always tied to and is relative to particular contexts. The holiday postcard which says 'Wish you were here' only has meaning if there is some shared agreement about where 'here' is. For the postcard writer, 'here' is a sign or index, pointing to a particular place or set of experiences which the reader either has to imagine or recall from memory. Similarly, one of the French bourgeois families, studied by Le Wita (1988), in using and referring to the grandparents' silver spoons, was creating meanings which were tied to a particular cultural context. As part of a small elite community, talk about the family silver reaffirms or indexes their heritage as a bourgeois group, calling up memories of 'a way of life' which are not so much 'French' as 'Parisian Bourgeois' and from a family located in a particular position within this community. Because language has this *indexical* function – always linking words to the particular context in which those words are spoken – meanings are local and situated. Indeed, language socialisation is the process of assigning particular forms of language to indexical meanings (Ochs, 1997). Just as the child learns over time to interpret, for example, when 'no' really means 'no', so the language student, resident in a new community has to learn how meanings are relative to that particular community, or network of interacting individuals.

The focus on local interactions and typical ways of communicating within a network or community as a way of understanding linguistic relativity does not mean that we should ignore the idea that language and culture are treated as abstract, homogeneous entities. People will go on talking about 'the Germans' or how Polish is a very 'direct' language and so on; and language and culture will continue to be used as symbolic and political resources to assert national identity. What is important is to recognise that these are ideological formations (Gumperz, 1996: 401) used in discourse to maintain group identity or to assert difference. This recognition is significant for language students, generally, but for language learners as ethnographers the task is to set aside these stereotyping assumptions and learn about local practices and the intepretive principles used by the community of which they have become a part or which they are studying. They can then compare these *situated meanings* with the ideologically formed generalisations commonly used to talk about language and national groups. It is the situated, conventionalised discourse habits of this group that they need to learn so that they can move from understanding differences in some general way to an appreciation of the relative and specific meanings of language use.

This engagement with 'otherness' on the ground is part of the decentring process which challenges negativity and anomie.

Participant observation is the most obvious means whereby students will learn about and possibly acquire the discourse habits of a community (see Chapter 5). Another ethnographic method is to use an approach called *ethnosemantics* (introduced to students in Unit 10 of the course). It is concerned with the cultural categories that people use to make sense of their worlds and it is a somewhat more formal and explicit way of drawing out these categories from the stream of speech in which they are embedded. The three elements of ethnosemantics are:

- recording of natural interactions and eliciting stories and anecdotes about key folk terms;
- the systematic eliciting of key folk terms – for example, by asking people to finish a sentence with the key word in it;
- a description of an informant's cultural knowledge based on this data collection.

The study by Agar (1991) that we referred to in the previous chapter is an example of an ethnosemantics study. He looked at the uses of the Viennese term 'Schmäh' – a word with rather different meanings in Germany. He dubbed this a 'rich' word 'heavily puttied' with associations which gives a particular insight into aspects of Viennese life. Similarly, Sophie, in her study of the *carnavaliers* in Nice, found that for the older men, a central concept was that of 'fierté' (pride) in their role. What this notion of pride meant to them and how it affected the way in which the carnavaliers' work was gendered became an important element in her ethnographic project.

So, current thinking about relativity takes an increasingly ethnographic view. There are universals and, indeed, we would not be able to begin the process of understanding different languages and cultures if there was not what Clark (1996) calls 'common ground' in the ways we think and the beliefs we have. But this common ground may not take us very far as any attempt to translate will show. The problem for the language learner is to find out where the common ground ends and this can only be done by learning, over time, from local contexts. Hymes' comments about ethnography in his own country, the USA, are equally relevant for the language learner setting out to learn about a new group or set of practices:

> The validity of knowing about persons, families, neighbourhoods, schools and communities in our country depends upon accurate and adequate knowledge of the meanings they find and impute to terms,

events, persons, and institutions. To an important extent, such meanings cannot be taken for granted as uniform, even within a single
city or school district, nor as known in advance. The overt forms
may be familiar – the words, the attire, the buildings – but the interpretation given to them is subject to shift, to deepening, to fresh
connecting up. (Hymes, 1996: 9)

Discourse, Text and Practice

We have argued, from different perspectives – studies of interaction,
notions of identity and the idea of relativity – that generalised abstractions about language-and-cultural practices are ideological formations.
These are certainly powerful abstractions in providing stereotypes of
national and linguistic groups but they are both unreliable and potentially dangerous if their ideological basis is not acknowledged. As we
have said, in order to understand how people can interpret each other
and the texts they produce, we have to study what people actually do
under specific local conditions. In other words, we have to understand
their practices.

So far, we have referred to both 'discourse' and 'practice' without
discussing how we are using these terms or their value in designing an
ethnographically based language learning project. This section looks at
recent theories on discourse and practice and connects them to texts –
both those studied within the tradition of Cultural Studies (see Chapter
2) and ethnographic texts, whether those of professional ethnographer
or the projects written by language learners. The purpose of this discussion is to see the links between some of the theory which is so influential
in Cultural Studies and the idea of language learners as ethnographers
and, in discussing some of this theory, to take somewhat further the
arguments initiated in Chapter 2. We suggested there some of the limitations of a textually based Cultural Studies and we want to consider
here how the relationship between discourse and practice contributes to
our argument for an ethnographically based cultural learning project.

Discourse, as we use the word in this book, draws on two broad
traditions of the term. The first, which can be characterised as the Anglo-
American tradition stemming from the functional linguistics of Firth and
Halliday, can be roughly defined as situated language use. Real-life interactions are recorded and written texts analysed. The main concern here
is a linguistic one: How do texts hang together? How is information
structured through syntax and prosody? How do styles of speaking call
up certain types of knowledge and assumptions about the world?

The second tradition, the 'continental one' can be defined more broadly as the systematic organisation of meanings and values in language . The study of discourse at this level focuses on how such meanings come to be produced and circulated (Foucault, 1972) and, therefore, on the ideological orders which determine language use. This tradition, with its emphasis on ideological orders, forms part of the critical approach mentioned above and tends not to immerse itself in actual language use but to remain at the level of social theory. Nevertheless, this tradition has been enormously influential in contributing to an understanding of how institutions are held together by talk and how such institutional discourse serves to determine the way in which people see the world. The language of institutions defines a particular set of concepts such as 'madness' or 'sexuality', a particular set of subject positions, such as 'the mentally ill', and a set of assumptions about what can and cannot be said. As Fairclough suggests: 'Discourse makes people as much as people make discourse' (Fairclough, 1989). Some recent studies in discourse analysis and sociolinguistics, such as critical discourse analysis, show the influences of both types of discourse – discourse as immediate language use and discourse as the production and circulation of knowledge. The issues that many theorists study today concern the relationship between the actual use of language in particular contexts and wider discourse formations (what Gee (1992) calls 'discourse' and 'Discourse').

Some of the language students used both discourse traditions in their ethnographic projects. For example, Rachel, who carried out her project with blind students at Marburg University in Germany, had to find out what discourses they used to talk about the fact that they could not see. The discourses used in relation to a disadvantaged group by the state or the media may be different from the discourses that the group uses about itself. The blind students' discourse was of independence, of cutting ties with their family, rather than reflecting the official, often patronising, discourses of disability. The ethnography student, as part of her study of what it means to be a blind student in Marburg, also observed and took notes of their language use in everyday interactions in the student canteen and residences. She was interested in understanding how they participated in conversations with their sighted peers and how they negotiated their different identities: as students, as having regional identities and as blind people. In this way, she drew on the two discourse traditions which are frequently treated as incompatible.

Students usually assume that people are free agents and are unaware of the power of discourse. The idea of discourse as language use often implies, simply, that the language user has the right to choose what he or she has to say, that in effect, language works autonomously. A more critical or ideological view of discourse sees discourse processes themselves as largely determining what people say. As Fairclough suggests, discourse is closely related to ideology. Within the Ealing ethnography project, we aimed to help students understand these two perspective – people choosing what they say and people being determined by what they say – and to see them constantly in tension. So, Quino, the little five-year-old growing up in Seville who Antonia studied (see Chapter 2), learns the discourses of Spanish catholicism which position him as a believer, but he is also an individual and creative agent who chooses to ask questions about the Christmas traditions and how the poor can manage to keep them up.

Although discourses are both oral and written, cultural studies tends to analyse written or media texts to bring out the ideological resonances of such topics as gender, popular culture, life-style and national and community politics. The close analysis of such texts alerts readers to the situated language use of media texts, political speeches and so on. They also create an awareness of the wider discourses which circulate and which constitute knowledge and power. As such, they bring a critical, analytical and ideological component into the language curriculum. However, there are two main difficulties in presenting text-based discourses in the tradition of cultural studies as a model for cultural learning. First, cultural learning cannot be limited to these text-based discourses. The discourses of texts do not make a life. As Tambiah (1968) says: 'Cultures and social systems are, after all, not only thought but lived.' Cultural learning needs to include the felt reality of everyday life, its bodily experiences and the mundane discourses of routine living. Secondly, cultural studies texts and approaches are not geared to the intercultural learner. As foreign language learners, students may 'read off' generalised values and beliefs from texts in an unproblematic way since cultural experience is limited to these texts. Discourses in texts from their own literacy world, draw readers into a dialogue with their own experiences. We bring to bear on a text both our memories of past events and thoughts and our immersion in the current flow of life and so a knowledgeable, highly differentiated and often critical and sceptical orientation to what we hear and read. For foreign language learners these same texts may reinforce difference or at best contribute to a thin, cognitively based knowledge of other conceptual systems. Text based discourses are an essential part of cultural learning but they need to be allied to the lived experiences

– the actual social practices which make individuals part of a group. To put it another way:

> You can use native speaker text in the classroom, but you cannot replicate the conditions of native speaker discourse. (Widdowson, 1995: 170)

As well as text-based discourses, language learners need to be immersed in the *practices* of a particular group. The practice of a group or a society can be defined as both the behaviour and the social and cultural conceptualisations that give meaning to this behaviour in different social contexts (Hymes, 1974). So practices include the everyday events which characterise our social lives and the folk models and ideologies which underpin them (Barton, 1994; Street, 1993). For example, the 'paseo' or regular evening walk down the main street of a Spanish town is more than a leg-stretching exercise before dinner. Traditionally, it was a way in which families could be seen together and young men and women could manage the business of early courtship without honour being lost (Gilmore, 1987). It is a social practice. Similarly, the bureaucratic negotiation of identity and acceptability in picking up a registered letter from the Post Office, the rituals of Sunday lunch or the formal introductions and chairing of a business or academic meeting are all practices combining functional behaviour and conceptualisations that give meaning to that behaviour, rooted in specific cultural processes and specific social contexts.

Of course all these activities include discourses. They are part of everyday practices and they are also used to talk and write about these practices. For example, a speech by a British politician about the need to tighten up regulations regarding housing benefit so that foreigners from continental Europe cannot exploit the system, is an example of one kind of *practice* experienced differently by those who hear it, depending on their political persuasions. The speech is made up of different discourses which may include the discourses of nationalism, the family, the economy and so on. But there will also be talk and writing about this speech which may draw on similar (supporting) or different (contesting) discourses. For some of the audience, the discourse of nationalism, keeping British resources for the British, calls up a system of values and beliefs which includes patriotism, fair play, the village cricket match and so on. For others, such discourses are representations of xenophobia, inequality and stigmatisation of vulnerable groups.

However, such a speech might produce other practices of which discourse is only a part. For example, there might be demonstrations against an unfair housing system, a fringe theatre play about the experience of migration, a row in a pub and so on. All these are different social practices involving activity, the physical and material world and so on, as well as discourses. Students need to be not so much aware of discourses as social practice as of practices which include discourse.

So 'culture' is more than discourse-based text. It is the lived experiences of groups and individuals as they act out their social roles and make meanings out of the ebb and flow of everyday life. 'Practice' includes the discourses of political speeches, gossip and so on but is not limited to them. To experience the practices of others, students need to interact with them and, in its most complete form, live in the new community, communicating in a second (or third or fourth) language and simultaneously participating in the practices of that community and studying its discourses. This may involve sitting in a university cafeteria, participating in a conversation about the kind of contact and relationships their peers sustain with their families and at the same time monitoring and mentally recording the way in which 'family' is being talked about and the different meanings and values attached to that concept by participants. It also means being aware of the physical setting and bodily presence of the others since all this is part of the event called 'chatting about families' as the section below discusses.

The relationship between discourse and practice is also important for language learners as they come to write their ethnographic projects. Here a rather different relationship between the two terms is offered by Bourdieu (1977). He uses the terms to distinguish between *discourse* – the process of analysis – and *practice* – the act of participation (similar to the contrast made by Habermas between *talk* and *discourse* (Habermas, 1987). The problem, as Bourdieu suggests, is that we can only study practice by bringing it to the level of discourse. The point here is that although an enormous amount of everyday life is carried out through language, it is only when we analyse and reflect on how it orders our daily practices, in other words, when we abstract it from those practices, as Bourdieu suggests, that we can see its power to organise our beliefs, values and meanings. Language learners as ethnographers face quite a daunting task in learning to make sense of the practices and discourses that surround them while abroad. But they are also in the enviable position of seeing those practices from the outside and so are able, as they lurk and soak, to carry out a form of running discourse analysis. They may do this, anyway, but, usually, only implicitly. The aim of the ethnography project is to make this process explicit. This is not to deny the importance of experiencing the practice – the sense of 'being there' – which is at the centre of the ethnographic experience. Students are encouraged to value this experience in their ethnographic texts in describing as vividly as they can the sights, sounds, smells and movements that they have observed and been part of.

The ethnographic projects are made up of practices brought to the level of discourse – in other words to a level where they can be analysed. They are also texts – a written document – subject to the same kind of critical analysis and deconstruction as any other text. As students draw patterns and themes out of the data collected on a group's practices, so they begin to find concepts, metaphors, comparisons and so on which begin to form a particular discourse for representing the other. These representations are then written up as an ethnographic text. Cultural learning occurs through the ethnographic text constructed at the boundary between ethnographers and their informants. This learning depends crucially upon the ethnographer's notion of *reflexivity* – the capacity to critically reflect upon your own practice as you carry out the business of 'translating hard work "in the field" into texts of cultural representation and interpretation' (Atkinson, 1990: 181). Sophie writing about the *carnavaliers* in Nice described some of this process when talking about what she thought a good ethnographic project should be like:

I suppose explaining about their life – cultures – a group's life – as clearly and as accurately as possible, really sort of explaining and sort of finding interesting ties between people I've interviewed – finding interesting concepts from them – loads of data – and verbatim data- then analysing afterwards – straight from the horse's mouth . . . and your own personal thoughts as well – reflexivity – how people accepted you as a researcher . . . trying to make comments of a reflective nature – myself – about the nature of each informant, and the source – where I got the information from – as to why it may or may not be a meaningful piece of data – either given or received and interpreted and what have influenced what I actually put in the main part as data.

We mentioned above some of the limitations of cultural learning based only on text, but where the text is produced by the students themselves then it becomes a significant element in the learning process, if it is treated with sufficient reflexivity. The act of writing (like the act of reading) is itself a construction of social reality . It is not a 'virtual culture' transmitted to the written page, but a rhetorical act of persuasion. As the writer selects a particular image and constructs an argument, they are using their 'ethnographic imagination' (Atkinson, 1990) to move from the observation of social practices to an intellectual representation of them. It is indeed an act of translation and in this process the writer's own discourses and cultural knowledge are implicated. For example, a student who chooses to write about bull fighting had to be reflexive about the language she used to describe this event. She had to be aware that her writing about it was constructing a particular view of it – not *the* view and she had to consider her own feelings about and judgements of the experience and how she could include this in the project without merely substituting evaluation for description. Chapters 5 and 9 take further the issues around language learners as producers of ethnographic texts.

Non-verbal Communication and Use of Social Space

In the previous section we discussed the need to think of cultural and social practices and not just discourses. Included in the notion of 'practice' are behaviour and activities which move us away from an overly linguistic view of 'language-and-culture'. This may sound something of a paradox since so much of this book is about the relationship between language and cultural practices. However, an ethnographic perspective is one which sees language and culture as inextricably interconnected *because* language is not viewed in a narrow sense and *because* culture is not seen as some abstraction. 'Culture is a verb' and implied here is human action in all its materiality not just as a speech act or abstract concept. Similarly, much of what makes up what Hymes calls a speech event is not speech at all in any narrow definition of the term. And although students may be studying such cultural themes as the notion of passion in Sevillano dance, it is of course the dance movements and rituals around the dance which are the subjects of the discourse. In a critique of the logocentric view of orality – a narrow view of communication as being only about words – Ron and Suzie Scollon suggest replacing 'orality' with 'somatic', from the Greek for 'body', making reference to the idea of the human body as the foundation of communication (Scollon & Scollon, 1995: 25).They give as an example the speech event of a casual conversation over coffee and suggest that a transcript of the conversation leaves out or marginalises important elements. These include the way people sit around the table; the way these positions were negotiated, even the buying of the coffee itself. Much traditional discourse analysis also overlooks all the bodily gestures involved with the interaction. In effect, except for language use, all the different ways in which people present themselves and use social space (Goffman, 1972) have tended to be ignored in discourse studies.

Much recent criticism of discourse analysis has centred on this logocentric view of communication. Short pieces of transcribed language abstracted from their physical contexts, it is argued, cannot make claims to represent face-to-face communication with all its complex modes. Discourse analysis lacks ecological validity (Cicourel, 1992). In other words, we need the wider context in which discourses are embedded if we are to understand them from an insider's perspective. If we are to make sense, for example, of how nurses run a ward, how a pétanque club functions or how transvestite prostitutes constitute themselves as a group, ethnographic studies and discourse analysis go hand in hand. The whole person is involved in cultural and social practices and it would be misleading to present 'wording' as the equivalent of 'meaning'. So, the language student while resident abroad, needs to combine an understanding and use of discourse with an ethnographic *eye* as well as ear. In fact, Foucault's original definition of discourse as the complex of signs and practices that regulate how we live did include this bodily and physical element but this aspect has become suppressed in the linguists' notion of discourse.

The original notion of discourse relates to Bourdieu's (1991) notion of *habitus*. This is a set of dispositions which incline us to behave in a certain way. These dispositions to move, talk, think and feel are learnt from our earliest years and operate below the level of consciousness. It is what we are socialised into and give us 'a practical sense or "feel" for the game' (Thompson, 1991: 13). To the extent that we acquire a particular habitus, we are ethnographers from the moment we are born:

> Our ability to learn ethnographically is an extension of what every human being must do, that is, learn the meanings, norms, patterns of a way of life. (Hymes, 1996: 13)

These dispositions to act, perceive and feel are 'regular' without being consciously governed by a rule:

> Through a myriad of mundane processes of training and learning, such as those involved in the inculcation of table manners ('sit up straight', 'don't talk with your mouth full', etc.) the individual acquires a set of dispositions which literally mould the body and become second nature. The dispositions produced thereby are also *structured* in the sense that they unavoidably reflect the social conditions within which they are acquired. (Thompson, 1991: 12)

The idea of habitus clearly has links with the new approaches to relativity discussed above and to the earlier section on interactional sociolinguistics. Provided that it is not used to make simple equations between, for example, a certain way of talking and behaving and a particular ethnic group, it is a useful reminder to students that cultural learning is about understanding otherness as a bodily as well as a linguistic experience. Becoming interculturally aware and competent assumes an understanding of the 'habitus' of others, including their bodily movements and reactions and their routine and ritual use of space. For this reason, early in the ethnography course (Unit 3), students are introduced to notions of non-verbal communication and social space, and methods for collecting data to make sense of them. For example, students read a home ethnography by Anna, one of the first students who participated in the ethnography programme. She studied the use of non-verbal communication and social space on the London Underground. Anna observed the many different ways in which, paradoxically, train travellers used their awareness of others to avoid any physical or gaze contact with them. Their fine-tuned adjustments – shifting an arm or tweaking a newspaper – were in reaction to other passengers and thus were part of a social event despite the apparent lack of social contact between them.

Travelling and the Intercultural Speaker

Anna's study of London travellers links to the final theme of this chapter – culture as travel. We have argued that there are a number of linguistic and cultural theories which underpin the notion of language learners as ethnographers. These are valuable both for staff designing a relevant programme and for students if they are to understand the process of cultural learning from ethnography. The whole ethnographic process from participation to writing, if carried out within a conceptual framework based on the theories outlined here, provides conditions for intercultural learning. This ethnographic journey from 'lurking and soaking' to wrestling with text both actively creates opportunities for learning and requires at least a minimal level of intercultural competence. The first enquiries that lead to finding informants are intense moments of intercultural contact so starting an ethnographic project draws students, early on, into negotiating with people from the new community. Similarly, the act of writing an ethnographic text is an intercultural journey because the writer is *committed* to translating cultural understandings from their own experience in the field into a text for readers without this experience. The metaphor of the journey is an apt one since intercultural learners and communicators, as we suggested in Chapter 2 are always travelling, always in-between.

Kramsch (1993, 1995), borrowing ideas from Bakhtin and Bhabha, conceptualises the intercultural learner as in a 'third space'. Here no participant in interaction is completely culturally or linguistically competent. Bhaktin has argued that even a 'native' speaker can never completely learn a language since it is made up of diverging, connecting and dialoguing discourses. In intercultural communication, therefore, native and non-native speakers are still learning their own languages and are meeting in a new space where both are non-native speakers. This is, perhaps, a marginal space where the experience of difference becomes central and where what was thought to be central – the nation, the national language, a homogeneous ethnic group, with its long historical additions and shared practices – begins to be marginalised. This is also the experience of the traveller more generally. So perhaps a useful metaphor for culture is not just as an inference making machine or as a verb, but as travel. Clifford argues that it is more apt to think of the ethnographer not so much in the field, dwelling in a place which is defined as separate and different from home, but as travelling and being with a group who are also travelling (Clifford, 1992). By this he means that the ethnographic experience abroad is not one in which the ethnographer is cut off in some remote island (physical or metaphorical) but is moving between the home world and the world abroad. This may be either physical travel (for example, students returning home for the Christmas break in the middle of their period overseas) or travelling between home and away experiences via satellite television, the internet or friends resident in the same place. Similarly the group the students are writing about may themselves be travellers, even familiar with the home of the student ethnographer, and if not physical travellers then part of the global village through international media.

Clifford argues that ethnographers and those they have contact with are both dwellers and travellers. There are always elements of continuity and discontinuity, of feeling at home and feeling displaced, of feeling at the centre and feeling on the margins. Clifford (1992: 92) says the question should be: 'Not so much "where are you from?" but "where are you between?"'. Those living on the borders, for example between the USA and Mexico, are a good example of those struggling between two countries. The metaphors of 'borders' and 'crossing' (Rampton, 1995), and the larger metaphor of travel remind the language learners as ethnographers that the experience of doing

ethnography is one of intellectual and emotional travel; that the informants they meet are also travelling and, like them, are hybrid creatures
full of their own difference and contradictions but not necessarily
inherently different in a pure sense; and that the process of becoming
interculturally competent is part of a journey which continues even
after they have returned 'home'.

Chapter 5
Ethnography for Linguists

We concluded the previous chapter with the metaphor of culture as travel in order to emphasise both the 'in-betweenness' of intercultural experiences and to make explicit the journey that language learners as ethnographers need to undertake if they are to become intercultural speakers. 'Ethnography' is an obvious choice for linguists to turn to because it combines extended communicative experience with the study of cultures, as we have already suggested. In other previous chapters, we have referred to some of the ways in which an anthropological and ethnographic perspective might contribute to cultural learning; in this chapter we step back a little to describe the ethnographic tradition and how its methods are relevant for linguists.

Ethnography in Anthropology

The concept of 'ethnography' has a specific history in European intellectual traditions and this section briefly recounts some of the meanings and the contests over meaning that have emerged in the past century of use, on the premise that they continue to underpin current usage though often in hidden ways. Different disciplines have their own preferred histories and lay special claim to the concept. We attempted to be conscious of these struggles and claims as we drew up a course based on 'ethnography'.

Social anthropologists in Britain have a well-defined myth of ancestry that gives a key role to ethnography in the emergence of the discipline. The story is told of Bronislaw Malinowski, a Polish émigré who went to the Trobriand Islands as an anthropologist to do what was then traditional survey type social research (Kuper, 1983). At the outbreak of the First World War he was treated as an alien subject and given the choice of spending the war in an Australian prison or of living in the Islands under the jurisdiction of a British Commissioner. He chose the latter and proceeded to make a virtue of necessity by then learning the local language, 'living with' local inhabitants and observing their customs and practices 'from the inside'.

On returning to the UK he presented this approach as a key to under-standing native ways of thought and proceeded to write a number of celebrated 'ethnographies' about the Trobriand Islands, their sexual customs, economic systems and beliefs (Malinowski, 1922). He obtained a lecturing post at the London School of Economics and became a 'founding father' of modern anthropology. Nineteenth-century anthro-pologists had worked mostly through surveys, either conducted themselves or, in the case of Sir James Frazer, from accounts by travellers, missionaries and district commissioners who corresponded with him. Malinowski's experience became the basis for a new tradition, that of ethnographic fieldwork; living with the 'natives' became a neces-sary rite of passage for entering the discipline of anthropology, and the core texts of the discipline became those ethnographies written by field-workers.

Students of anthropology in British universities today are still exposed to these early texts, though now often framed by current theoretical and ideological perspectives, while new fieldworkers continue the tradition and provide new ethnographies for anthropology courses. Anthropology claims a special prerogative over this sense of ethnography, as the expe-rience of living with 'other' peoples and learning their language, then reporting on their findings in large academic monographs. Students and researchers using the concept in other disciplines are frequently made to feel that they are not 'proper' ethnographers, especially if their 'field' experience is restricted to their own society or to brief studies.

Other disciplines have, nevertheless, made their own claims to the term. In the USA the 'ethnography of communication' tradition, that emerged out of a combination of anthropology and linguistics, has estab-lished its own credibility and its own literature. As we have briefly discussed in Chapter 3, the ethnography of communication can be carried out in our own society and on a specific event or set of events such as the classroom, the courtroom, a religious service or a community meeting. Students on the ethnography course can choose to write a project that focuses on a particular speech event and one of their assignments is to undertake a mini-classroom ethnography of one of their own classes.

Anthropology itself has recently become more self-conscious and critical of its early heritage, in particular the colonial overtones of Malinowski and other 'founding fathers' and has now begun to explore the nature of the ethnographic account itself (Fardon, 1990; Asad, 1980). Asad and Dixon (1985), for instance, have critiqued the ways in which the metaphors used by anthropologists both in their fieldwork experi-ence and in writing it up, to represent apparently technical issues, such as landholding arrangements or leadership, are actually located in

Eurocentric politics and epistemology. They cite a description by Frederick Barth, of Pathans in Swat, northern Pakistan, where tenants' 'loyalty is for sale to the highest bidder', and landlords may 'slough off dependants' at will, but also provide followers with 'the spoils', and distribute 'the loot'. Here, they argue, images from European culture are being invoked which may not be appropriate to the time or cultural group under consideration. Barth, they claim, represents Pathans as though their social relations were entirely 'contractual between highly competitive individuals always concerned to maximise their interests'. Asad and Dixon argue that these metaphors are inappropriate for translating the concepts of exchange and power embedded in Pathan society, in which class, hierarchy and constraint may be more appropriate ways of understanding social relations than the language of utilitarian individualism derived from Barth's own society. Such critiques may apply to many accounts by anthropologists, and current training in the discipline requires students to be sensitised to the biases and ethnocentrism of the language they use to describe other cultures (cf. Fardon, 1990).

Clifford and Marcus (1986) in their highly influential volume *Writing Culture* have focused on the writing up of such accounts in equally critical vein. They argue that anthropologists have paid too little attention to the process of how they write their field experiences: many treat writing as a transparent vehicle for the experience itself, whereas close analysis of their texts demonstrates how much their message was dependent on the form of language and rhetoric they adopted. Indeed, Thornton (1983) went so far as to say that what defined anthropology as a discipline at the turn of the century, as it struggled to differentiate itself from travellers' tales, missionary accounts and commissioner reports, was not the experience itself – these people had often experienced longer and deeper encounters with 'natives', and knew their languages better than the anthropologists – but rather the way in which it was represented in text. The academic discourse, including the tradition of the monograph, with its classic layout into chapters based on economics, politics, religion, was itself constitutive of the discipline. In this sense ethnography is only one component of the anthropological tradition while conversely, other disciplines may use ethnography in different ways without having to locate it in the discourse of anthropology or its myth history.

For language students, data collection and analysis and the writing of the ethnographic account are equally important. They are, of course, familiar with the idea of translation but the challenge for them is not only to translate from one language to another but to present cultural practices observed in one society in terms of their own and be reflexive and critical about the process at the same time. This is a kind of cultural 'translation' as they compare the new practices with their own and find ways of writing about 'the other' which acknowledge their own role in the interpretive process. Since they are not training to be professional ethnographers, they are not expected to take on a fully critical perspective nor to read the theories of ethnographic writing in any depth. But they are expected to take on the habit of interrogating the way in which they undertake the translation process and to use this interrogation as part of their cultural learning.

Fieldwork

Reflection upon the nature and experience of fieldwork has also led to some revision of the meaning of ethnography within anthropology. Todorov (1988) has suggested that there is a fundamental contradiction at the heart of the ethnographic enterprise although he believes that this contradiction can be used in a productive and illuminating way. On the one hand, the ethnographer claims validity because he or she has some 'distance' from the ideas and beliefs of the people under scrutiny. Members of a culture often do not realise what they are taking for granted. The classic introductions to anthropology state that you do not ask a fish to tell you about water; it is so immersed in the medium that it does not realise it is water. Only by exposure to another medium – 'taking the fish out of water' – can we identify the nature of the medium we take for granted: the outside ethnographer by dint of distance from the culture can draw attention to its fundamental tenets and epistemological presuppositions – the assumptions it makes about knowledge, how it is defined and legitimated and who has rights over it.

An example from the work of Evans-Pritchard (1937; cf. also Singer & Street, 1972) brings this point home, through reference to a 'classic' figure from post-war British anthropology. Classic texts of this kind were used on the Ealing Ethnography course as the best way of introducing teachers and students to the tradition of ethnography, both as a rich source of detail and as a necessary baseline before introducing recent critical perspectives. Evans-Pritchard claimed that by coming from outside of Zande society (a people in the Southern Sudan with whom he lived during the 1950s) he was able to see what they took for granted and therefore did not articulate – namely that witchcraft accusations are not so much about individuals and their supposed wrongdoing, as about maintaining social cohesion and creating sanctions against those who would bring disorder and chaos to their neighbours by breaking the moral code. Zande did not talk in this way about witchcraft but Evans-Pritchard argued that his 'outsider' view provided a perspective that enabled people to understand witchcraft in a new and more meaningful way.

The same principle applied to members of his own society, whose views of witchcraft tend to be based in exotic and dramatic accounts of European medieval witchcraft as 'primitive' and 'unscientific'. By describing the social processes involved rather than attending to the truth or falsity of accusations or their 'scientific' validity – the perspective many European observers brought to bear – Evans-Pritchard was able to 'make sense' for his own society too of practices that otherwise appeared meaningless and 'irrational'. It was his distance from both Zande society in the first instance, and then from his own society, that enabled an alternative perspective to be brought to bear that went beyond the representations of witchcraft dominant in either society.

There is, however, according to Todorov, a contradiction in the way that anthropologists value such 'distancing'. For the same anthropologists who celebrate distance in ethnographic accounts require their colleagues to have familiarity with the local culture, derived from proximity and close, everyday interaction: in anthropological circles it is important to 'know your people' well and not simply to remain at a distance. Evans-Pritchard's credibility derives as much from his claim to intimate knowledge of everyday Zande life as to his 'distance' from them as a European. This tension between distance and proximity is the defining feature of ethnography according to Todorov.

When ethnographers go to the field, they separate themselves from their home culture and enter a strange and alien one. When they leave that culture in turn, to return home, they go through a further separation and have to re-enter their home culture, and it is here that the travelling metaphor persists. At this threshold point, the returning ethnographer can see their own culture with the eyes of a stranger: the familiar becomes strange, a concept emphasised in Agar's (1980) classic account *The Professional Stranger* (cf. also Stocking, 1983). And it is at this point that the language students write up their ethnographic projects. They bring with them not only their piles of notes and transcriptions from the experiences they have lived through but a sense of 'a feel for the game' from these experiences. At the same time, they are back home, returning to a society which is a part of them and yet is distant. In this way, the writing up of the project is a translation not only of language but of the whole social person. (See Chapter 10 for the students' account of writing up on their return.)

Gradually, however, the sense of distance, too, lessens as the ethnographer enters into closer proximity to their own everyday norms and beliefs. The likelihood is that they will return at some point to the culture they have studied and the process will happen again. Indeed, they will most likely be always mentally moving between different cultures, always shifting between proximity and distance in any cultural setting – always travelling, as Clifford suggests. This, then, is the essence of the ethnographic experience; proximity and distance held in tension simultaneously.

The experience involves three fundamental concepts: epistemological relativity, reflexivity, and critical consciousness. Epistemological relativity (linked to the linguistic relativity introduced in Chapter 3) involves recognising one's own assumptions about knowledge, and how it is legitimised in one's own society, so as to be able to view the knowledge of other societies with a more open mind. Since assumptions about knowledge are frequently hidden and naturalised, it is easy to simply impose them on other people as though they were universal. The discipline of anthropology in particular has been concerned with this relativity of knowledge and anthropologists would argue that doing ethnography involves attention to such epistemological levels and not just issues of technique and method. For this reason, early on in the ethnography course, students are introduced to the idea of cultural knowledge and the extent to which sharing it defines a community. They are asked to draw out the cultural knowledge required to make sense of one small incident in a restaurant in which a diner leaves money, presumably as a tip, on the table and one of their companions scoops up the money into their pocket while the original diner is away from the table. Issues of 'tipping', 'stealing' and 'friendship' are raised in this discussion – all of them culturally relative concepts.

Reflexivity, as we have already suggested, refers to the ability to reflect critically on the way in which one's own cultural background and standpoint influence one's view of other cultures. Lack of reflection, for instance, on the metaphors we use for describing other ways of life can, as Asad and Dixon (1985) showed, serve to impose our own views on them in subtle and hidden ways. So, for example, one student in Seville, Toni, reflecting on her view of bull-fighting after six months in Spain was able to understand it within the context of Spanish cultural practices even though she did not like it.

Critical consciousness, introduced in Chapters 2 and 3, represents a newer tradition in anthropology and views ethnography not simply as a convenient tool for studying and researching but as itself a product of particular dominant societies at a particular period. The ways in which we observe and then write up those observations need to be considered critically if they are to avoid the ethnocentrism of earlier periods of academic work. The study of foreign languages as part of liberal education emphasises their role in combating ethnocentrism but a critical perspective goes one step further. It alerts all those whose studies involve linguistic and cultural crossing, not only to recognise and relate to difference but to see that, in turn, these differences are themselves embedded in political and ideological contexts, as are our own views and ways of knowing. For language learners as ethnographers, this means not only questioning how the values and perceptions of the group they are studying came to be produced but how their own views and writing come to be valued in particular ways. A good example of this from the first cohort of students was the critical way in which one student came to understand the 'performance' aspects of identity among the inhabitants of Seville (see Chapter 10).

Ethnography for Linguists

The original questions asked by those designing the 'ethnography' course at Ealing were whether aspects of these subtler notions of ethnography could be developed among teachers and students working in different disciplinary traditions and for whom ethnography was not in itself a primary focus of their academic study. The objectives of the project included: 'the development of new approaches and methods in structuring the learning experience and the feasibility of these approaches in language courses'; in other words, using ethnography to develop 'intercultural speakers'. Bourdieu (1977), writing on the shifts between the 'language of familiarity' and 'outsider-oriented discourse', on the relationship between practice and discourse, provides a way of linking the anthropological debates to those in language studies. For Bourdieu, as for Todorov, there are problems of familiarity and distance: the native speaks a 'language of familiarity' in everyday life, but when questioned by a stranger, such as an ethnographer, tends to shift to a more self-conscious and 'constructed' language. An important theme, therefore, for the language student, is the close attention to the language of everyday talk and how it compares with the more constructed language used by informants in interviews and ethnographic conversations.

The ethnographer, at the same time, is constructing questions and working within a universe of reference that is alien to the native. The ethnographic account runs the danger of forgetting this process: 'it is understandable, then, that the anthropologist should so often forget the distance between learned reconstruction of the native world and the native experience of that world' (Bourdieu 1977: 95). This, however, does not undermine the enterprise. What a training in ethnography does is precisely to draw attention to such dilemmas, which implicitly lie beneath all cultural encounters (including those of students on year abroad schemes) so that students and ethnographers are sensitised to the differences between their own and their informants' discourse.

Central to the ethnographer's understanding, then, is sensitivity to the ways in which information is elicited, organised and circulated in the community being studied and how this might be different from the observer's own speech community. In order to understand these processes, the ethnographer must attain communicative competence in the culture under consideration. As we have discussed in Chapter 2, the concept of communicative competence refers not only to language skills but to understanding of the rich nuances of a culture and the appropriateness of when and how to use specific linguistic forms. This is congruent with that reflective sensitivity to proximity and distance to which Bourdieu and Todorov refer. Dubin (1989) points out that this view of 'communicative competence' has sometimes been highjacked by technical language trainers in the foreign language teaching tradition to imply simply acquiring a set of 'competencies': 'it is apparent that over time there has been a shift away from an agenda for finding out what is happening in a community regarding language used to a set of statements about what an idealised curriculum for L2 learning/acquisition should entail; a shift from how people in a particular culture use language to what elements comprise communicative behaviour' (Dubin, 1989: 174). For Dubin, as for us in the Ealing project, competence has a much broader and richer connotation. It is this meaning of competence that the ethnography course was concerned to facilitate for language students, combining their sensitivity to language nuances and variations with sensitivity to cultural nuances and variations. In the tradition of reflexive ethnography outlined above, this requires deep self-consciousness regarding the influence of their own background and their position as cultural mediators in their interpretations of these processes.

In designing a course to facilitate this competence, we were working always with a tension (that we hoped was a creative one) between theory and practice. On the one hand, it was important to help students understand what ethnographic perspectives could contribute by exposing them to what other ethnographers had done and to what ethnography meant at different periods and in different disciplines. On the other hand, the students were themselves going to experience the ethnographic reality of living in a different culture and speaking a foreign language for a lengthy period. Some of the theoretical and methodological issues raised in the course before their departure abroad would only make sense once they engaged in that experience. However, a key assumption of the whole programme was that the experience itself might remain relatively superficial and unreflective without that prior course work.

The linking point between these two aspects of the programme was the 'project' – an ethnographic report on some aspect of the host culture which students would research and begin writing while abroad and complete during their first term back at Ealing at the beginning of their fourth and final year. The ethnographic project would also contribute towards their final degree grades. This writing process was conceived not just as a summative assessment exercise but as an integral part of their making sense of the experience abroad. It depended, then, on their ability to relate the conceptual and methodological content of the course to their own lived experience and in this sense, also, they were learning to become ethnographers since that process is at the heart of the ethnographic enterprise, as Clifford and Marcus (1986) point out. The writing was more than simply a project report, of the kind required in Area Studies modules or for library-based projects. It required developing at least some of what Hammersley describes as the major rational for ethnography – 'developing theory through the study of critical cases' (Hammersley, 1992: 20). This sounds rather daunting for students who are not specialising in anthropology, but what it amounts to is using a concept such as 'boundary maintenance' to find significance in an observed activity and to write this up as a case. It is a way of seeing more, and of relating small and apparently unimportant behaviour to wider notions that help to structure social relations.

Mitchell's essay (1984) on case studies represents a particularly influential example of the use of ethnographic 'case studies'. Rather than applying 'enumerative induction', as in much scientific and statistical research, as a means of generalising and establishing the 'representativeness' of social data, Mitchell advocates 'analytical induction':

> What the anthropologist using a case study to support an argument does is to show how general principles deriving from some theoretical orientation manifest themselves in some given set of particular circumstances. A good case study, therefore, enables the analyst to establish theoretically valid connections between events and phenomena which previously were ineluctable. From this point of

view, the search for a 'typical' case for analytic exposition is likely
to be less fruitful than the search for a 'telling' case in which the
particular circumstances surrounding a case, serve to make previously obscure theoretical relationships suddenly apparent . . . Case
studies used in this way are clearly more than 'apt illustrations'
Instead, they are means whereby general theory may be developed.
(Mitchell, 1984: 239).

This view represents one of the basic tenets of the ethnography course
at Ealing and provided the rationale for the ethnographic 'project' or
'case study' that students were asked to undertake during their year
abroad. Their projects can be viewed as 'case studies' in this sense of
the term: as telling accounts of specific aspects of the culture they inhab-
ited that address the theoretical issues they raise in an analytic and
reflective way. This rests on an assumption that there are 'patterns' to
be found in social life that are often so taken for granted by participants
that they remain unnoticed. The stranger-ethnographer can elucidate
these because of their initial distance, with the help of appropriate
training and reflexivity, and by bringing to bear questions derived from
general theory. Assessment of the 'success' of student accounts rests,
then, on the criteria set out by Mitchell rather than on the descriptive
detail alone, or on a mechanical list of 'competencies'; the case studies/
projects are analytic expositions not inventories of exotica. So, the ethnographic case study discourages students from generalising about a
'culture' and instead leads them to find concepts and patterns which
account for the many, small and often banal aspects of social life
which they observe and hear about from day to day.

These concepts and patterns allow the student ethnographer to write
about a particular group or event at a more general level than just the
highly detailed and locally grounded account which provides the texture
of the case study. So, Antonia could write about the varied and subtle
connections between religious and eating practices in such a way that
more general patterns could be identified. But these more general
patterns or principals must always be embedded in specific and local
circumstances. The ethnographic writer can then claim that these general
patterns exist, that there is some kind of theory or set of concepts, *in*
the particular contexts studied:

> Case studies allow analysts to show how general regularities exist
> precisely when specific contextual circumstances are taken account
> of. (Mitchell, 1984: 239)

Generalisations are not about 'a culture' or even a whole group but are patterns or concepts which only stand up to scrutiny because all the circumstances in which they are found, in any one study, have been taken account of. We can say that the early socialisation of young Catholic children in Seville makes profound links between religion and eating in contexts where a young child, such as the five-year-old Quino, talks about 'bread' in the Bible and equates it with the bread on the table at breakfast, lunch and dinner. It is because of this incident and numerous others that connect with it and resonate in various ways, that Antonia could begin to see the significance of a wider pattern. By worrying away at these interconnections, like a dog with an old slipper, some general principals about Sevillano social practices began to emerge.

This summary gives a picture of the 'academic' framework within which the course designers approached 'ethnography'. How to mediate these debates to students trained in different disciplinary traditions, and more concerned with the practical application of ethnography than the academic debates about it, was the central pedagogic issue. It was probably this aspect that was the most difficult to accomplish. Students in the British educational system tend to be wary of 'theory' and have probably had little experience of explicit attention to it prior to university. Moreover, those studying language courses (where there is little or no accompanying literary or cultural studies) may also find most of their course work geared to technical skill acquisition and not be emotionally or intellectually familiar with the theoretical and methodological emphasis necessary in the kind of programme described here.

We document in the following chapters the ways in which the teachers and students involved in the Ealing ethnography project engaged in this process and the extent to which it was successful and replicable. We consider how the application of ethnographic perspectives helped clarify if not resolve questions of pedagogy in language learning; of the relationship between language and culture; and of how to make sense of the experience of living abroad that language courses perennially raise. We begin, in the next chapter which forms the beginning of the case study element of the book, by documenting the process by which the tutors themselves became involved in learning about ethnography, in learning how to design an ethnography course and in teaching that course to language students. We argue that the process itself drew upon the very principles – proximity and distancing, reflexivity and the application of theory to specific cases – that are described above as the bases of our conception of ethnography.

Part II
The Ealing Ethnography Project:
A Case Study

Chapter 6
Teaching Ethnography

We have argued in Part I that language-and-culture learning is an integrated process and that, when learners have the opportunity to immerse themselves in a community where the language they are learning is spoken, the traditions of ethnography in anthropology offer a perspective which can ensure that the experience is a rich and not just a superficial one. The challenge we set ourselves, as indicated in the preceding chapter, was to adapt those traditions and insights to the needs and perspectives of students and their teachers who saw themselves above all as 'language people' (Evans, 1988). Our purpose was, however, not simply to stop at the experimental stage. We wanted to show that the approach was generalisable, and the argument about generalisation from case study outlined in the previous chapter applies not only to the work of the students – their ethnographies – but to the 'language learners as ethnographers' project as a whole. It was thus part of the rationale of the project that a curriculum development of this kind would be generalisable to other circumstances if it could be shown that existing language specialists – whatever their qualifications and training – could adopt the principles and methods of the course. It was important that, although as a funded project there was extra support from colleagues with previous experience of ethnography, there should develop an approach which any linguist teaching advanced learners in a comparable situation could adopt.

Ethnography as Staff Development

At the outset of the project, the teachers involved had no previous knowledge or experience of anthropology and only rudimentary knowledge of ethnographic methods. They had a relatively short period of time in which to prepare to teach ethnography and several areas of development to consider:

- learning about relevant approaches in anthropology through guided reading and team discussions;

- learning about methodologies of ethnography;
- considering ways of selecting, adapting and presenting these ideas to students.

This was pre-course activity, but later the actual teaching and evaluating of seminars and supervision of projects would prove to be no less essential as staff development.

Because the planning and teaching of the ethnography course ran parallel with their own development as ethnography teachers, there was an organic relationship between the two, springing from the interaction of all participants in the project, including the first cohort of students. It is not intended that the following should be the process adopted in other circumstances, not least because we hope that this book will help others to prepare in a different way. It is not a prescription for learning to teach ethnography, but rather a case study of the experience of two members of the Ealing ethnography team, which will illustrate what was involved and provide readers with a basis for comparison of their own learning.

The first issue to be faced was that of legitimacy, and the rationale for language teachers attempting to equip themselves to teach ethnography. Would it not be more appropriate to draft in a professional anthropologist to teach the course? However, the purpose was not to take up another academic discipline, but to work across discipline boundaries, engaging with new perspectives on cultural understanding which enhanced linguists' existing knowledge on conceptual and epistemological levels. Since language programmes typically draw on a variety of discipline areas to explore the target culture, most language teachers in higher education are in fact accustomed to this breadth of approach, while also developing specific research interests in just one or two areas. Indeed, it is the norm to have to bridge disciplines to a greater or lesser extent, and this breadth and flexibility is an existing strength which language teachers can bring to a project developing an expertise in ethnography.

Furthermore, language teachers are ideally placed to select the topics and areas of interest to which they can bring anthropological perspectives since they know what is appropriate and necessary for students during their period abroad. We were aware of the extent and type of knowledge about cultural issues language students already possess, as well as being conscious of the ways in which they have acquired this knowledge. The course also builds on areas students have already examined (e.g. notions of national identity; French or Spanish family life;

political and educational systems) but to which they have usually been introduced through factual, positivistic perspectives, either in the traditional Area Studies approach to culture or in the language classroom. Often, cultural issues and cultural knowledge are an illuminating but *ad hoc* part of the students' learning, which they acquire by chance rather than by design. In an Area Studies course, the focus is usually on history and institutions, and the approach text-based rather than experiential. In language classes the approach may be more experiential and interactive but it is generally unsystematic in exploring issues connecting language and cultural practice, and is based either on texts or on the teacher's own experience. The teacher is regarded as somebody with prior knowledge of the target culture from an insider perspective, and cultural information is transmitted by her from that authoritative position. In contrast, ethnography allows language teachers to take cultural learning into a new realm by exploring cultural processes rather than delivering information about culture. It provides an important methodological and conceptual basis both for enhancing teachers' own understanding of cultural processes, and for providing students with opportunities to take a more active role in their cultural learning.

Finally, and most importantly in the Ealing project, the teachers' lack of experience of ethnography was an advantage. They were like their students in the sense of being already familiar with issues of language and culture, and needing to carry out fieldwork with limited professional resources. This meant that their own learning experience helped them to be realistic about what they could expect from students, and to make decisions about what was feasible. They were to acquire first-hand knowledge of the challenges. The remainder of this chapter is written from the two teachers' insider view of trying their own hands at an ethnographic project.

Fieldwork at First Hand

Our previous experience of curriculum development projects had generally been grounded in text-based research, but in this case there was an experiential element too. There was a phase of reading introductory works on ethnographic methods (e.g. Agar, 1980; Hammersley & Atkinson, 1983), parts of which were subsequently recommended to students, but we then chose to do ethnography as well as read about it. This gave us a similar experience to that of our students, and when during the course, a student assignment in data collection, ethnographic conversation, or self-observation was devised, we first carried it out ourselves before using it. This was not unlike a frequent exhortation to language teachers to make temporary departures from their area of expertise by learning a new language from time to time, with the intention that they will again experience second language acquisition and the issues involved. What we shall concentrate on here, then, is precisely this experiential, exploratory aspect. In particular, we felt it desirable to undertake ethnographic projects of our own, in order to gain first-hand knowledge of the problems waiting for the researcher in the field rather than simply referring students to existing accounts. The experiential nature of cultural learning is a fundamental dimension of the course, and we felt we should develop and reflect upon our own ethnographic skills before attempting to teach students to deploy them effectively and reflexively. Although this is not the only way to prepare for teaching ethnography, if time and circumstances allow, it is the ideal. In order to represent this, we shall describe two projects which were similar in several respects and which gave rise to fairly typical problems.

As we shall see later, during the ethnography course students are asked to carry out an ethnographic study of some aspect of their familiar environment in order to make them realise that this too can be analysed from an ethnographic standpoint, that ethnography is not just a means of understanding what is new but also of 'making the familiar strange'. This is called 'the home ethnography' and done during a vacation period. Those involved in teaching the course carried out a similar project with the same practical considerations of time constraints. We had to do fieldwork in an accessible environment, and decided to focus on an aspect of the workplace. Making contact with informants in the workplace was the first step of the learning process which engaged us at once with some of the practical considerations and ethical issues of ethnographic research. Framing the project sensitively so that informants understand why someone would like to learn about their lives is a challenge which the most self-confident students can find intimidating, and it was not different for us.

Ana Barro began discussing her research with two caretakers working in the same university building, while Shirley Jordan took a more formal route, negotiating access to a larger group of female cleaning staff through embarking on conversations with their supervisor. We were, therefore, able to carry out participant observation in our own environment after or before working hours, 'hanging around' with the caretakers for an hour or two after work, or with the cleaners during their early morning tea break, and learning from them about aspects of their working lives. The locale in itself instantly involved the process of 'making strange'. We discovered the limitations of our perceptions of what we had so far thought of as our own environment, and further-more while working with these informants, we had the experience of being caught between the position of insider and outsider in different parts of the university community.

The participant observation, conversations, note-taking and analysis lasted for about a term during which we had meetings with the profes-sional anthropologist member of the research team to discuss work in progress. By the end we had gained valuable experience in fieldwork, data collection and analysis, and written ethnographic accounts which could be used in teaching. One of these, 'It's Not My Job', explored how two caretakers came to define their own roles and responsibilities, going beyond their official job description to become 'care-takers' in the broader sense (through their pastoral role as advice givers to students, their inter-action with academic staff, and their management of social and symbolic space within the university). The account drew on concepts of bound-aries, exchange, reciprocity and hierarchies. The second study, 'We're Just Nobody, We Aren't', drew on a similar complex of concepts to explore the cleaners' perceptions of themselves in relation to students, supervisors and academic staff, and the strategies they had developed for interacting with these groups. For our purposes here, however, it is more useful to focus on the process of doing ethnography than to give detailed accounts of the findings.

The experiential learning in the process can be best represented in extracts from a reflection on doing ethnography written soon after:

> Initially we had believed that researching a group in our own place of work was an easy solution, but it also presented some difficul-ties. Our informants were people we worked with and encountered on a daily basis. We already had a relationship with them outside that of ethnographer and informant, and so negotiating a new role for ourselves as 'ethnographers' was not easy. Our relationship with these groups was complicated by existing notions of hierarchy; we were both conscious that we were 'representatives' of academic staff, and in the case of the project with the cleaners, informants were acutely aware of ways in which staff might perceive them. They also harboured their own strong perceptions of lecturers, and their knowl-edge of the researcher's role as 'one of them' meant they never really accepted her in her capacity as an ethnographer. Her procedure of using the supervisor as 'gatekeeper' to the group was to create misun-derstandings in the complex web of relations which fieldwork entails;

a member of academic staff apparently descending on them as 'objects of study' and imposed upon them by their immediate hierarchical superior was a source of anxiety for all concerned. The research situation was therefore politically delicate and involved the researcher in discovering and dealing with fragile relationships, sometimes in a poor state of repair. In this ethnography, it was precisely these relationships which became the main focus of research, whereas at first the researcher just saw them as an unfortunate barrier, getting in the way of what she 'really wanted to look at'. This process of letting go was a valuable lesson in flexibility and in using informants as teachers (see Agar, 1986b) rather than grafting on one's own preoccupations.

Sharing experiences of fieldwork was important and feelings of insecurity were common to both of us. It took patience and perseverance to develop what we felt was, literally, a new way of seeing, and our professional anthropologist colleague urged us to express our doubts both in field diaries and in our meetings. One of us suggested it was 'like being in deep and fast-flowing water and having to build my own raft!' The best analogy to describe part of our learning process came from a shared recent experience of learning to drive. The learner is self-conscious and overwhelmed. There are so many skills to acquire, so many aspects to be alert to, so many things to do at once that it seems hard to prioritise. Participant observation is similar in terms of its simultaneous demands: how do you observe *and* participate *and* decide what to take notes on at the same time? When can or should you take rough notes, and if you don't, how can you be sure your memories of the encounter will be sufficiently detailed and accurate? In the end, all your technical skills and heightened perception have to be combined into a synthesis which is instinctive and flexible enough to respond to different and constantly changing contexts. In addition, learning how to monitor, handle and respond to fieldwork situations are only a part of research; such skills must be interwoven with and directed by conceptual knowledge in the discovery process.

Training 'the ethnographic eye' is, then, a little like acquiring road sense, that combination of multiple skills and alertness to the environment which seem so elusive when one first sits in the driver's seat. This analogy is helpful to students who encounter the same uncertainties and frustrations, and are sometimes doubtful about how their learning will all fall into place in the end. From the start of the course they are asked to spend a long time doing what seems mundane, or recording what seems obvious, and it is only when they have sufficient data that some of their apparently banal jottings will come to make sense, revealing patterns and directions in their research. In the same way, our own experience of fieldwork taught us the importance of patient observation. We were perhaps even less willing than students to do these observations because we wanted to produce a conceptually rich piece of work and tended to go into the field and immediately draw out the concepts, pre-empting the data. This unfamiliar territory was also a threat to us as academics, although in retrospect this was one of the most useful aspects of the fieldwork. What was on the page seemed raw and unsophisticated. Was the data valid? Was there enough going on or should we try to make something exciting happen? What exactly were we going to be able to write about? What right did we have to invade other people's jobs, feelings and experiences? In addition, despite previous experience of writing academic essays, lack of familiarity with anthropological discourse meant that our writing was under constant scrutiny. Draft accounts were not always reflexive enough, not always conceptually grounded enough, not always meeting the demands of the discipline; it felt as if we had to develop a completely new voice.

Much of this is common to all learning, although particularly heightened by the experience of fieldwork and the constraints of time and place. On the other hand, there was the exhilarating feeling of setting out on new territory. We attempted to transmit this to students during the ethnography course itself, and having undertaken fieldwork meant that we could do this honestly and realistically. Students expect of their teachers not only enthusiasm, but also authority in the discipline. In this case, authority and credibility was a function of being open about how recent the learning experiences were. Students encountered a different notion of the teacher and her role in a new kind of learning environment which was exciting and often unpredictable, requiring all participants to deal with unexpected issues on the spot. The experiential nature of the course has already been highlighted and it was important that students saw this as a two-way process. It was not a case of handing down the experiences for them to undergo, but of participating in them oneself. There is a valuable point to be made here about the nature of cultural learning as a perpetual process: it is not something one can acquire and transmit, but something one continually learns by doing, by developing a different way of looking at things.

In sum, it was this experience of carrying out an ethnographic project, more than an increasing familiarity with anthropology as an academic discipline, that provided a solid grounding for teaching. The projects enriched the approach to teaching the methodological part of the course, to integrating the methodological and conceptual aspects, and to conducting individual tutorials with students engaged in research and usually struggling with the relationship of data and theory. Thus the writing up of our ethnographic projects was important. It demonstrated that ethnography is not to be equated simply with experience in the field. There is a temptation to get a feel for fieldwork and data collection, and to go no further. This is a mistake, since concerns about organising materials, thinking through issues of style, tone, the balance between description and analysis, and particularly the ways in which claims are made on the basis of data, can later be shared with students and compared with their own experiences.

Generating Teaching Materials

These projects also fed directly into the course in more tangible ways. Extracts were incorporated into the units, either to focus on specific issues, or for students to carry out more general critiques of them as examples of ethnographic writing. There was also material from field diaries, covering every stage: deciding on the project, gaining access, locating good informants, the problems of participant observation, data collection and analysis. A good example was Shirley's strong concern that her informants felt she was 'spying' on them. In this case what started off as a vague sense of unease became a valuable asset in her teaching. The whole problematic issue of finding gatekeepers – people likely to give access to informants – and gaining entry to a group was well illustrated by these experiences. She consequently felt equipped to prepare students for this, or encourage them to avoid it by not picking a group which was too external to their lives. In many ways, then, what started off as research problems became opportunities to enhance the course for teachers and for students.

Three specific examples of how material from these projects was integrated in the course units, which will be described in more detail in Chapter 7, illustrate the relationship between staff development and teaching. In a unit on 'ethnographic conversations', students carry out an assignment which requires them to identify and approach suitable informants, striking up conversation and if appropriate, explaining about the ethnographic project. Part of the follow-up to the assignment involves students working in small groups and sharing their experiences to see if they can answer the question 'What makes a good informant?'

Their findings are then compared with general criteria for good informants (Spradley, 1979) and also with findings from the project on the
cleaners. As part of this project the teacher concerned analysed the ways
in which her various informants interpreted both the research project
and their own role within it. Her comments covered issues such as the
importance of flexibility on the part of the researcher, since different
strategies of information gathering were required for different informants, and the need to abandon a priori assumptions about what would
be important in their lives. She also illustrated how some extremely
willing informants may ultimately be less helpful than those who
appear more reticent. Her most helpful informant was in fact the least
self-consciously involved, the least ready to present herself to the
ethnographer and relatively indifferent to the latter's presence during
the tea breaks.

Some of the students' findings can be related to this extract, and this
also leads them to consider the different skills required, and data derived,
when researching within a group as opposed to conducting ethnographic
conversations with one informant. Finally, the exercise is an important
reminder that the ethnographer is not the only one to have an agenda.
In this case, some informants turned to the researcher as a possible source
of information about academic staff, supervisory staff or other groups
of cleaners. Others responded to her as 'biographer' since they had
decided that writing about them meant writing about their private
histories, not their working lives: '. . . they would try to give me what
they thought I wanted, attempting to make themselves interesting as
individuals, whereas I was interested in the functioning of the group
as a whole.'

The second example relates to the unit on local level politics and
reciprocity where students explore the symbolic aspects of exchange
and look at the ways in which favours, gifts and other exchanges structure our everyday relations, and allow us to achieve and maintain an
equilibrium. These concepts formed an important part of the ethnography on the cleaners who felt they were giving a valuable service to
members of academic staff – often a personal service, since they were
prepared to undertake certain special favours not strictly within the remit
of their job, such as emptying and cleaning the coffee cups – but getting
little in return, sometimes not even what, in one of the readings for the
course, Bailey (1971), is referred to as 'the gift of good manners'. This
lack of reciprocity was one of the major factors which influenced the
cleaners' perception of themselves as a marginal group in the university community.

The third extract from staff projects is used to illustrate ways in which students may be helped to make sense of their raw data by uncovering connections and patterns within it. Indexing and analysis should ideally be constants throughout fieldwork, and students are encouraged to consolidate their notes, regularly and methodically transferring rough jottings into permanent notebooks in which data coding and interpretation are bound up with one another. However, entering into a meaningful dialogue with their data can give students as many problems as data collection itself, and they are occasionally tempted to dismiss illuminating material simply because they feel unable to account for its relation to the main categories and concepts guiding their projects. The scatter sheet from Ana's 'home ethnography' which is reproduced below (see Figure 2) shows how a conceptual diagram or 'visual map' can be a valuable method of organising and understanding data. This scatter diagram depicts an early stage of indexing notes in categories for analysis once the initial field notes had been carried out. The numbers in the circles refer to the page numbers in the notes. According to the clusters of references, the writer was able to organise data into categories and check back with informants before the final writing up of the project.

Here, headings and sub-headings form a cumulative contents page – some conceptual and some relating to purely descriptive phenomena – are jotted at random onto a single sheet. A 'mental map' of connections is then established which can often reveal previously unrecognised patterns, point to gaps in the research, and enable the ethnographer to give more coherent and persuasive accounts of the data.

Students also use longer extracts from staff projects for critique, just as they do with the home ethnographies of previous students which have been integrated with the course material. They are asked to concentrate on key questions:

- What anthropological concepts does the project draw on?
- How is it structured?
- Can examples be found of where the writer is reflexive about her data?
- How does she combine generalisation and detailed examples?
- How does the writer use the detailed language of her informants to make general points about their sense of identity?

This is one important way of making students aware of the considerations they will be expected to account for in their own ethnographic writing.

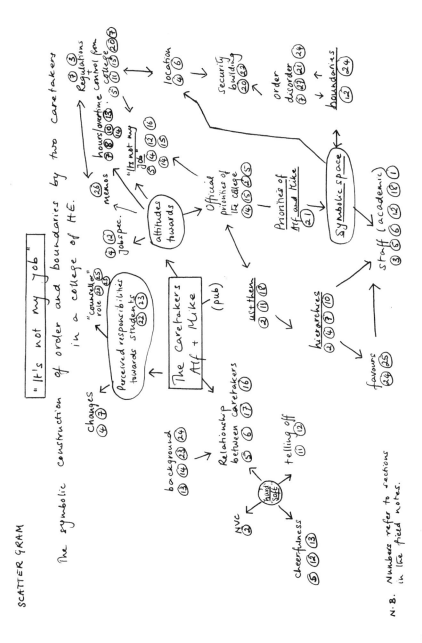

Figure 2

Evaluation and Generalisation

As pointed out earlier, it was one of the basic questions of the Ealing project to determine to what extent teachers with no background in anthropology or ethnography can acquire in a relatively short time complex anthropological and ethnographic concepts and methodologies, and employ them in teaching non-specialists. This was part of the research 'umbrella' to the project, an evaluation of its generalisability.

One way of answering this question was itself through use of ethnographic methods. Evidence was acquired through open-ended interviews involving the linguists and our anthropologist colleague, through consideration both of their teaching on the course and their participation in course team meetings, through analysis of the ethnography projects described above, and through informal discussions throughout the period of the project.

We have described above how the linguists learned about anthropology through seminars and tutorials with our professional anthropologist colleague, by reading, and through doing ethnography projects. It is also important to emphasise that we learned through supervising students on their projects, and through the actual practice of having to teach sessions on anthropological topics.

Although the initial approach was to focus on teaching students 'how to do ethnography', it was soon agreed that 'ethnography' could not be taught in a theoretical vacuum. Methods were meaningless without something that the methods were trying to find out. Students were already rooted in issues of language and culture and were anticipating some of the experiences they would encounter through living in a foreign country. The topics chosen reflected this context: for example, 'Local Level Politics', 'National Identity and Local Boundaries' and 'The Family'. The curriculum also responded to the students as linguists, and units and tasks were introduced, for example 'Language and Identity', 'doing compliments', which required observation and analysis of micro-linguistic data and the exercise of power through discourse.

This combination of factors required us to focus on epistemological issues, questioning taken-for-granted assumptions about the 'ordinary' and the 'natural' in daily life. First we, and then our students, were learning to see that apparently trivial surface concerns are deeply rooted in cultural assumptions about knowledge and experience. We were also learning to move beyond stereotypical conceptions of 'a culture' towards recognition of 'cultural processes' (Street, 1993) and meanings changing over time and context. Teachers and students were learning to be reflexive about the observer's position as both 'inside' and 'outside', as they move between their own cultural context and that of their informants. Indeed, the teachers felt that the main learning and adapting process had less to do with content knowledge than with the process of developing new perspectives; less to do with cultural knowledge than with frameworks for understanding cultural processes.

We felt that curriculum objectives were not simply achieved by content knowledge of the discipline of anthropology, but through the actual interactive process of teaching. We took what we deemed appropriate in terms of anthropological knowledge and perspectives and adapted it to teaching methods with which we were familiar: photocopying selections for students; finding short pieces that focused the issue; linking a theme to some activity; asking students to engage in some concrete task on which to report in the classes. Our aim was to start from their observations, and help them to understand the way meaning is constructed. What we developed, then, was a mix of the features of traditional anthropology and sociolinguistics and traditional language teaching, mediated through our own personal backgrounds, our own project experience and, most strongly, the experience of teaching the course as a team.

In the judgement of the professional anthropologist in the team, those teaching the course achieved considerable success in internalising many of the perspectives outlined in earlier chapters, and the evidence from student ethnographies and interviews suggests this passed on to them also, as we shall see later. With respect to generalisation, there is evidence that other teachers in language departments come with backgrounds and interests sympathetic to this kind of work and can adapt to teaching ethnography in the ways that the original volunteers did. Shirley Jordan joined the team later, wrote an ethnography project of her own, as we have illustrated, and began to join in teaching course units. Similarly, colleagues at other universities and language departments have liaised with the Ealing team and are introducing elements of the ethnography project in their own institutions. The finding appears to be that it is not simply a matter of individual 'personality' but rather a combination of background and teaching experience. All of the teachers stressed that this is not a matter of making a clean break with previous approaches but rather a 'change process' at levels of epistemology as well as of curriculum and pedagogy. Language specialists have international and cross-cultural experience and intellectual interests in social and cultural questions. In the Ealing project this was combined with an interactive, student-centred, and exploratory style of teaching, which is likely to facilitate successful adaptation to an innovative course such as this.

Chapter 7

Developing the Principles for an Ethnography Course

Some Fundamental Principles

In Chapter 6 we described some of the ways in which language staff can develop themselves as teachers of ethnography. In this chapter, we describe how a course for introducing students to ethnography can be designed. In order to do this, we have had certain fundamental principles in mind. First, there need to be elements both of ethnographic method and of anthropological, and, to a more limited degree, sociolinguistic concepts. The aim is not to try to train students as anthropologists and therefore it is necessary to be highly selective in making decisions about both content and approach. However, a narrow skills based approach, teaching only ethnographic methods, is not appropriate. As we have said, methods of data collection and analysis cannot be taught in a vacuum separate from a conceptual framework which informs these methods.

Secondly, as with issues of staff development, it is important to take account of the fact that students' background is in modern languages: and we have outlined in the previous chapter some of the implications of this in terms of their factual knowledge of the country where they are to reside and the somewhat *ad hoc* way in which cultural knowledge is often taught. A third principle stems from these first two. This involves making the course as student-centred as possible, working from students' own experiences, building in weekly 'tasks' of data collection and analysis from which conceptual work can be drawn and ensuring a strong cyclical element so that ways of thinking and looking are frequently revisited from different angles. In this way, the conceptual elements talk to the students through their own experiences.

The culmination of the course before the Year Abroad, and the major means by which the course is assessed is the 'home ethnography'. This gives students the opportunity to try out some of what they have learnt in a small-scale project based on a group activity or set of practices which are part of or close to their own world. It is also part of the process of learning about their own socially and culturally constructed worlds before they undertake a study within a community quite different from their own.

The rest of this chapter uses examples from the Ealing ethnography course to draw out the general approach for an introduction to ethnography for language learners. Chapter 8 then describes some of the concrete detail of the programme over years two to four and a particular session on the course. Before looking at the examples, we give an overview of the whole course (see Figure 3, following).

The units cover the following areas:

1. Preparing for fieldwork
The period abroad is introduced as an opportunity to go out into the field, on the analogy of the anthropologist's fieldwork, and study some aspect of a community in a systematic way.

2. What is an ethnographic approach?
Some of the fundamental principles of ethnography are introduced: ethnography as a holistic method; data as always interpreted in context; the notion of reflexivity.

3. Non-verbal communication and social space
These concepts are used to introduce students to methods of observation. Goffman's work is introduced along with some of the anthropological studies of how people make meaning out of their use of space.

4. Shared cultural knowledge
The idea of ethnography as 'thick description' is introduced. The difference between description and interpretation is used to focus on the idea that we draw on our social and cultural knowledge in order to judge and label experiences.

5. Families and households
The idea of the 'family' as a cultural construct is introduced and the role of cultural knowledge is illustrated by looking at kinship terms, and, more sociolinguistically, by the analysis of family conversations.

6. Gender relations
The focus in this unit is on gender and language, both the discourses around gender and female and male interaction.

7. Ethnography of education
The concept of education as a process of socialisation is introduced. Culturally organised patterns of classroom behaviour are related to wider issues of education as a means of social reproduction.

8. Participant observation
This is the first session to focus on specific methods and it introduces the key method of participant observation. The tension between being a participant and being an observer is explored and practical help is given in how to locate informants and take field notes.

9. Ethnographic conversations
Alternative methods to observation are discussed. Some techniques for informal ethnographic interviewing are tried out and problems raised and discussed.

10. Ethnographic interviewing
In addition to trying out some ethnographic conversations in a foreign language, more formal interview methods based on cognitive and linguistic anthropology are used to elicit key cultural words and their semantic associations.

11. Data analysis 1: From data collection to analysis
The relationship between data collection and data analysis is explored. Two ways of drawing out concepts from the data are introduced and students are reminded of the importance of reflexivity in data analysis.

12. Data analysis 2: Further interpretive analysis and organising data in the field
Further practice in interpretive data analysis is given. Ways of organising field notes and other data are introduced. The importance of writing a field diary is stressed.

13. National identity and local boundaries
The period abroad is designed to immerse students in a different cultural experience and so questions of identity, of what it means to belong to a nation are particularly salient. In this unit, the concept of boundary is used to explore ethnic and national groups.

14. Language and social identities
The relationship between language and social identity is introduced, drawing on sociolinguistics and the ethnography of communication. The use of different varieties of language, styles of talking and code-switching illuminate the political economy of language.

15. Local level politics
The central role that small 'p' politics plays in the formation and maintenance of social relations is discussed. The notion of exchange is related both to students' own gift-giving habits and to wider social issues of honour and shame.

16. Belief and action 1: Symbolic classification
The distinction between the symbolic and functional is explored by looking at eating habits and the different ways in which what appears as 'natural' is classified symbolically.

17. Belief and action 2: Discourse and power
Aspects of the ethnography of communication, critical linguistics and the analysis of ritual language and rhetoric are combined in looking at some aspects of institutional discourses.

18. Writing an ethnographic project
Recent work on writing ethnographic accounts is used to highlight the constructed nature of ethnographic texts, challenging positivistic assumptions of objectivity in writing. Students are also helped to think about some of the tensions they will have to manage in writing their ethnographic project in the foreign language but using many of the Anglo-American concepts of the ethnography course.

19. Butterfly unit
This unit contains guidance on assessment, the home ethnography and the ethnographic project while abroad. As a butterfly rests on different flowers, so the elements of this unit may be used at different times in the course, depending on how the overall programme is structured.

Figure 3   Overview of the introduction to ethnography course

In the rest of this chapter, we look at three major aspects of the ethnography course and illustrate them with detailed descriptions of course content and approach. These three aspects are:

- looking at everyday life culturally and ethnographically;
- developing a conceptual framework, focusing on the symbolic aspects of social practice;
- developing an ethnographic method.

Looking at Everyday Life Culturally and Ethnographically

Motorways and pubs

In Unit 2 of the ethnography course students read a short student ethnography on motorway workers (Raeburn, 1978). The writer's question was: Why do men choose to work as itinerant motorway workers? Although there are obvious incentives in terms of pay, there are also strong social and cultural reasons for opting for this kind of life. These include the notion of freedom shared and maintained by the group which contributes to a sense of group identity. This, in turn, is reinforced by a set of 'rules' of acceptable standards of behaviour and celebrated in the act of taking such a job.

These themes fit into an ideology – a set of values and assumptions which legitimise the group's social position and provide a means of resistance to the prevailing values and norms in society. A similar theme is pursued in Willis' classic text on working-class schoolboys, *Learning to Labour* (1977) and Agar's study of independent truckers in the United States (1986b), both of which the students are introduced to during the course. This theme was reworked as a home ethnography by one of the students in his participant observation of motor-cycle despatch riders.

These studies are all examples of one aspect of everyday life: work and what it means to those who labour. Ethnography is the study of the everydayness of things, such as fairly routine jobs, and requires an ability to see and 'read' everyday life as a cultural phenomenon. By this we mean the ability to ask and attempt an answer to the following questions:

- What is going on?
- What meanings does it have?
- How does it come to have these meanings?

What is going on?

This question assumes the capacity to see and hear the fine-grained detail of everyday practices. Drawing from anthropology the idea of making the 'invisibility' of everyday life visible and of making the taken for granted strange, the language learner as ethnographer needs to develop new ways of seeing and hearing. 'Culture' is being acted out in the most mundane interactions and habits and the challenge is, first of all, to notice it.

This is a perspective on one's own cultural world. The culture of one's own everyday life when contrasted with a different cultural group or when abroad takes on a new significance. Much of the everyday life of other groups is not seen at all. It is literally invisible to outsiders if they are little more than tourists. However, what is seen may either be noted as 'ordinary' and likened to one's own experiences and so not attended to, or seen as extraordinary and exotic and labelled as such. To challenge both of these tendencies, students need to learn to see and hear the worlds they inhabit 'at home' before, during and after participating in others' worlds while abroad. We take up below issues of ethnographic methods for seeing and hearing.

What meanings does it have?

This next question assumes a capacity to find out the common-sense knowledge which accounts for the routine and familiar. For the motorway workers, this shared cultural knowledge included assumptions about the freedom such a job offered and the roving life-style that accompanied it. Gradually, out of the accumulated layers of data, both from observation and informants' comments, patterns and regularities begin to emerge. These take the ethnographer beyond individual responses to a cultural interpretation.

A particular routine or activity does not have an isolated meaning but is itself embedded in other meanings which in turn are part of larger structures of meaning extending out, like the circles of a whirlpool. So the motorway workers' dismissal of office life is part of a set of assumptions that celebrate their tough, unpleasant work as worthwhile. These assumptions in turn, link to the ideology which sets them apart from what they describe as 'dead' middle-class life.

Yet an awareness of these embedded meanings still raises questions about the nature of evidence and the basis on which cultural interpretations are made. An ethnographer cannot assume that they have captured *the* meanings, as if there was one fixed or essential set of meanings which define aspects of culture in some unproblematic way.

Understanding cultural meanings is a process of recognising the inter-action between one's own ways of meaning and one's understanding of others'. This 'reflexive' attitude towards understanding others is funda-mental to ethnography and assumes being analytical about one's own cultural knowledge and identity as well as those of 'others', as we have suggested in Chapter 5.

These issues of evidence and interpretation as raised by ethnography are immediately relevant to language and culture learning and to students who identify themselves as 'linguists'. They raise questions such as: On what basis is this interpretation made? What is the evidence for categorising in this way? How does such a generalisation come to be in place? It is this constant questioning of evidence and judgements that constructs resistance to stereotyping. Without this questioning habit, cultural information can simply be used to reinforce existing assumptions and stereotypes. Asking the question of any data or text, 'What meaning does it have?' involves the student in both affective and cognitive change. Simple clichéd stereotypes and attitudes sit uncomfortably alongside this interrogative mode. However, trying to see the meaning in observed behaviour also requires cognitive effort since it involves students in a constant process of conscious interpretation. As such, the student linguist becomes an 'interpreter' not in any narrow sense of transmitting messages from one language to another but in the broadest sense of making mean-ing out of the most mundane practices of everyday life.

How does it come to have meaning?

This final question assumes a historical and critical perspective on everyday life. For example, why do itinerant motorway workers come to share the values they articulate? Are their representations of their lives simply facts or do they need a deeper reading in which they are presented as facts but are, at another level, constructs, myths, imagined strengths and pride fashioned out of a need to sustain a sense of group identity and worthwhileness in gruelling jobs? In this reading of the group, both the factory, the office and middle-class life are invested with metaphors of boredom and death against which their roving life on the motorway is pitted.

But where do these metaphors come from? The ethnographer needs to bring some idea of social class and the ideologies that maintain class positions to an understanding of the motorway workers' lives. Why is it that certain values and ways of living come to be dominant and how far is their resistance to these dominant values itself a way of colluding with them?

The example of the motorway workers illustrates some aspects of what we are calling cultural learning. To begin the process of cultural learning students need 'an ethnographic imagination' (Atkinson, 1990) which involves both a constant questioning process and the ability not just to read *off* from behaviour or texts a particular interpretation but to read *into* data and texts. The contrast between 'reading off' and 'reading into' is a contrast between simple generalisations and stereotypes: 'motorway workers are tough', 'motorway workers do the job because the money is good', and a rich, complex interpretation of others' lives which includes context, history and theoretical sensitivity. An 'ethnographic imagina-tion' is at the heart of cultural learning. It implies a continuous process of observation, questioning, analysis, conceptual development and reflexive writing, and the capacity to enter into at least the suburbs of another group's world, and so move beyond the boundaries of our own. In the early stages of the ethnography course, the discussion of 'Motorway' and other exercises helps raise many of these issues and introduces students to the nature of ethnographic work and the processes involved: its concentration on small-scale local events and knowledge, the extended and systematic periods of data collection, and an increas-ingly focused set of questions. For example, in 'Motorway', Raeburn narrowed down his study to why people chose the job rather than looking more generally at life on the motorway.

Two sessions later, in Unit 4, students are introduced to the notion of shared cultural knowledge and are given a number of incidents to discuss (see Figure 4).

One theme that runs throughout the discussions is the relationship between description and interpretation. At this early stage it can be quite a challenge for students even to recognise that they regularly conflate description and interpretation. For example, students are quick to interpret what is going on in the 'money on the table' incident as an example of someone leaving a tip and one of their friends stealing it. They have to be encouraged to question these assump-tions, to consider on what basis they have come to this conclusion and to slow down the interpretive process, learning to describe what they see first and then interpret it. The other four incidents are treated in the same way. The point that is constantly emphasised is that it is worth looking at the small, detailed and apparently trivial things of life and that this means slowing down, taking time, not jumping to conclusions. Smallness and slowness are worthwhile values to pursue when trying to understand the unfamiliar or in making the apparently familiar strange.

Discuss the following incidents:

1. Four people sitting together in a restaurant get up from the table, having paid the bill and leave a few coins on the table. As three of them leave the restaurant, the fourth goes to the 'Ladies'. When she returns, she scoops up the money left on the table. What is going on? (adapted from Singer, n.d.)
2. You bump into someone you know in the street but have not seen for months. What inferences do you draw from her leave-taking remark: 'You must come and see us sometime'?
3. You are invited to a recently opened Chinese restaurant where all the dishes are based on snake. What is your reaction? If you are less than ecstatic at the prospect, how do you account for your reactions?
4. How would you explain what a 'honeymoon' was to someone newly arrived in Britain from a country where marriage practices are very different?
5. You take along a friend from France to your little brother's school fête. She sees a woman standing with her head in a cardboard frame while schoolchildren and adults throw wet sponges at her face. On enquiring, she finds out that the woman is the school's headmistress. How do you explain this behaviour? How far can you generalise about this behaviour?

Figure 4   Extract from Unit 4

The data used to help students understand the difference between description and interpretation comes from their first attempt at participant observation. They are given the assignment shown in Figure 5.

In the next session, students, using the handout (Figure 6) to guide their discussion, report back on their observations. A typical description would be: 'Two women were standing near the bar and a man rudely interrupted them by leaning between them and asking for a drink.' But they fail to see that this is part description and part interpretation. The latter depends on the women's reaction and any other observed behaviour and history of relationships (or not) between the women and the man. The interpretation includes an evaluative element in which the behaviour is considered rude according to the norms of the observer.

Assignment: Hanging around a local bar

The PURPOSE of this assignment is to get more practice in making observations and taking notes in a setting with relatively easy access but which is complex enough to have different things going at the same time.

You will begin to learn:

- to analyse the raw material you have collected in terms of culture and social organisation;
- to collect and use adequate evidence for the inferences, hunches and assertions you make from your observations.

Location

You should go to a place:

- where you can observe unobtrusively and where you will not feel odd or awkward;
- where you can observe different types of patron groups, interactions between patrons and employees, division of labour among employees.

Ideally we would like everyone to go to a *local pub*, but if you do not feel comfortable with that you could alternatively go to a coffee bar, tea room, etc.

Procedure

1. Go to your chosen location. Spend about *half an hour to an hour* there, depending on how much is happening. You could stop when nothing new appears to be going on.
2. See what you can see, hear and learn by just hanging around as a patron. *Do not formally interview anyone.* In your notes, however, try to indicate questions that occur to you which you feel cannot be answered without interviewing people. What limitations did this cause?
3. If you can take notes unobtrusively while you are there, fine. If you think it is too difficult to do so, *write down everything you can remember as soon as possible.* This means within a couple of hours: if you leave it much later, or even until the next day, you will inevitably find that you have forgotten large chunks. The loo is said to be a popular refuge amongst anthropologists. It is essential that you note the time, date, etc. of your visit.

4. Look through your notes a few times. Make a note of any *further thoughts* you may have on your material.
5. Draw *a quick map* of your chosen location, clearly labelling the major objects and areas of activity.

What to look for:
1. Social organization, including:

   • the different categories of patrons who frequent the place while you are there;
   • the division of labour among employees;
   • any patterns in the interactions between patrons, between patrons and employees, between employees.

Other things to think about:
1. Identifying typical routines of activity, (i.e. recurring sequences of behaviour).
2. Anything which strikes you as unusual, how do you make sense of it?
3. Do you see any inappropriate/unacceptable behaviour? How do other participants deal with it?

(With acknowledgment to D. Campbell of Michigan State University)

Figure 5   Unit 4 – Shared cultural knowledge

Although, as Geertz (1973: 20) says, 'cultural analysis is guessing at meanings', these guesses must at least be informed by the kind of evidence required to give an interpretation of this small example. Geertz borrowed from the philosopher, Gilbert Ryle, the notion of 'thick description' to illustrate the process from description to interpretation (see Chapter 3). In our example, 'thin description' would be one that details what is observed. The 'thick description' would have to account for the context in which the 'interruption' occurs (if that is what it was), an understanding of relationships in public, in pubs, this pub in particular, and of these people in particular, in order to come to an interpretation of this incident as an example of boorish behaviour, an attempt at the beginning of a chat-up, a ritual game played out before, etc. etc.

A 'thick description' might include themes of 'belonging' or exclusion enacted and re-enacted in public and private places, such as pubs, common rooms, at parties and so on, where social roles are negotiated and where stereotyped judgements are frequently formed and expressed.

Assignment: Hanging around a local bar

Guidelines for discussion:
Compare notes: What was written down/what not.
Groups to look at/report back on one specific aspect/issue.

1.1 Characteristics for differentiating between different groups
1.2 Patterns of interaction, e.g.
    gender relations
    joining a group
    ordering a drink
1.3 Typical routines, e.g.
    method of entering/leaving
    people at the bar
2. What was particularly interesting?
2.1 Did anything odd happen? What made it unusual?
2.2 Was there any inappropriate/unacceptable behaviour? Any taboos involved?

What previous knowledge (i.e. interpretive resource) do you need to make sense of what you observed?
What is the evidence for your conclusions?
What constituted a pattern? How was it identified?
How did your hunches change during the visit?

Figure 6

Looking at everyday life culturally and ethnographically means looking at the group or the community and so, by implication, the boundaries that constitute the group as such.

Groups and identities

Because of the dominant western construction of people as free-wheeling individuals, it requires analytic effort and imagination for students to view themselves as socially constructed as a part of a group. In addition, the period abroad is designed to immerse students in a different cultural experience and so raise questions about themselves as individuals and as representatives of a group, a 'people', a 'nation'. Questions of identity and of national and group allegiance are therefore important issues both in ethnography and for modern languages students more generally and one of the aims of the course is to encourage students to think ethnographically about identity.

For this reason, one of the key units in the course is the unit on national identity and local boundaries (Unit 13). For many students the distinction between national and ethnic identity is not clear. As Warner (1994) suggests there has been a long tradition in Britain, as elsewhere, of seeing 'home' and 'native place' as one and the same. Home, heritage, identity and women, she argues, have been interconnected in a 'romantic nationalism'. This idea takes on particular resonance at times of loss or when a nation is at war when 'keeping the home fires burning' is the ideological work women must do to maintain the tradition and stability of the nation.

The nation, it is argued, is only an 'imagined community'(Anderson, 1983) since it is interconnected with many other 'nations' and is itself made up of different ethnic groups. The community is an imagined one because it is a construction of commonality out of difference. This is a mythical, symbolic and ideological process as much as a material one. It is concerned with how a nation represents itself to itself. For example, every time Britain or the British are mentioned or a map of Britain appears in the media, in textbooks or other discourses, a statement is made about Britain as a united political, economic and cultural entity, or to put it more directly – 'There ain't no black in the Union Jack' (Gilroy, 1987). In other words, the red, white and blue of the British flag, although an apparent symbol of national unity and pride, is unrepresentative of British people. Indeed, its co-option by fascist British groups such as the British National Party makes the point all too strongly.

As the nation is represented as a unified whole, so there is pressure to make the political unit the cultural unit. The government speaks for us as a people. So the nation, the ethnicity of the majority and what is called our cultural heritage, are bonded together in a set of political and symbolic representations. Many of these themes are introduced in Forsythe's 'German identity and the problem of history' which is used as the focus for discussion in this unit. She concludes her paper in this way:

> When I first set out to investigate German identity, I thought of it as something solid, possibly even threatening, but unquestionably there (. . .) But from within the image is rather different (. . .) My thesis in this paper has been that there is a connection between the elusiveness of Deutschland as a geographical and political entity, the ambiguousness of Deutsche as a category of people, and the seeming fragility of Germanness as a personal and collective identity in the late twentieth century. (Forsythe 1989: 154)

Central to her argument is the way in which German, Germanness and foreigners are categorised. This focus on the language used to classify and on the negative stereotyping of 'Ausländer' as symbolically polluting, looks forward to the Units on Belief and Action later in the course (see below).

The assignment for this unit on national identity and local boundaries requires students to analyse the BBC programme 'The Essential History of the UK'. This is one of a series on the 'Essential History of Europe' transmitted in 1992. It is ambiguous both in its title and treatment, leaving the viewer to interpret 'essential' as either meaning necessary and representative or to treat it as ironic. The students are given a series of questions which require them to read into and not just read off from the visual images, interviews and commentary. The programme can be read on a number of levels: as factual presentation, as an outsider's view of Britain (the narrator is French) or as a complex text in which commentary and visuals are often contesting each other.

Video: *The Essential History of Europe* **(1992: 28 mins)**

View the video both for its overt and subliminal messages.

1. The notion of the UK as isolated and protected is presented along with the commentary that Britain is 'reassuringly well-regulated and orderly'. Why this connection? Or is no connection intended?
2. The narrator says 'we' are 'conservative by necessity'. Again, who is she describing? Are these 'national' values of nostalgia and conservatism part of our experience or a myth?
3. Do you see any irony, and is any intended, in the visual images of the white, male schoolboys and masters and the commentary on 'the spirit of unity and tolerance'?
4. The programme is an outsider's views in two ways: it is framed by the French narrator and it is a piece of journalism, drawing on quotes and imagery to make an argument. Compare this with what an ethnographer might do to try and get an insider's perspective. Does the French narration justify the stereotyped views, i.e. that to an outsider, a community has to represent itself in clichés and stereotypes – a representation that it would not make to itself?

Figure 7   Example from Unit 13 (extracts only)

Applications

The conceptual themes and ways of looking at every day life discussed in this section are designed, as we have suggested, to develop 'an ethnographic imagination'. Students are encouraged to focus on the idea of a 'group' at a local level and to connect data gathered as rigorously and systematically as possible to analytic concepts and wider historical and critical perspectives.

The cluster of ideas around 'group', 'identity' and 'boundary' proved beguiling for many students in carrying out their home ethnographies. One student, Gary, made a study of his own group of friends living in a village in Yorkshire. To his surprise, he found that the boundary that marked out this group as a friendship group was considerably more blurred than he had supposed and that there were many shifting and contested identities even within this small group. Another student, for her ethnographic project abroad, worked on issues of Spanish /Catalan identity (following studies of Catalan identity by O'Brien, 1994 and the work of Woolard, 1989) by looking at code-switching among a small group of residents in Barcelona. She traced some of the ways in which code-switching is used as a resource to maintain ethnic identity in a multilingual community.

As well as giving students a specific sense of direction in choosing topics associated with identities, the three units referred to in this section, 2, 4 and 13, had an impact on the way in which students managed the early stages of the period abroad and on the discourses of 'otherness'. For example, one group in Spain, when visited by one of the lecturers, did not use any of the usual clichés about Spanish people. They were more cautious in how they judged others and more tolerant of ambiguity. For instance, they talked a great deal about the 'performance' aspect of everyday lives in Seville but were able to be reflexive about this and analyse its functional and symbolic significance.

Developing a Conceptual Framework

Once students have started to think ethnographically and can begin to relate detailed observation to cultural patterns, they need to develop a conceptual understanding of the cultural patterns observed, and an awareness of the culturally constructed nature of social practices. They also need to address the questions of what evidence, collected through ethnographic methods, can be considered to be valid knowledge of a particular cultural scene and how it might be written up in a project. The notion that our social practices are symbolically structured and lived is reiterated throughout the course, and is built into the teaching units in a rigorous but also holistic manner rather than being 'taught' at a particular stage or in a particular unit. This section uses examples from the units *Gender Relations* and *Belief and Action* to elucidate students' experience of the process of cultural learning and ethnographic analysis.

In order to help unravel some of the epistemological issues that are raised in the process of cultural learning, the incorporation and use of students' own data to complement the set texts proved even more valuable than we had initially anticipated. By seeing themselves and their informants reflexively, as cultural beings who are as open to interpretation as other cultural products, abstract concepts such as 'exchange' or 'socialisation' are brought to life in a more immediate way, and students turn the 'ethnographic gaze' on themselves and the cultural scenes they are familiar with.

Gender relations

Quite early in the course, in Unit 6 we introduced the topic of *Gender Relations*. At this stage, the main focus is on practising observation and elicitation skills; getting a feel, in other words, for what is involved in an ethnographic approach. This unit highlights the cultural analysis of identities through the dimension of gender. It draws on anthropological investigations into the ways in which men and women are perceived and symbolised, while the sociolinguistic input relates to the study of how gender affects interactions, power relations and language use. The aim of this session is to make the connection between an ethnographic approach to gender and students' own notions of how gender impinges on their own lives, to see how they have been constructed as men and women themselves.

Gender provides an accessible and manageable context for capturing the 'thick' kind of data needed for cultural interpretation. The topic of gender is featured in most GCE A-Level and university language textbooks and has been foregrounded as a topic of interdisciplinary critical enquiry in many departments of Languages and Humanities. There is a wealth of material available to students but, on the whole, they are less likely to have encountered an ethnographic perspective. Our approach complements these materials, in encouraging a reflexive examination of the notion that gender roles are not natural and unproblematic facts, but a culturally constructed and contested dimension of social reality.

Aspects of gender studies are also a popular choice for project work abroad by students working on area studies courses. Project tutors are often asked to supervise students who want to study gender relations, e.g. the changing roles of women in Spain, but who face the obstacles of a lack of methodological training or a focus for their research. One outcome of a training in cultural interpretation through ethnography is reflected in more focused project proposals. One example of a student project will suffice here: the ritualised language and behaviour of courtship among young couples in Sevilla. This project was narrowed down in the end to a study of one street, looking at how relations between young men and women are 'choreographed' as a semi-ritualised chase, how age-sets delineate gender and family allegiances and how the transition is made from informal to formal courtship (noviazgo). Data were collected mainly through participant observation (she shared a flat with two Spanish students, both of whom proved to be invaluable informants) and informal interviewing with older as well as younger members of the community. The student's own role as a 'catch' by virtue of being a foreigner who is flirted with, but who, like many foreign women, would almost never taken to be a serious girlfriend, was a useful methodological position to start from and used to advantage, highlighting the differences in the young men's ritualised behaviour.

Materials used for the session

The pre-session assignment (see Figure 8) is designed to encourage this kind of focus and to practise 'making strange' in a familiar environment. This approach draws on sociolinguistic work on female/male interactions (Tannen, 1990, 1993; Fishman, 1983; Coates, 1993, 1996).

Observe a mixed gender informal conversation (e.g. in the Common Room) for about 10 minutes. Take detailed notes of interactions. You might find the following aspects of particular interest.

1. Who initiates/changes the subject of conversation?
2. Who does most of the talking?
3. Who is doing the listening?
4. Who is maintaining the conversation?
5. Do men/women interrupt more?
6. Are there any differences in pitch/loudness?
7. Any other observations about how men/women participate in the conversation in different ways?

Figure 8   Assignment from Unit 6

At the start of the session students pooled their data and discussed some of the methodological and ethical issues involved in collecting this data. They then worked on drawing out patterns of tacit rules needed to understand this kind of interactional behaviour in a particular context. Factors that were taken into account included age, occupation, etc., and several groups argued, for example, that age and ethnic background were important factors in interpreting their data. (The 'Languages' Common Room is a meeting place for many different nationalities, so the discussion broadened out into the different communicative styles of French, Spanish students, etc.)

A number of related issues arose also in relation to the problem of generalising and making plausible inferences from their own anecdotal data. As one student commented on her data: 'How can we know that it is really gender assumptions that made this guy interrupt all the time and not just his forceful and jokey personality?' In the ensuing class discussion the main point that was made was that, in fact, we cannot know. All we can do is to find patterns that occur according to certain contextual clues and try to provide a cultural interpretation rather than one final truth. The importance of context in framing interpretations is easy for students to understand in theory. In practice, however, it really needs to be seen operating in numerous and varied processes of moving from raw data to pattern-finding and interpretation in order to become an intellectual habit. The student's question also reflects one of the most difficult aspects of cultural learning that emerges in class discussion: distinguishing between an individual's psychological make-up and idiosyncracies and socially generated patterns. Again, this is a complex question which has no simple explanation; but the assignments, by encouraging the search for patterns, can help students to relate individual data to broader concepts.

The next stage was to relate these first-hand observations to Fishman's (1983) article 'Interaction: The Work Women Do', which they had been asked to read and annotate before the session. Fishman presents a case study of recorded interactions between 10 couples over an extended period of time. Among her findings is the claim that women do more of the 'maintenance work' in conversation, for example through the use of questions to elicit a response from their partners. By relating two sources of information, their own data and Fishman's case study, students are practising triangulation of data (taking into account more than one source of data on the same topic), while observing how gender is interactionally accomplished.

Interestingly, the subjects of Fishman's study – the couples who were asked to record all their interactions over a certain period – also raised the issue of the value of their data. To them, the recorded fragments of conversation seemed banal and certainly not worthy of 'academic' interest. The thought that 'nothing's happening here' is a phrase echoed by many students while carrying out their observations until they see that something of interest to an ethnographer is happening all the time.

Observing detail

One of the ways in which ethnography may be a useful tool for understanding cultural patterns is through a heightened sensitivity to the detail of interaction, even when it seems insignificant, in order to tease out the deeper meanings that underlie social behaviour. The wide-ranging and abstract concepts seen in the unit on gender relations can be observed in the practices surrounding us all the time, in everyday contexts. This unit looks at only some sociolinguistic aspects of gender relations, in a very focused way. The primary aim is for students to engage in a reflexive analysis of the impact of gender on communicative styles, while taking into account their own cultural processes and responses. One student reacted to the article by Fishman and subsequent class discussion with the following comment taken from her class diary: 'The idea of women's work really hit home. I realised that I did it, my mother did it, etc. I was actually able to point it out to the two males in my family.'

The use of case studies such as Fishman's is useful insofar as it allows students to see how theory can be applied, and how issues arising from a topic such as gender relations, when linked to theoretical propositions in a case study, can help make sense of abstract notions.

Students often point out one of the dangers of doing assignments such as the Common Room observation, and of generalising about gender on the basis of research such as Fishman's. They are naturally wary of making reductionist and possibly inaccurate interpretations, particularly when based upon their own experiences, when thinking about their socialisation, in contexts that are all too familiar. Triangulation of data, in which one type of data collection is used to help make judgements about another, is one way of minimising this risk, as is a focus on detail and context. Recognising a resistance to generalisations about our own cultural processes can engender a greater degree of caution in generalising about others' experiences also. The more detailed the raw data that generates a theoretical interpretation, the more of an insider account it is, the more elusive that analysis becomes. This is well illustrated in Cowan's study (1991) in Greece. She examines the social organisation of everyday activities such as going out to a coffee house in central Macedonia, to concentrate on how 'dominant ideas about female sexuality, moral virtue and autonomy are embedded in the practices of everyday sociability'. Her research shows that 'it is through mundane but recontextualised acts like drinking coffee that such ideas may be contested' (p. 180). On the surface, women's roles may seem unchanged, but by examining the detail of interactions and getting to know her informants over an extended period, Cowan finds many alternative discourses to contest local gender ideologies as well as acknowledging the ambiguous and contradictory dimensions of their everyday realities. By consistently practising detailed and reflexive data analysis of this kind, students become more adept at relativising and nuancing their interpretations.

One of the primary intellectual challenges, then, is generated by a dynamic of familiarity and distance, accompanied by a greater awareness of the context-dependency of data analysis. The 'rawness' of the data from the weekly assignment provides a useful contrast to the published studies students read. By re-enacting on a micro level the trajectory from data to theory to text, we see how we are socialised, how we can interpret ourselves, as well as members of the target culture, as sources of cultural knowledge. It is naturally much harder to see ourselves as having a 'culture' than it is to talk of other people's cultures, because nobody likes to have their rich and intricate world view reduced to a set of explanations. This raises particular difficulties when cultural meanings are represented in a textual account which by necessity must leave out much essential information.

The selected readings also provide a useful set of parameters (what are the sorts of theories people might be applying to a particular area of research?) and familiarise students with a language in which to discuss topics such as gender, an academic discourse which language students may not have encountered before. This process helps students to translate action and anecdotes into an account of cultural patterns that may emerge within a group. Students may ask how to account for differences in behaviour or attitudes while also trying to draw out patterns. In trying to address this question, it is important to emphasise a bifocal approach, in other words, keeping the ethnographic gaze on both the particular and the general. This is one of the most challenging aspects of the course for language students who are testing out ethnographic methodologies and trying to apply abstract concepts about the cultural construction of reality to raw data.

Applications

Let us consider some examples in detail. The student who carried out a project in Spain on the *Sevillana* dance, explored gender as one of the dimensions of shared cultural knowledge that operated on both a local and a general level. She was also interested in exploring the ways in which gender roles related to aspects of the broader sociopolitical context of contemporary Andalusian society. On a local level, she examined some of the stylised statements about gender as manifested in the ritualised movements of the dance and the configurations of space and gesture. She then went on to look at the elements of competition between couples and same sex groups which in turn revealed rivalries and alliances between different neighbourhoods and regions. This student's account explicitly acknowledged the fluidity of symbolic meanings, through a careful examination of the manifold ways in which the ineffable quality of *gracia*, which determines whether a dancer performs well or not, is expressed and used by the members of the groups she chose to study. This critical distance was also reflected in her comments on the difficulties of reaching a definitive interpretation of people's cultural practices.

In the project report, she did not attempt to present a 'typical' case of what the dance and the rituals surrounding it meant to local individuals, but focused rather on an attempt to capture the 'telling' detail (Ellen, 1984) which could then be linked to a symbolic interpretation. This highlighted the interrelationship between different facets of these practices, to include a recognition and discussion of the contested meanings attributed by cultural insiders to particular sets of behaviours. As a result, it was perhaps more tentative in its propositions and conclusions than other types of projects, in raising questions about the instability of cultural identity rather than offering a set of assertions about Andalusian identity based on the more usual outsider perspectives.

Another student focused on gender in a rather different setting to look at issues of identity among a group of transvestite prostitutes, again in Spain. His research led him to interrogate his data, derived mainly from extended ethnographic conversations and a lot of 'hanging around' to find out about how the prostitutes see themselves in relation to the outside world, essentially mainstream society, and to their customers. In the process he had to ask himself reflexive questions about his own identity, his attitudes to marginalised members of society and unconventional sexual identities, involving both affective and cognitive aspects to the research, that eventually became an integral part of the written project. The kind of questions he had to ask in relation to his informants were the following: How can I deconstruct or present my data in such a way as to show the normative value of their beliefs? And crucially, how does my presence affect what they reveal about themselves or how they present themselves to student ethnographers? What can I count as evidence in understanding their lives, and how can I write about them in a way that is faithful somehow to how they see themselves? All these questions are typical of ethnographic thinking and research, relating to the epistemological and methodological issues that are part of the broader debate initiated by 'writing culture' (Clifford & Marcus, 1986).

As mentioned above, a reflexive approach to course topics such as gender relations, is an important feature of ethnographic methodology as illustrated by the student who chose to study the French pétanque club referred to in Chapters 1 and 2. As the club was almost exclusively male, her experience of trying to gain access to her informants and negotiate with 'gatekeepers' was clearly affected by the fact of being a female student. This had to be taken into account when considering how her informants treated her and what kind of information they allowed her to obtain.

The leap from a study of male/female interaction in a Common Room in a London university, to, for example, a 7000 word project on a trans-vestite scene in Spain is considerable, but in both situations there are common features which significantly link the two kinds of experience. First, an openness towards and acceptance of conflicting detail and the different 'voices' of informants. Second, an awareness of the need to move outwards from isolated details in order to make connections between data and concepts that will reveal the different levels at which lived data translates into a fabric of culturally constructed patterns.

Symbolic classification

At a later stage in the course, the units on *Belief and Action* – 16 and 17 – take a deeper plunge into the cultural interpretation of symbolic classification. Anthropologists and others have shown how the meanings which are normal and natural to ourselves are culturally determined and patterned. The ways we classify the mass of experience of our worlds serve not only functional purposes but intellectual and moral ones too, that inform our cultural patterns, e.g. what we eat, how we dress, the signals we communicate, and how we manage social relations generally.

In the classroom sessions dealing with these topics, we begin with an introduction to notions of symbolic order explored through the topic of

food and the rituals and discourses around food and eating, to examine
some of the ways in which the 'why' and 'how' as well as the 'what'
of cultural practices can be explored ethnographically. Everyone thinks
of food and eating when they think of culture, but this is often done in
a superficial way which does not extend to an examination of the
contested nature of food and the variations from one group to the next
in terms of rituals and the symbolic meanings around food. To start this
process students are given an assignment (see Figure 9).

Some interesting questions which arose out of the assignment feedback were: Why does some food provoke collective expressions of
disgust? Why are some eating practices considered 'unnatural' (e.g.
eating horse meat in the UK). Are there tacit rules concerning the combination and sequence of certain foods?

Exploring what is structured and symbolic about food leads to an
emotive realm of feeling about what is good to eat and what is
'disgusting', all of which is of course culturally constructed. Differences
in food habits are particularly prone to discourses of 'otherness', at its
most benign in foreign language textbooks. Students thus begin to question their own assumptions about what they eat, about taste and about
what is common sense or natural. They begin to look at the kinds of
food they would and would not eat, the existence and changing nature
of food communities, the 'cultural' associations of food (e.g. as working
class, trendy, or connected to religious beliefs) and in particular their
role in defining and creating social boundaries or hierarchies. From this
analysis, they begin to appreciate that a meaning given to an item of
food as, for example, 'edible' or not is arbitrary and is the result of socialisation into a particular food community.

This assignment then leads into broader discussion of how we classify otherness (us/them; good/bad, clean/dirty, etc.) which, although
open to criticism that the world does not come to us in simple oppo-
sites, does provide a useful grid for exploring the variability of symbolic
values and for exploring how *language* itself plays a vital role in
constructing our world view. The following extract from one class diary
illustrates how one student related to this assignment:

> One example that was extremely helpful to me was the reason for
> not eating dogs or human flesh. I wouldn't eat them, but I have
> never tasted them and I cannot say that they are harmful. If I don't
> eat them it is because there are some 'rules' that tell me not to do
> it, but these 'rules' have been created by Us. There is not one reality,
> we create that reality, and there are almost as many realities as there
> are people.

Assignment: Belief and action: Symbolic classification

Eating habits: Taste or symbol?

1. Over the week try to engage as many of your friends/contacts/ teachers/family/friends, etc. in an ethnographic conversation about their eating habits.
2. Don't elicit information in an interview, but try to work the conversation round to eating habits. Ideally, they should not feel that they have been specifically questioned. But if you prefer to make your interests explicit, then mention that this is a subject you are looking at as part of your course. Talking about your own eating habits is a good way to get people talking about theirs.
3. Elicit as much as you can about:
   - what animals they consider edible
   - what part of the animal they are happy to eat/would never eat (e.g. liver, tongue, lungs, etc.)
   - what meat they would consider eating, if their normal food was not available (zebra, dog, sparrow, etc.)
   - what vegetables they would never eat
   - their feelings if someone next to them was eating a food they would never eat.
   - other interesting perceptions that emerge out of all these questions, elicit as much as you can about their reasons for eating/not eating certain foods.
4. Try to construct some 'value' patterns or classifications from the data you have collected. You will be asked to draw up a chart or diagram with others.

Concepts behind the task

1. 'Society is constructed out of feelings of affinity and estrangement' (Lincoln, 1986).
2. 'It is culture which constitutes utility' (Sahlins, 1976) and not the other way round. In other words we don't do things for practical reasons and then find a meaning for them. The symbolic meaning is what underpins our practical endeavours.
3. 'The rituals and discourses around food help to construct the borders, structures and hierarchic relations that constitute society itself' (Lincoln, 1986).

Figure 9

The rather abstract idea that cultural and social groupings can be constructed and maintained in part by shared food cultures becomes accessible to students when they look at their own data. The intellectual excitement that comes from eliciting, organising and interpreting one's own data brings the experience of seeing everyday culture as interesting to study much closer than simply being presented with a set of polished and 'expert' studies. Much of the value of this assignment on the classification of eating habits lies in the fact that it takes students through the whole ethnographic process in a condensed form – from eliciting data through an analysis of that data to its 'translation' into a verbal or written account. Thus it provides a valuable experience in understanding and dealing with any classificatory, or semiotic, system that they may encounter in different contexts of research.

The notion of symbolic classification has led to some interesting recent projects. For example, a project on vegetarianism in Spain which examined some of the linguistic and behavioural markers of difference between the 'normal' meat-eating Spaniard, and the vegetarian, still very much a minority. Another project, described in Chapter 9, also drew on ideas introduced in this unit for a classificatory framework. In this case involving the classification of students in a German university according to physical appearance.

At a more abstract level, the students can be encouraged to think about relating their findings to notions of symbolic cleanliness and pollution. For this kind of analysis we draw also on Mary Douglas' *Purity and Danger* (1966) which discusses the moral and emotional commitment of social groups to seemingly functional actions. This is summarised in the observation that 'Dirt is matter out of place'. In other words, something that is seen as dirty or polluting in one context is quite acceptable in another. This, in turn, relates to some of the discourses about food which can be linked to ideologies of inclusion or exclusion (e.g. racist discourses about foreigners' food). One student applied this notion to a different context in her project work abroad on racist discourses in a German Hall of Residence. She showed how expressions of 'pollution' and 'contamination' carry a powerful normative value and a moral commitment which serve to position others negatively. Her informants were both foreign and German students. In a suggestive example of how language and discourse are primary vehicles for symbolic classification, she based her research on the notion that terms such as 'Ausländer' are heavily connoted in a variety of ways that reflect also on German concerns about what it means to be German. For this she also drew on Diana Forsyth's study 'German identity and the problem of history' mentioned above.

Developing an Ethnographic Method

In previous sections, there have been several references to ethnographic ways of thinking or an 'ethnographic imagination'. This requires the capacity to observe and record some aspects of everyday life and to 'read' this data in interpretive ways which are themselves constantly questioned. For example, something as commonplace as the layout of a supermarket or a town or village market can be systematically documented and analysed in order to discover the underlying pattern behind the classification of consumables. We may conclude that goods are displayed in a supermarket according to semiotic principles concerning ritual pollution; but on what basis have we concluded this? Are the findings based on one data source or several? Did initial analysis inform subsequent data collection? How far is the interpretive analysis based on more general conceptual categories? And do we present our conclusions as general facts, a particular case, the writer's own view or . . . ?

The last section of this chapter illustrates some of the ways in which the conceptual frameworks introduced above are linked to ethnographic methods so that students can begin to ask and answer some of these questions for themselves. The course is structured so that the more conceptually based units and the methods units are integrated, reflecting the necessary relationship between conceptual thinking and data collection, analysis and writing up which gives ethnography its special character.

Participant observation

Participant observation (PO) is the first of the methods units introduced on the course, some weeks before the students embark on their 'home ethnography'. Participant observation is generally recognised as *the* essential method for doing ethnography. As the name suggests, it is a method involving simultaneously both participation and observation. Hymes, 1996, has suggested that we are born ethnographers but the process of being an active participant observer wears off after a time, as we start to take for granted the world around us. So, on one level the method of participant observation (PO) is a common-sense one – we take part in and observe the world around us all the time, but at another level it is fraught with difficulties because we have lost the habit of doing it actively and have to learn it again. And in doing so we are faced with practical and ethical difficulties (Spradley, 1980).

Some of these issues are raised through reflecting on two short tasks students have already completed. One involves 'Hanging around in a local pub', mentioned above, and the other an observation of one of their own seminars. Typical issues raised are:

- difficulties with observing in a disciplined way what is all too familiar;
- practical difficulties of noise and note-taking;
- theoretical issues of what to record or focus on;
- ethical concerns to do with 'using people' or deceiving friends or eavesdropping;
- and most important of all, issues around the validity of the data: 'How much is you being there affecting things?'

This latter point is taken up by referring students back to the notion of 'reflexivity'. Being part of the social world we study and explicitly acknowledging that our interpretations of others are that and no more – not a positive fact – is central to any process of cultural learning. As students report back on the PO study of some cultural practice with which they are relatively familiar, such as ordering a pint of beer or doing a piece of translation in class, they begin the process of inhabiting some data and interrogating the relationship between themselves as data collectors and the data as they have recorded them. The notion of them-selves as participant observers will give students both a role and a purpose when they start their period of residence abroad.

As part of this session, different types of PO are introduced: from the complete participant who makes no systematic observations, to the complete observer where there is no interaction with informants. Between these two ends of the spectrum come the participant as observer and the observer as participant and it is in this middle ground that students are encouraged to stay. Gary's home ethnography was about his own group of friends and he was therefore, as part of that group, a partici-pant who took on an observing role. As he wrote in the reflexive section of his project: 'Although rather reluctant at first as I thought "nothing ever happens", after three weeks of "making strange", close observation and many a drunken night out running off to the toilet to scribble down notes on beer mats, I eventually learnt that there was much more happening than meets the eye, and that I did not know these people as well as I thought.'

Another student, Anna, chose to do her home ethnography on the London Underground. In this situation she was primarily an observer as participant since she was a passenger like those she observed but the interaction with others was minimal. The avoidance of interaction among passengers became the focus of her study as she charted the work done by underground passengers to avoid their social space being invaded.

Observing and participating in the everyday practices of a small group prepares students for the process of being socialised into a new community when abroad. Part of this socialisation is 'language socialisation' (see Chapter 2) whereby students learn how to manage interactions, understand the functioning of politeness and issues of 'face' and, more generally, make sense of the different roles and values ascribed to various language activities in the new community. However, the object of the cultural learner is not necessarily to become 'as if' a member of the new group. PO implies some distance as well as considerable involvement, as we have discussed in Chapter 5. The capacity to distance, to reflect as well as be reflexive and to draw out the perceptions and reflections of informants may lead the student ethnographer beyond the 'lurking and soaking' aspects of PO to more focused ethnographic conversations or interviews. For this reason, there is also an introduction to the principles and practice of ethnographic interviewing.

Ethnographic interviewing

Participant observation will provide much of the data for a 'thick description' of a particular group or event, but however carefully and fully observations are documented, they only give partial access to the meanings experienced by informants. Ethnographers can make interpretations but they are only based on their own cultural frames. For example, how can you be sure from your observation whether someone is winking or blinking? (Geertz, 1973). At some stage it may be necessary to engage with informants in an ethnographic conversation or more formal interview to find out how they are describing and interpreting their world.

One of the most difficult aspects of the methods element of the course is to help students unlearn their preconceptions about the interview as a research method. They have to replace their image of the white coat and the clipboard with something that is much closer to a focused conversation. This does not mean that ethnographic interviews are unstructured, unprepared encounters. Quite the contrary, as students learn in Units 9 and 10. Ethnographic interviews are carefully structured in a number of ways. First, they are carefully prepared for and a checklist of themes which might be covered is used as a guide. Secondly, they are shaped by the informant in the sense that he or she will, in their responses be setting up topics for the interviewer to pick up later. Thirdly, they are structured over time so that early interviews will range over many areas and later interviews will be more focused. Fourthly, in more formal interviews used in more cognitively orientated ethnography (Agar, 1985; Spradley, 1979) informants may be asked a series of questions around particular concepts which have emerged as salient. For example, the notion of *allegria* is presented by Sevillanos to outsiders as something important for them. Such a concept can be used as the basis for eliciting narratives about how the people of Seville express *allegria* in their everyday lives and what meanings it has for them.

Students are given a step-by-step guide to interviewing based on Spradley's (1979) *The Ethnographic Interview*. They then have an opportunity to practise and observe others trying out this new approach in their first or dominant language. At this stage, students tend to raise a number of questions about ethnographic conversations and interviewing:

- How do you reach a stage when you can ask people if you can talk to them in a more focused way ?
- How to 'capture' the information? Should they take notes, tape-record or simply try to remember ?
- How should they cope with such interviews in the foreign language, given that they will be non-native speakers?

After a discussion on the relationship of PO and interviewing, on the advantages and disadvantages of tape-recording, but leaving the fears about their own language competence until they have attempted an ethnographic interview in a foreign language, other more complex issues have to be raised about the nature of the data they are collecting. These are raised by Briggs in his study of interviews as a research method in anthropology. He argues that the way interviewing is used acts as a hidden filter and blocks our ability to hear the data as a piece of socially constructed material:

> If I were to put my finger on the single most serious shortcoming relating to the use of interviews in the social sciences, it would certainly be the common sense unreflexive way in which most analyses of interview data are conducted. (...) Questions and answers are presumed to have obvious significance. (Briggs, 1986: 102)

Briggs is arguing here that the conclusions drawn from data collected in interviews are not unproblematic facts. The questions are asked in particular ways and construct and constrain the answers. A different question would produce a different response and so different data. So any interview data is jointly produced and is as much the product of the interviewers' social and cultural world as it is of the informants'. This idea of reality as socially constructed (Berger & Luckmann, 1966) is a theme that runs throughout the course and is fundamental to the process of cultural learning (see Chapter 3). Students have to learn that data from informants are partly produced by them, the researchers, because they ask certain questions, follow up on certain themes, foreground certain concerns in the way they ask questions and so on. They also need to appreciate that any item of data is situated in a particular context. By asking an informant, for example, about their life as a blind student in Marburg, the category of 'blind student' is the one that the informant is being asked to identify with and represent their views on. At other times and in other contexts, that same category may be de-emphasised and the informant might present quite a different aspect of themselves. For example, they might be part of the student community which is on strike because of government underfunding or they might be single parents or jazz musicians. In any of these cases, they would present themselves in different ways depending upon the particular group identity that was in focus.

Working within this reflexive frame of mind, the ethnographer can resist the easy generalisations and stereotyping which are a commonplace reaction when people are confronted with cultural differences. It also helps them to think about their own cultural worlds. They ask a particular question because it seems significant to them – is part of their way of believing, acting and valuing and so on. So, every interview can deepen the language learners' understanding of themselves as cultural beings as well as teaching them about others. This approach may also, paradoxically, help them not to stress the ethnic and cultural differences in their informants – not necessarily to see particular behaviours or opinions as French or German. Instead, they need to realise that ethnic and cultural differences (and identities) may be unstressed and what they are observing is not so much French, for example, with a capital 'F' but to do with particular personalities, social positions and biographies rather than Frenchness. Discussing these issues at this data collection stage also raises another common theme in the course, the interdependence of data collection and analysis which we shall consider below.

Some of the most common difficulties experienced by students when they first attempt ethnographic interviewing are given in Figure 10.

- Difficulty in getting started.
- Using closed or leading or overly direct questions, e.g. 'Doesn't it give you a bit of a buzz if your horoscope says you are going to . . .? or e.g. 'Are you doing French commerce?'
- Using questions which are not obviously leading questions but where assumptions are built into the question by the ethnographer, e.g. 'What did you achieve in doing your degree?' Where the commonplace assumption that there *is* achievement enters into the way the question is asked.
- A tendency to start a new topic of conversation, once the informant has given one response, so the ethnographic conversation becomes more like a formal interview.
- A tendency to ask direct questions rather then find less interventionist ways of continuing the interview, such as nods, uh huhs or even silence.
- A tendency to feed back to the informant an interpretive summary of what they said rather than working with the informants' own words.
- A difficulty in picking up on the informant's style – for example her use of metaphors to describe a key event.

Figure 10   Common difficulties

Throughout the process of learning to interview, thinking reflexively about the data collected and reflecting on the cognitive and interpersonal demands of doing ethnographic conversations and interviews, students are continually reminded of the attention to language which such a technique involves. In some ways it is like the most demanding kind of listening comprehension that they might be familiar with or the multiple skills required in simultaneous interpreting. Their informant will, if all goes well, be relaxed and talking freely and informally in a local vernacular which may still be relatively unfamiliar to the student. The capacity to listen in a highly focused and intense way, attempting to record, either mentally or on tape, the exact words of the informant; to follow up wherever appropriate with questions; to keep open a tracking channel so that, periodically, a quick scan can be made of the check list to decide what areas this interview might still try to cover – and to do all this in a foreign language – emphasises yet again the inseparability of language and cultural learning in the field and the skills and intellectual demands placed on students.

Once they have worked on ethnographic interviews in their first language, they are given the task of doing one in the foreign language. Interestingly, the fears about their own competence in interviewing in the foreign language are quickly laid to rest. They find that ethnographic interviewing requires relatively little productive competence because the whole point is to give the informant control of the interview and because questions so often use the informant's own language.

Students were asked to transcribe a part of their interview and comment reflexively both on the way in which they had framed the informant's responses and on the themes that those responses suggested. The opening few turns from an interview between a male Spanish student learning German and a female German student in Britain for her period of residence abroad, shown in Figure 11, illustrate the very first steps in a reflexive process in which data collection and analysis are combined:

The example in Figure 11 shows a student who is just beginning to think about the way in which he could elicit data from an informant. He noted from this first attempt at an ethnographic interview that his opening question produced only a short answer and he also commented on the value of simply repeating back the other's words to encourage expansion. However, although he is beginning to learn some of the possible techniques, he still opens the interview as if it were a socio-logical survey rather than an ethnographic encounter and comments on her utterances from a psychological perspective (she was trying to justify herself) rather than asking questions like: 'What does it mean to say you "cannot stand" to be kissed by your family?' Discussion of this kind of self-reporting in the sessions begins the process of moving students towards a cultural and social orientation and helps them to see how data collection and analysis are inextricably linked together.

Recording and analysing data

As we have suggested, the process of collecting data and analysing it is an interconnected one. However, all the stages of an ethnographic study from an initial 'foreshadowed problem' (Malinowski, 1922) to the writing up are all interdependent:

> The process of theory construction, hypothesis formulation, cate-gorisation, data production, coding and interpreting are inextricably bound-up with one another. (Ellen, 1984: 285)

This is well illustrated in Shirley Jordan's narrative account of her first ethnographic venture, discussed in Chapter 6, on a group of cleaners at

Original German + English	Comments about interviewer	Comments about informant
Ich möchte herausfinden, ob es viele körperliche Kontakte innerhalb der deutschen Familie gibt Zum Beispiel küßt du deine Mutter ? I should like to find out is there much physical contact in the German family. For example, do you kiss your mother?	Perhaps I shouldn't have asked this Q. so early	
Nee, gar nicht No, not at all	I was a bit troubled by her reaction – short answer	
Und warum ist das? And why is that? *Weil ich es als Kind gehaßt habe* Because I hated it as a child *Ja?* Yes?		
Ja, also mein Vater wollte		She was justifying herself but she knew my opinion was completely different
mich immer küssen und das habe ich gehaßt. Ich konnte das nicht leiden, weil meine Oma mich immer küssen wollte. Tatsächlich! Yes, my father always wanted to kiss me and I hated that. I couldn't stand it because my granny always wanted to kiss me. Really!		
Tatsächlich? Really?	short reaction to show interest	

Figure 11

the university. At first she planned to undertake a 'topic-based' study on cleanliness (Zaharlick & Green, 1991 discuss the difference between a topic-based and a 'comprehensive ethnography') but once she had started 'lurking and soaking' she found she had to rethink her research problem according to the informants' concerns.

This discussion of student interviews (in Units 9 and 10) highlights a number of the issues around recording data, specifically note-taking. After two sessions on ethnographic interviews and conversations, students are introduced to the discipline of note-taking. In addition to developing a systematic approach to note-taking, for example acquiring the habit of labelling each note with date, time and place so that it can be easily indexed and referred to, students are introduced to the different kinds of notes which they may accumulate – from 'head notes' which are those memories, impressions and perceptions which never get written down but influence the analysis, through 'scratch notes' which are the rough, often seemingly chaotic field notes that are a first attempt at documenting observations, to more analytic notes, as the raw data is continuously reread and interpreted (Sanjek, 1992).

As the notes are gradually processed and themes begin to emerge, so the ethnographer moves from initial recording to consolidation and analysis. As further data are collected, the preliminary analysis is then reviewed and adjustments made so that the ethnographer constantly toggles between recording and interpreting. This process of consolidation 'facilitates a constant cumulative dialogue with your material' (Ellen, 1984: 283). Ellen suggests writing up a 'cumulative contents page' in which key descriptive themes are brought together. In the process of doing this, connections and patterns can also begin to emerge and cross-referencing may be helpful. For example, in a home ethnography on despatch riders by Chris, leather clothing was an important element in the way in which the riders designed their image for the public and managed the tension between their very controlled working practices and the free wheeling 'Easy Rider' image which they conveyed to the world outside. As part of his field notes, he started to bring together a list of events and themes (see Figure 12).

Undoubtedly, for most students the most difficult aspect of data analysis is moving from initial themes to more conceptual categories and relating these categories to some of the concepts introduced during the course. At this stage, students are shown the scatter sheet from Ana Barro's ethnographic study of the porters at the university, 'It's not my job' (see Chapter 6). Students are also given an example from Agar's (1986b) study of self-employed long-distance truck-drivers in America,

---

Events:
Radio traffic, road traffic problems (constant), breaks, pick-ups, deliveries, problems, petrol, lunch, meetings, work, maps, the file.

Themes:
Rush, hassle, stress, boredom, frustration, excitement, exhilaration, self-containedness, capable, durable, knowledge of streets, amount of money, amount of work around, sense of sharing problems, distribution of work, watching people, remarking on different customers and staff.

Figure 12

Independents Declared. He was interested in finding out the extent to which the trucker lived up to the image of the free-wheeling independent cowboy mythologised in American narratives. There are obvious links here with the student ethnography on despatch riders. The study was carried out over nine months and the data collected during 40 days on the road, attending meetings, hundreds of conversations and 17 extended career history interviews. The interviews came to be the core data and it was to this data that Agar made himself accountable, drawing on the rest of the data to illuminate and enrich the interview data.

His conclusions centre around the tension that the truckers live with: the tension between imagined freedom and the very real dependency which is their 'lived experience'. They are dependent on the carriers who give them work, the mechanics who keep them on the road and the regulatory officials who keep them on a bureaucratic treadmill. Given the cowboy image that they project publicly, Agar asks why their accounts of trucking life are, in the main, so negative. He concludes that they represent worst case scenarios. In other words, these events happen but the frequency and awfulness of their experiences are overstated. This is, Agar argues, a rhetorical device in which the informant over-dramatises the consequences of the situation in order to make it a good story for the ethnographer.

In coming to his conclusions, Agar discusses his methods and the ways in which the concepts he is working with are 'grounded' in the data (Glaser & Strauss, 1967). The descriptive themes at the early stages of analysis are interpreted in terms of concepts which are then grouped together in categories. Through a continuous process of comparing different descriptions and different concepts, broad categories are decided on. For example, in his study, Agar has a chapter called 'Getting Underway' which consists of a number of categories: 'Load and Unload', 'Lumping', 'Manoeuvring' and 'The Driver's Log'.

The terms Agar uses for categorising the data are a combination of terms drawn from the literature, for example 'dependence'; terms used by the informants themselves, for example 'lumping'; and his own terms, for example 'road life'. Yet none of these concepts are brought in from outside and imposed on the data, nor does Agar simply present the voices of the truckers or describe their lives as if the events they described could be presented in an unproblematic way.

Agar's study can be used to sum up some of the key concerns of this part of the course:

- collect data in an intensive and extensive way and collect lots of it;
- organise the data systematically and do this as part of a daily routine;
- be reflexive about the data, questioning how it came to be produced (as Agar questions why the accounts from truckers are so negative) and your own initial assumptions about it;
- be steeped in the data, reading and rereading, constantly searching for further illumination;
- be accountable to the data, so that concepts are grounded in the data and the data is not simply used to illustrate a point. (The difference between a 'telling' and a 'typical' case, Ellen, 1984);
- use questions and comparison to move from description to conceptualisation;
- look for patterns but also take account of contradictory evidence;
- go for a story line or central phenomenon which draws your ethnography together.

At the end of the 1993/94 course, one student wrote: 'Thanks again for helping me to develop skills by which to open my eyes and mind, and experience many weird and wonderful aspects of life I might otherwise have overlooked.' This brief quotation illustrates many of the principles upon which the Introduction to Ethnography course is based: an intellectual openness, specific skills of data collection and analysis, the making strange (and 'wonderful') what had seemed ordinary and uneventful, and a sense of process, of things not being finite but in a constant state of development. To sum up, therefore, the course aims to give students experience of:

- looking at aspects of their lives from a constructivist perspective – seeing practice and discourse as socially constructed and not as a transparent piece of reality;
- collecting data, lots of data, organising them and grounding their interpretations in the data;
- applying case study principles to make sense of apparently disparate and seemingly 'trivial' data by making conceptual connections more apparent;
- developing a reflexive habit so that data are constantly questioned in relation to the conditions under which they came to be produced and in relation to the students' own practices; developing a resistance to easy generalisations and stereotypes;
- engaging with the everydayness of their own and others' lives and identifying the patterns and symbolic systems within them;
- tolerating ambiguity and complexity – both intellectually and emotionally;
- presenting information to others as an integral part of the process of learning to 'translate' meanings from lived experience to a textual account.

Underlying much of these experiences, was the pedagogy of the course, the assumptions about learning and teaching and the roles of student and teacher. For many students, the course did not follow an accustomed pattern and indeed the experience of taking the course was something of a culture shock. In the following chapter, we describe some aspects of the ethnography classroom.

Chapter 8
The Ethnography Class

In this chapter we describe what took place in one fairly typical ethnography class. The class we have selected is based on concepts of local level politics and reciprocity (Unit 15), and is designed to help students conceptualise politics as a part of everyday life. In particular, we explore the notion that the role of gifts and exchanges in social interaction provides a useful entry point for understanding the cultural patterning of local level politics in different communities. Students as newcomers to the country will find themselves having to negotiate quite a number of routine and bureaucratic exchanges, so the notion of 'exchange' is a useful one to have covered in the course. These early intercultural encounters can be crucial both in creating or confirming stereotypes or, more usefully, as opportunities for cultural learning. It is in contributing towards the latter that concepts of exchange and reciprocity are helpful.

As this is one of the later sessions in the course, it is intended not only to introduce new concepts, but also to have a synthetic function encouraging students to relate the overarching theme of exchange to other areas already explored (e.g. shared cultural knowledge, gender relations, the family) and to demonstrate how it may be functional in the interpretation of any interaction. Finally, although this course unit does not have language as its main focus, the basic concepts of exchange and reciprocity are given a specifically linguistic dimension at the end of the session through a short exercise, related to a pre-session reading, on the pragmatics of compliment giving and receiving. In this way, students are again reminded of the linguistic basis of the more general cultural concepts introduced to them.

Introduction: Local Level Politics

The term 'local level politics' is useful in drawing a distinction between the high-profile politics of statesmen, and politics on the micro-level, involving the small taken-for-granted details of behaviour which form part of the fabric of our everyday lives and govern the way we manage our relationships and interactions with others. The class is intended to encourage students to analyse how patterns of favours and obligations constitute the 'social glue' which holds a community together, and how, if we look beyond the purely functional, this reciprocal behaviour is used to create and maintain social links and boundaries on a deeper structural level. Whatever the form of exchange, be it material (money or gifts) or non-material (greetings, pieces of information, politeness or compliments), exchanges carry potent messages, and detailed observation of interactions from this perspective is one of the ways in which students explore how reciprocity, obligation, reputation maintenance, power and negotiation of status are routinely worked out.

As in all the sessions, students are expected to relativise their own practices. It is therefore important to introduce them to the workings of exchange in different contexts and in different types of society, which in turn helps to uncover fundamental similarities in the symbolic notion of exchange. By shifting our focus between the familiar and the strange, and by 'making strange', connections may be seen between the apparently exotic practices of the Potlatch or the Moka (see below) much studied by anthropologists, and what students may define as the more mundane customs of returning a dinner invitation or doing favours for one's neighbour down the road.

Mauss's distinction (1954) between 'gift societies' and 'commodity societies' is useful here. These have been linked by anthropologists to states of inalienability (gift societies) and alienation (commodity societies), and the materials selected for this unit lead students towards a consideration of how the commodification of society depersonalises transactions, converting social relationships into economic ones, and how bureaucratisation impinges upon social structures. As individuals become less involved with others in face-to-face relations of mutual interest and interdependency, their relationships with institutions play an increasingly vital role in the organisation of their lives. Studies on what could be referred to as alienation-avoidance strategies include, for example, research on the strategies adopted by tenants on a London council estate. They find many original ways of adapting and adding to the identical rooms and facilities made available by the state to stamp their own identities on their flats (Miller, 1989).

A good point of comparison with the students' own world is provided by the many anthropological studies of patron–client systems in rural areas of southern Europe (e.g. Davis, 1992; Delamont, 1995). Such systems rely more heavily on establishing personal links as a means to get things done, and are in some respects closer to gift societies. Anthropologists have examined how clients typically bypass direct dealings with state bureaucracy by inviting patrons or 'fixers' to intercede on their behalf, rewarding them with gifts, favours or support at elections, and in turn reinforcing their respective statuses and the prevalent power relations. Of course, patron–client relationships are also present in less explicit forms in the bureaucratic encounters of complex urban environments where there is an overlap between different systems of exchange and varieties of reciprocity. For example, just as patrons and clients may call themselves 'friends', the hospitality motif also functions within the state bureaucracy. This is most obvious in the German represen-tation of migrant workers as '*guest*workers'. So although clear-cut distinctions have been made between exchange systems in traditional and modern urban societies, such distinctions may not be so obvious (Herzfeld, 1992).

Students are asked to consider the different types of exchange within their own lives. These may range from the brief, impersonal ones they routinely enter into when purchasing or selling, or when dealing with bureaucracy rather than with known individuals (e.g. when they pay the 'council tax' in return for certain local services), to those on a more intimate scale with friends, neighbours, family and colleagues at work, where issues of status, power relations or reputation may be obscured by sheer familiarity.

The primary focus of this session, however, is less the institutional (although students may well need to be aware of how 'exchange' oper-ates rather differently in institutions abroad) than the local and interpersonal, and we concentrate on what may broadly be defined as 'gift exchange' as an element of the politics of daily life. Gift giving may seem like a very small manifestation of social and economic life, but a gift, like a pebble dropped in a pond, creates many ripples or reper-cussions. As Davis suggests in his discussion of the important political and emotional consequences of exchange, 'A simple gift has meanings which can involve class, social mobility, matrimony, patronage, employ-ment, manufacturing processes, issues of style and of changing rituals or conventions of gift giving.' (Davis, 1992). And, as we have suggested above, gift-giving is no more peripheral in advanced capitalist economies than in, for example, the Trobriand Islands. Cheater, in drawing this comparison, concludes that 'An industry [the gift industry] with a turnover of over one billion pounds annually is not an ephemeral spec-ulation in a passing fashion. It is securely founded on structural relationships in society.' (Cheater 1986).

Before this class, students were given three short texts and, as usual, an assignment, so they arrived in the classroom prepared to contribute with examples from their experience which they had been able to develop to some degree using the concepts encountered in the readings. Each aspect of the session is discussed in detail below, but firstly we need to account for what really happens in the classroom. What gives the ethnography sessions their specific 'flavour'?

Ethnography in the Classroom

As teachers we certainly feel that teaching and learning in the ethnography classroom is special; but special in what sense? Trying to provide a 'thick description' of what we actually do in classes revealed only a few concrete modifications in our routine teaching practice, such as the presence, on many occasions, of two members of staff, or the reliance on informal dialogue and small group work. On the face of it, however, the type of activity (the use of texts, videos, assignments and various exercises to generate discussion) is nothing radically different from what is taking place in many modern languages classrooms. The 'special' factor, then, is generated not by any lesson plan or activity type, but by the unpredictable and explicitly heuristic flavour of classroom interaction. For the success of a session, teachers are heavily reliant on students contributing raw data for analysis. Students, in turn, are asked to undertake open-ended tasks of an experiential kind, for which there is no 'right' or 'wrong' answer. As one of them put it, 'Sometimes this class seems quite unusual to me. I think it's because it's so different from all my other subjects [. . .] there doesn't seem to be a clear right or wrong.' Other student comments pinpoint issues such as increased involvement ('I think that [. . .] I am still waiting to be "lectured" and taught, when really it is for me to think on'), growing confidence ('. . . this is one of the things that I feel I am learning from the classes – to use my initiative more and have a go at things'), and the advantages of an informal atmosphere ('I enjoy the way the class is organised, it's very informal and you can pretty much air your own views').

A further contributing factor lies in the cultural mix of students which the ethnography programme typically attracts. A high proportion of exchange students come together with home students in a rich melting pot of native and target languages and cultures. Linguistic issues and examples of differing cultural practices and values therefore emerge naturally from almost every class activity – and this extends to students' responses to classroom practice itself.

Our conclusion, then, is that it is both the substance of our discussions and the nature and level of student contribution which makes this classroom different. In other classes, the students' opinions may be elicited, but their personal experiences are usually illicit diversions from the subject in hand, and although personalisation is routine in language classes, the offering of such details is somewhat 'staged' since the primary objective here is the honing of language skills. Part of the excitement of the ethnography sessions lies in the way the personal (in this case, starting with the gifts students gave or received) is shown to have some validity as part of a wider study of cultural practices. Hence the comments, 'We all learn from each other', or 'I think this is encouraging to the students, they like to know there might be some validity in their interpretations'. The real key to the difference of a session is in this notion of the students taking their lived experiences as sources, using their own beliefs, attitudes and actions as data for discussion, and learning to be reflexive enough to bring their own cultural practices to the level of discourse. Gradually students acquire the tools to transform the 'anecdote' about personal experience into an illuminating example of cultural practice. There is consequently a real feeling that the sessions belong to the students: 'I think that an ethnography course is made by the contribution of the class, by everybody's ideas and thoughts'. As we shall see below, this was extended in later years to the question of assessment for the course.

The notion of student experience as source has a further repercussion for the atmosphere of a session, since classes become a forum for learning how to deal with other people's personal experiences: 'It's good that we can discuss these things objectively in such a way that no one feels offended or worried about speaking out'. Students are expected to show diplomacy and empathy as they direct group discussions or listen and respond to their peers, skills which they will certainly need when eliciting data from informants in the field. As one student commented apropos of class discussion, 'I feel this [. . .] has been very helpful for me in developing my skills concerning interaction within a team (or group) and as a result it has developed a critical awareness within myself that I feel I didn't have before.' So this is an important, if intangible, part of each session, and one in fact which fits in particularly well with the theme of reciprocity we will be discussing here.

A Typical Session: Local Level Politics

The session outline is given in Figure 13.

Session outline

1. Introduction of local level politics. A brief lecture and informal discussion based on two pre-session readings developing the concepts of 'reputation' and 'moral community'.
2. Group work based on the data collection assignment. Students compare their charts and write up two examples on overhead transparencies to present to the class. The discussion is further developed through the British Repertoire of Exchange.
3. Discussion of culturally variable conventions, rituals and taboos surrounding practices of exchange.
4. Viewing and guided discussion of video excerpt, 'Ongka's Big Moka'.
5. Brief, informal lecture on the relationship between 'face' and social relationships leading into discussion on compliments.
6. Group work on an article on compliments using questions on a handout. Followed by feedback to the whole class, focusing on cross-cultural aspects and the usefulness of looking at compliments as part of an ethnographic project.
7. Brief information on how past students have used 'exchange' as an organising theme in their ethnography projects.

Figure 13 Session outline

Making strange: Introduction and discussion of readings

As we have mentioned, students had been asked to read two texts about exchange before the session: 'Tis the Season to be Jolly – Why?' (Beattie, 1962) and the first chapter from Bailey's *Gifts and Poisons: The Politics of Reputation* (1971). They had also undertaken an assignment drawing on examples of their own practices of exchange. Before discussing these key introductory texts, the session was framed by making a link between exchange and politics, two terms with which students are familiar in isolation, but not accustomed to connecting or viewing from an anthropological perspective.

The students' own familiar experience of learning about politics in area studies classes (e.g. focusing on election campaigns, political institutions or current affairs in their target country) was taken as the starting point in order to make a distinction between this macro-level and the micro-politics we were to explore in ethnography. Students were first asked what they understood by the term 'local level politics' and several of them came up with familiar examples such as 'office politics' or 'sexual politics'. We rapidly arrived at an understanding that this was politics with a small 'p', politics at work in the everyday life of smaller, more private units which could usefully be looked at from an anthropological or sociological perspective.

Following this preamble, our exploration of exchanges and the cultural and symbolic meanings they embody was embarked upon by throwing out Bailey's pithy statement which serves as a leitmotif for the session that gifts are the channels along which social relations run (1971). This complex notion was clarified as the session progressed, and the initial puzzlement it generated was clearly due to the students' rather literal interpretation of the term 'gift'. This interpretation would also turn out to be one of the session's richest and most heated areas of debate since it was clear from the start that 'gifts' and giving had immediately positive connotations for students. Emotionally and morally they were to cling to a rather straightforward approach to this facet of their social lives, maintaining that gifts were often freely given with no real notion of reciprocity (or anything else) behind them; they were simply synonymous with getting and giving pleasure. The examples they initially raised tended to revolve around established rituals such as birthdays, Christmas, or the symbolic giving of Valentine's Day, where the messages of the exchange were relatively clear within that particular cultural context. But the notion of gifts also needed to be broadened to incorporate other exchanges (Bailey speaks, for example, of 'the gift of good manners'), so one of our aims was to encourage students throughout the session to add to the most obvious exchange of material resources, other less tangible ones such as favours, greetings, pieces of information, politeness, compliments, or even an often unrecognised element such as time, which is routinely referred to as a commodity in English and other Western languages (see Chapter 4 on language and metaphor).

The fact that exchange is all-pervasive meant that there was a wealth of fresh, recent data from the students' own experience to unpack. However, much of this tumbled out without real consideration of how such exchanges are negotiated and achieved in interaction (i.e. not as 'thick description'). Getting to the symbolic, 'making strange' and unearthing latent messages about reciprocity or status maintenance proved to be especially difficult because of the sheer familiarity of this aspect of their behaviour. The two readings provided some help here. Both were discussed by the class as a whole before small groups were formed for the discussion of the assignment.

The first reading, 'Tis the Season to be Jolly – Why?' (Beattie, 1962) is a short article which offered a useful starting point since it begins with the culturally familiar (Christmas), and its initial examples are easy to relate to: why do we feel this annoying sense of obligation to put 'great-aunt Mary' on our Christmas card list? Why do we accept invitations to dismal parties from people we don't really like? This is in turn related to unfamiliar cultural practices among, for example, the Maoris or Trobriand Islanders, drawing out some of the universal principles at work. A distinction is drawn between gifts (which create social relationships) and purchases (which create only economic ones), and the article's conclusion is that gift-giving takes place because people 'want to be indebted to one another'. Not only the content, but the way in which the article develops, clearly helped the students to move from assumptions of morality and personal judgements to seeing things as social practice, although at this stage of the session the teachers were predominantly responsible for advancing the discussion, and many of the students were in 'note-taking' mode.

The notion of voluntarily becoming indebted allowed us to raise at an early stage ideas of exchange as a guarantor of 'belonging' in a community, and helped to explain the widespread preference for personal services, accompanied by the abiding suspicion that one's interests will be less well served by large organisations and faceless bureaucrats than by family and friends (in her study of French bourgeois culture, for example, Beatrix Le Wita (1994) has shown how services are provided as far as possible by those in, or close to, the family network). It also allowed us to account for the persistent attempts of politicians, or even high street stores, to represent themselves and their services as warm, familiar, caring and personal. The promise of greater intimacy re-introduces the moral element into the wider economic and political systems. By the same token, to 'clean the slate' and pay back everything one owes to a person is one way of signalling that any relationship with them is over, as with divorcing couples engaged in dividing the spoils.

The second reading, from Bailey's *Gifts and Poisons*, further broadened the scope of debate. As it is more complex, students had been given some prepared questions we had designed to guide them through it. The reading investigates what Bailey describes as 'small politics', political processes seen at work in the everyday and the interpersonal – for example, when we indulge in gossip, engage in one-upmanship, or generally go about our business of making friends and influencing people. The manipulation of public opinion in small communities is illustrated as one end – perhaps the most intimate one – of the political spectrum, with the same principles of competition and alliance running like a thread throughout. This provides students with an excellent example of the kinds of things at stake in our exchanges, through exploring their relation to issues of identity, power, role and status (status being described as a bundle of roles a person possesses, and the self as a set of reputations 'which spring from belonging to a community'). The initial vignette sketched by Bailey of housewives in Valloire was a useful concrete example which captured the students' imagination. Bailey describes an important mechanism these women have developed to preserve their reputation when they are on their way to the shops. They are effectively caught between two stools in this situation: if they stop to chat with neighbours they will be branded as 'gossips'; if they pass by without chatting they may be branded as 'haughty'. The solution lies in going to the shops with their apron on, the apron becoming a powerful signifier or 'laconic sign' indicating that they are busy and politically offstage, not available for exchanges. This example was linked to notions of frame and metacommunication encountered earlier in the course, two connected concepts which help students perceive the contextual as a crucial factor in cultural interpretation. Seemingly small exchanges can have important political and emotional consequences and can lead to large judgements about people, as the example of the housewives shows. What is at stake in these incidents, Bailey suggests, is the crucial management of social life, 'how to manage social space so that one is neither lonely nor overcrowded; how to preserve one's individuality and identity and self-respect while at the same time serving the interests of the community to which one belongs' (1971: 3).

The link between exchange and reputation is an important one and students were keen to relate this to many of the seemingly insignificant interactions they are engaged in on a daily basis, all of which trigger off signals about them. All members of a community are constantly manipulating, negotiating their reputation and status, and responsible for safeguarding or damaging the reputations of others. A key reason for much of the care taken in our interaction is, then, that any reputation is fragile, and that in a sense our reputation is a gift from others (one student remarked that a solitary castaway on a desert island would not have, or need a reputation). Another raised the example of a 'normally very friendly' teacher he had seen walking briskly along the corridor with a pile of books and deliberately not making eye contact with students. He suggested she may have been signalling her temporary unavailability, giving off the message 'I'm busy and on my way to teach'. It would be inappropriate to draw from this a conclusion that the teacher is generally 'unapproachable', yet the threat of such an interpretation is there. In terms of their role as participant observers, it is important for students to recognise that such small but significant 'contextualisation cues' (Gumperz, 1982a) are entirely dependent on shared cultural knowledge for their correct interpretation.

The point was made that membership of a community does not depend on having a good reputation, just on having a reputation (even if it is a negative one) and therefore fitting in to the existing system of social relations. Here the class was also encouraged to relativise what constitutes a 'good' reputation, and teachers pointed out that this debate can usefully be linked to the wealth of anthropological literature on honour and shame in the Mediterranean where factors such as chastity, or the fulfilment of family obligations may weigh far more heavily in the balance than material wealth or the nature of one's employment (Gilmore, 1987).

The discussion of types of role relationships was further focused by briefly drawing on Milroy's (1980) sociolinguistic studies using categories of high and low density personal network structures. Students were asked how reputations in small rural communities may be negotiated and managed differently from reputations in urban communities (the former being both more crucial and more difficult to maintain given the tighter web of social connections involved). Milroy isolates two network types, according to degrees of contact between individuals. A high density network structure would be typified by a small community where the man who plays the church organ may also be your next door neighbour, the teacher of your children at a local school, and a member of the same rambling club. By contrast, in urban contexts it is more common to have dealings with an individual in only one capacity, and to have single roles *vis-à-vis* one's acquaintances, who in turn may be strangers to each other. As Frankenberg (1968) points out, at the rural end, status will determine how people behave when they meet; at the urban end, it will dictate whether they meet at all.

One student illustrated the specificity of high density network structures through the example of popular TV soap operas in Britain which, whether in rural settings (Emmerdale Farm; the Archers) or urban ones (Coronation Street; East Enders) rely entirely on the peripeteia of such small-scale community relations. Here, systems of exchange reflect the greater degree of interconnectedness among protagonists, and gossip and the making and breaking of reputations constitute the backbone of such familiar dramas. Anthropologists have referred to groups of people who, like those from the soap operas, share a distinctive set of values and beliefs for what constitutes appropriate behaviour within their community, and who are prepared to make moral judgements about each other, as 'moral communities'. There was some discussion of this term and interestingly, it was the handful of students who came from a small village or rural community who had particularly useful contributions to make on the role of gossip and reputation as they perceived them and were able to isolate the differences between how they know people in, for example, a college environment, a big city, or a small village.

Bailey's thesis is particularly useful in its stress not just on reputation, but on the finely tuned, dynamic work of reputation maintenance. For example, he affirms that all exchanges carry the seeds of co-operation and competition, that claiming to have acted in the public interest is usually a hypocritical claim, or that people 'run hard in order to stand still', since it requires much skill and energy simply to maintain the status quo, to preserve the balance of reputations, and to keep people in the places they have always occupied. This latter concept was usefully unpacked with the help of some contrasting examples of all female and male/female interaction described by Tannen (1990) as 'symmetrical' and 'asymmetrical' connections, both of which are instrumental in achieving and maintaining a kind of status quo between participants. Here women she had observed on a videotape discussing their respective college grades are said to be involved in a kind of 'one-downmanship', the goal of which, according to Tannen, is to 'reinforce symmetry', 'to keep the scales even by lowering one's own side'. This is contrasted with a second 'game' of one-downmanship (this time said to be reinforcing asymmetry) which Beeman (1986) encountered in studying patterns of interaction in Iran. This game is described as 'intensely hierarchical in nature. By portraying himself as lower in status, an Iranian puts himself at the mercy of someone more powerful, who is thereby obligated to do things for him: It invokes a protector schema.'

Tannen suggests that women may also adopt such a position 'so that men will take care of them'. This allowed students to make connections with the kind of mixed gender interactions they had explored earlier in the course, and reflect again on complex issues of social hierarchies and identities established and maintained, in part, through the constant compromises and adjustments enacted in practices of exchange.

The main stumbling block for students in this session was what several of them referred to as the 'cynical' nature of the reading from *Gifts and Poisons*. In particular the class resisted the notion that gift giving can be something more than arbitrary or altruistic, or that it may be regarded, symbolically, as a kind of poison in as much as it invokes a heavy burden of obligation. Students' emotional resistance to this more sophisticated interpretation of gift giving was fierce, and this is not an untypical episode of ethnography sessions where they are required to distance themselves and conceptualise aspects of their own behaviour. They share a tendency to make sweeping value judgements based on very personal feelings about cultural issues, and resist seeing themselves as cogs in a community whose beliefs, attitudes and actions are culturally constructed. To contest such a view, they are particularly keen to point out their own differences from, rather than similarities to, other individuals and practices. It can be difficult for students to abandon such moral individualism, to step back and see how their feelings might fit into a pattern, or examine why such feelings are there in the first place. This session, then, highlighted some of the difficulties they encounter in relating lived experiences, particularly their own, to anthropological concepts.

Pooling data: Presenting assignment findings to the class

Collecting and interpreting raw data can be a considerable challenge for students accustomed to the more traditional approach of drawing on text-based material as a starting point for their work. Most of the ethnography sessions therefore provide opportunities for analysing such data, for comparing them with data obtained by other students, and relating them to anthropological literature. Testing interpretations or claims through combining several data sources ('triangulation') is an important aspect of the student projects, serving to guard against hasty value judgements or one-dimensional versions, and often throwing up useful disconfirming evidence.

For their pre-session assignment, students had been given a table to complete. This entailed looking back over the previous week to think of several examples of gifts, favours or other exchanges in which they had been involved. They were then asked to try to think about the wider implications of these interactions, to interpret any messages involving rights and obligations and to look beyond the immediate gift or favour by considering the moral and symbolic aspects. As usual, students were asked to bring their data to the session for discussion. On the pre-session assignment sheet (Figure 14), we have included some examples of students' initial findings which show them beginning to scratch the surface of their own practices.

Gift / favour / exchange	Relationship symbolised	Obligations	Wider implications
Information regarding possibilities for work in Teaching English as a Foreign Language (TEFL), and offer of 'Recommendation' to a contact who controls such posts.	Teacher – Student Guide – Looking Experienced – Learning Insider – Outsider (*vis-à-vis* TEFL).	Thanks for information. Thanks for offer of help. Reply/decision whether to take up/explore offer Follow-up by teacher (either positive or negative). Owing a 'favour' back/ wanting to give a favour back.	Teachers assessment of compatibility of student (i.e. me) and language school: must be suitable. I must believe this + trust judgement. No immediate exchange is evident. What gain for teacher? Favour in return stored for future 'collection'? Satisfaction in arranging a beneficial exchange (Beneficial for school +me).
Lending £1.00 to another student who needs change to pay someone else £1.00 that he owes them.	Friendship. Trust. Fellow sufferer from change – related problems (at times) (sympathy).	To try to help (me). To say thank you for that help (him). To say (sometimes) when it will be returned. To say back (sometimes) that it doesn't matter – either today or tomorrow will do. Prompt reimbursement and thanks. Accept thanks.	Shared conception of value (symbolic) of money – despite nominal amount. Confirmation/realignment regarding degree of friendship/trust/sympathy. Do you need to say it will be paid back by a certain time? Depends on relationship. How much 'dare' one borrow? What explanation need be given? When is it okay to remind somebody about an outstanding debt?

Figure 14 Pre-session assignment sheet

The next step was to discuss findings in small groups, where students pooled their data and attempted to look beyond the anecdotal for patterns and structures which they could relate to broader concepts of exchange. Each group selected two examples which they wrote on a transparency and one student from each group presented this to the class. The ensuing discussion was an attempt to modify and refine ideas about reciprocity and obligation, to expand the notion of exchange and to reflect on more and more varied examples, either hypothetical or real. Some of the most telling examples included the student who had felt suspicious and embarrassed about a gift she had received; the student who had subverted the obligation to receive (by rejecting the offer of food from a host), and the student who had returned a gift. Analysing such scenarios allowed us to draw out concepts of moral expectations, and make the point about the hidden messages contained in gifts quite successfully. Staff also offered examples from their own experience to be analysed by the students. One member of the teaching team drew on the interaction between herself and a student who came into her office for a French oral examination. After being invited to sit down in the chair designated for candidates, he proceeded to produce two glasses and a bottle of champagne from his bag. What might the intended messages have been? What was at stake for the participants? The scenario is laden with messages which were perhaps easier to discuss objectively since the students themselves were not involved.

Further impetus was given to the discussion by handing out the British Repertoire of Exchange (Davis, 1992) (see Figure 15) This allowed students to consider how the apparently altruistic and moral (e.g. donations or alms-giving) may belong to the same repertoire as the self-interested and immoral (e.g. bribery, burglary, mugging or shoplifting) as two 'poles' on a continuum of exchange relationships. Confronting students with the idea that mugging and charity are two ends of the same continuum is, of course, deliberately provocative and is designed to disturb students out of their complacency about the way the world is.

Davis's repertoire serves as a useful *aide-mémoire* for varieties of exchange relationships over and above the most obvious, with terms including institutionalised practices such as banking, mortgaging and commodity dealing, and examples of transactions like pawning, prostitution or swapping which may not immediately spring to mind. The exercise reveals how broad and pervasive exchange is and provides an opportunity to reflect on cultural differences. Several class members raised the problem of the presence of mugging and theft on the repertoire,

Part of the British Repertoire		
alms-giving	expropriation	reciprocity
altruism	extortion	renting
arbitrage	futures trading	retailing
banking	giving	robbery
barter	huckstering	scrounging
bribery	insider dealing	shoplifting
burglary	insurance shopping	
buying / selling	marketing	simony
charity	money-lending	social wage
commodity-dealing	mortgaging	swapping
corruption	mugging	theft
donation	pawning	tipping
employment	profiteering	trading
exploitation	prostitution	wholesaling

Figure 15 British repertoire of exchange

and the notion that they constituted a form of exchange at all was contested. These terms were retrieved by the suggestion that a con-man, for example, who engages in a negative (because unreciprocal) form of exchange, is only able to con at all because there exists a shared concept of exchange. This makes it easier for him to convince people they will be getting something in return. Students were particularly ready to contribute on this point, and soon arrived at their own conclusions about theft as non-reciprocal and de-personalised, a form of taking but with no relationship between participants, thus denying the social dimension of all exchanges as well as the fact that they are usually consensual. This in turn led to a brief discussion concerning the widespread discourse about a 'crumbling society', and a 'loss of community spirit' which is commonplace in all areas from media reporting to corner shop gossip, and which is a response to increasing levels of petty theft, joy riding, etc. Interestingly, students pointed out that such activities are frequently referred to not just as criminal, but as 'anti-social', and that the idea of young offenders engaging in community service or doing some work for their victims as recompense is increasingly popular. Through exploring the implications of theft, students again highlighted in their own way the essential fairness and equilibrium that are normally nego-tiated through exchange.

One particularly problematic area was the notion of altruism consti-
tuting an exchange, and much of the debate revolved around this. 'What
about giving to charity?'; 'What about anonymous donors?'; 'What about
Ghandi and Mother Theresa?' Is there indeed such a thing as a 'free
lunch'? (Or if someone pays for your lunch, is there automatically some
obligation on you to reciprocate in some way?) We asked students to
consider at this point whether that virtuous feeling they get when they
give money to charity could be the pay-off in the exchange. They were
encouraged to give us their thoughts on, for example, being a blood
donor and whether blood donors should be paid as they are in the
United States (the overwhelming consensus was that they should not).
A good tactic is to draw on an example which is either contemporary
or related to something local. At the time of writing, the latest Comic
Relief operation (a massive media promoted effort to encourage donations to aid for the Third World) was about to take place. This mediatised
example of giving to good causes as a form of exchange relationship
was particularly useful to us since it drew out all the normally hidden
mechanisms at work and made them explicit. Anonymous donors
pledged money to the appeal and in return there were regular progress
accounts broadcast. Viewers were also rewarded with a clear and tangible
'dénouement' to the narrative of their own generosity as they watched
footage of the recipients with celebrities and saw how their needs would
be met. In addition, the private, personal pleasure of giving was made
consensual by the appeal, so that giving had become a nation-wide
activity, thus uniting the nation further and reinforcing a shared
identity as a generous nation. Storing and exploiting examples of contemporary or local practice is an important aspect of the sessions; it keeps
the teaching fresh for us and for the students, and reinforces the message
that 'the field' is all around us, ready for observation by the 'ethnographic eye'.

Another example of how we attempted to achieve this feeling of imme-
diacy was by asking students to interrogate classroom practice and
consider what exchange relationships were at work there and then, in
the context of the session. Having been asked earlier in the course to
undertake a classroom observation, they were now less reticent and were
more prepared to make statements about this aspect of their university
lives. So we learned that when the students come into the classroom
they had certain expectations of what we should be giving them. We in
turn had our expectations. There was a discussion of a much larger chain
of exchange, starting at government level (which determines, for
example, how many people there are in a class and what can be taught

there), and with the tax payer who pays for the students to come and study. Lecturers are employed in order to give students something and they in turn will give back to society. When do they feel they haven't had their money's worth? How do they feel on these occasions? The recent surge of educational new-speak describing students as clients has more than just metaphorical value, since through the student loan system they are increasingly likely to have to pay ever larger amounts for the educational services they receive.

Conventions, rituals and taboos

During the break students were asked to read a very brief extract from Barley's *Native Land* (1990) which touches on two aspects: notions of appropriacy in gift giving, and our habit of deliberately detaching gifts from the monetary sphere. Certain scenarios were used to get the discussion going again. For example, most people would be surprised to be given a gift as inappropriate as a dishcloth or a bin-liner for their birthday. Why are such things not culturally acceptable tokens of affection? What might be your reactions if you were the recipient and how could you account for them? Would you expect your partner to need to ask you what you wanted for your birthday? Why is there the potential for such embarrassment when the message behind a gift is misinterpreted? This led to discussion of how we know when to start giving and what it is appropriate to offer on a given occasion. The list of considerations students drew up highlighted the complexity of giving: what should be the type or price of the gift, and how should it be made to look? Should we accompany the giving of the gift with any kind of ritual? How would you feel if you found a price tag still on a gift? Would you tell the giver? If the gift was expensive, how can you be sure the giver did not leave the tag there deliberately? How would you feel if you had inadvertently left a (cheap) price sticker on a gift? Why can it be so disappointing to receive a gift of money or a cheque, and why is it that we often 'convert' money to gifts by offering gift tokens, which are often considered more acceptable? The point made in the extract from *Native Land*, which echoes Mauss's earlier work, is that giving a gift is like passing on a bit of the self, and that the real gift is the feeling which urged us to give in the first place so the material gift is merely a 'token'. Hence the popular aphorism 'it's the thought that counts'. The discussion also touched on the stringent rules we apply for keeping sex or love separate from money, which was usefully contrasted with African practices involving dowries or bride prices. In a small way, students were able to relate this to their own experience, from the discomfort experienced when a would-be suitor attempts to pay for a dinner (the practice of 'going Dutch' has gradually become an accepted avoidance tactic for the sense of obligation this may create) to the taboos around prostitution. Finally, in terms of fieldwork, a further exchange relationship mentioned was that which is struck up between ethnographer and informant: what might the ethnographer give the informant in return?

The debates outlined so far, generated by texts and by the students' own data, allowed them to make connections between their own social practices and those prevalent elsewhere. They developed or abandoned some of their initial assumptions according to the additional material they encountered, although on the notion of whether 'pure' altruism really belongs to the dance of indebtedness or stands outside it, the class had to agree to disagree. In fact, the exchange of views about this became rather intense, with several students presenting examples of their own selfless practices of giving, and another group attempting to theorise these practices to fit them into a paradigm of exchange. This episode had to be curtailed in order for the class to move on to the video analysis, but it was a useful reminder that 'making strange' of one's own practices can be an uncomfortable exercise. The ethnography classes often draw on personal experiences and deeply ingrained beliefs, and students were reminded that the diplomacy, tact and empathy they are expected to draw upon in the classroom should be carried with them into fieldwork.

Video excerpt: 'Ongka's Big Moka'

The next part of the session was a short video excerpt taken from a documentary called *Ongka's Big Moka* from the BBC's Disappearing World series. It concerns practices in a non-capitalist economy among the Kawelka in the Western Highlands of Papua New Guinea, practices through which power and influence is asserted by one community over another, not by warfare but by the obligatory exchange of gifts. This small community of around 1000 people is largely structured by a complex system which involves investing, collecting, giving and receiving pigs. A great deal is at stake for everyone involved, and particularly for Ongka who is the most prominent leader of his community and has the honorific title of 'Big Man'. As such, he is responsible for the Moka, a huge and highly ritualised gift-giving ceremony which has involved him in years of preparation, persuasion, negotiation and fixing in order to accumulate a sufficiently large gift. Ongka gains a lot for his group from the Moka: prestige, honour, as well as reconfirmation of his own honorific status as Big Man. The recipient is the leader of a neighbouring group, and also a local government official. He suspects the Moka is coming but does not know when or how big it will be. Ongka's idea is to provide such an enormous Moka that the neighbouring community will be overpowered and, in accepting the gift, will admit their lower status. Their Big Man will also be under obligation to pay Ongka back and do him favours; an overwhelmingly big Moka will be extremely worrying for him. It will take him years to reciprocate by making his own Moka and meanwhile he will remain in debt to Ongka. The notion of exchange as a way of winning a victory over a local community may be regarded as a metaphor for the rituals of exchange and gift giving in modern urban society.

A brief introduction was given to contextualise the excerpt and relate it to the concepts we were examining. Students were asked to consider the following questions: what differences and parallels were there between the exchange system and reputation presented in the video and the exchange practices in their cultural world? What were the difficulties involved in interpreting unfamiliar practices such as these? This is one of the most 'exotic' examples used in the course materials. Some students found it difficult at first to draw out any similarities, and were simply struck by difference. This was also translated by a degree of amusement at, for example, the idea of pigs as an essential commodity and conferers of status ('If you don't have pigs you are rubbish' claims Ongka). Some students were struck by the apparent incongruity of other elements of the gift: 600 pigs, rare birds, face paint, but also a truck and a motor bike. Other aspects of the value system of Ongka and his group were commented upon as 'odd', such as the fact that this Big Man spends days walking around and cajoling people to feed pigs into the Moka system, but he could well afford transport as he has a large bank account and is very wealthy in terms of dollars. Watching Ongka preparing for the ritual of the mini-Moka and stuffing his woolly hat with straw to give height to his head-dress also caused amusement. Finally, the sheer scale of the gift was hard to relate to. It had taken Ongka five years to assemble the gift and arrange the Moka, and it was the most important thing in his life.

After the viewing there were five minutes for group discussion, then comments were shared with the class. A central issue was the idea of ritual humiliation which was usefully related to the commonplace description of a recipient as 'overwhelmed with gratitude', and since the video neatly encapsulated the ambivalent nature of gifts this was a fine occasion to re-introduce Bailey's idea of 'gifts and poisons'. The difficulty of establishing the intention behind gifts came up again, and notions of using them to challenge, to humiliate or to assert one's superiority seemed more acceptable to students. The excerpt and discussion of it were an important way of relativising their own practices, including those which are used to frame gift giving with ritual and ceremony. Students are well used to seeing documentaries on television about apparently exotic practices, and it helps to seek out any universal principles which may be at work. A further reading, provided as follow-up work for students who wish to pursue exchange in their project, includes a discussion of the Indian potlatch practice in British Columbia and bears much similarity to the video (Leinhardt, 1964). In particular, both illustrate how the whole social system is organised around intricate systems of exchange relationships. To abolish the potlatch, as Leinhardt points out, would be 'to destroy the system of ranking in the society, the relations between tribes and their chiefs, even the relations between friends and kinsmen' (Leinhardt, 1964: 81). Similarly, without the Moka, the relations within Ongka's community and between it and neighbouring communities, would simply collapse.

'Face' and social relationships

The last part of the session shifts to looking at how social relationships are managed through day-to-day interaction. The concepts of 'face' and 'politeness' (Brown & Levinson, 1987) are used to alert students to the detailed, fine-grained way in which we acknowledge the other's face or reputation, accord them certain status and mark our relationship to them. Brown and Levinson's notions of positive and negative face needs and wants determine what kind of politeness strategies we use in, for example, greetings, making requests, offering invitations, commenting on others' appearance and so on. Strategies that attend to positive face needs stress solidarity and familiarity (as do the Tu, Du, Tú pronoun forms) while those that mark negative face needs stress deference and relative distance and formality (as do the Vous, Sie and Usted forms). Reputation and the 'gift of good manners' are inextricably linked to face and politeness issues and one of the most obvious ways in which face is managed is through the giving and receiving of compliments.

Group work on compliments

Students are asked to read the paper by Joan Manes on *Compliments: A mirror of cultural values* (1983) and to relate the findings to their own experience of giving and receiving compliments. They work in groups, comparing their own experiences both with each other and with Manes' conclusions. Their findings are then related to the wider issues of face and politeness and, outwards, to the concepts of exchange and gift. Manes looks at compliments as a way of establishing solidarity (although they can also be used to show deference). And although she does not explicitly discuss how compliments function as part of an exchange system, this is implied in her discussion of when compliments are given (for example when someone has a new acquisition) and how they are routinely responded to (by down-playing them). From an anthropological perspective, compliment giving and receiving are part of the give and take of gifts which help to develop and define social relations and to reinforce certain ideologies (as in Manes' examples of American English compliments which feed into assumptions about the value of physical appearance and newness).

Comparisons are made between the methods which linguists use to study compliments cross-culturally and how compliment giving can be studied more ethnographically. While linguists tend to use questionnaires to elicit how people think they give and receive compliments or collect data through notes or tape-recording focusing only on the act of complimenting, an ethnographic approach would be to collect complimenting data as part of a wider focus on social relationships within a group. In this way, complimenting is described more thickly, taking account of the context of relationships and situations in which compliments circulate.

Exchange in ethnography projects

The session ended with students being encouraged to consider how the concepts we had been looking at might feed into a future project. The project looms large at the back of their minds right from the start and they frequently express concern at the 'leap into the void' they will face with fieldwork. We therefore attempt to foreground quite explicitly in each session the ways in which concepts or approaches under discussion may be put to good use by students in making sense of cultural interactions encountered during their period abroad. To use exchange as an avenue into investigating politics is to open up new possibilities for language students who often want to base their project on the political or economic matters introduced in area studies. An ethnographic approach to politics on a micro-level provides a much broader range of options and implies a more rigorous set of methodological and conceptual considerations. We looked briefly with the students at how a simple task like the assignment described here could form part of their fieldwork, perhaps giving a starting point for looking at what exchanges or gifts mean within another cultural group. What gifts or favours have your informants received or given recently? What favours are they waiting to have returned? What are the expectations or degrees of reciprocity there? How can exchange be shown to be part of the 'social glue' of that group, related to concepts of identity, boundaries or community?

Links to Ethnography Projects

The work covered in this session was indeed followed up more systematically in some of the ethnography projects, which ranged from more sociolinguistically focused pragmatic work on compliments, to studies which were more anthropologically orientated. Several examples are outlined below to indicate the often innovative ways in which students were able to marry the concepts encountered in the class to their own naturally occurring data collected in the field.

One 'home ethnography', carried out in the students' home environment during a vacation, explored the ways in which employees of a major high street store accomplished the complex range of exchanges taking place at the customer service desk of a local branch. These ranged from purely economic exchanges (purchases, refunds and exchanges of goods of the same value) to the more interpersonal dimension, the carefully balanced verbal exchanges with the customer, at this sensitive part of the store, where factors such as trust, politeness and face became important. Here issues of staff hierarchy, control, customer relations and the store's reputation were seen to underpin interactions in specific ways. The student (an employee of the store) and her colleagues found themselves operating in situations where they were caught between personal decisions and judgements, and statutory company policy. The public's perception of this well-known store and the employees' duty as ambassadors for the store provided a very specific set of tensions between commodity exchange and social exchange, and an interesting frame for a localised study of exchange at work.

A rather different focus was provided by a Spanish student, based in Ealing, who undertook his home ethnography in Spain, examining the ritual and discourses surrounding a major gift-giving ceremony, Twelfth Night (*Reyes*). The term 'home ethnography' was taken to its literal conclusion as the student concentrated predominantly on roles and relationships within his own family. Drawing on concepts from the session on exchange and from an earlier session on families and households, the student was able to 'make strange' and gain new insights into this familiar aspect of his life. Far from Twelfth Night being a simple exchange of gifts, his research led him to the persuasive conclusion that it was one of the very powerful ritual ways in which his family re-confirmed its identity as family and, through notions of duty, expectations, and degrees of reciprocity, re-confirmed hierarchical relationships within it.

'The Other Side of the Stream', a third home ethnography, explored the minutiae of everyday exchanges (favours, greetings, gossip, hospitality and 'neighbourliness') in an isolated hamlet. The student discovered that the hamlet was divided into two 'factions': her informants, who lived on one side of the stream, and 'them up there' who lived on the other. Through her observations and ethnographic conversations she was able to develop a sensitive account of small-community relations by drawing, predominantly, on concepts of boundaries and by charting the many exchanges which not only served to ensure the cohesion of these distinct groups, but which occasionally resulted in the symbolic boundaries between them being negotiated and crossed.

The projects described above are first attempts, carried out in the students' own familiar cultural environment. These home ethnographies are pilot studies intended, in part, to increase the students' confidence for fieldwork abroad, which often results in more adventurous flights of the ethnographic imagination. For example, Chris, on a six-month placement in Cadiz, eventually chose to focus on an aspect of exchange which was treated only fleetingly in the session, that of prostitution, and his fieldwork was carried out among transsexual prostitutes in the city bars, as we have mentioned in previous chapters. He found that exchange was an important element in the conversations he had with his informants, and a crucial part of their value system. The prostitutes defined themselves as different from mainstream culture largely through their more honest and up-front management of sexual exchange, and through the way they transferred the values of the marketplace to transform sex into an economic activity in a very explicit way. Putting a price on their services and making themselves into commodities was seen by them as being less hypocritical about social exchange. The student gained many insights not just into the cultural patterns of this group, but also into those they were reacting against and subverting. In addition, he was forced to be particularly reflexive about his own values, attitudes and preconceptions and the ways in which these may have affected the data obtained.

Sophie's project on *Les Artisans*, a group of *Carnavaliers* in Nice, is again a good illustration. The main theme was the notion of boundaries, exclusion and membership rules, but she also explored notions of reputation and reciprocity as a secondary issue. Here the student attempted to tease-out the foundation for a *carnavalier*'s good reputation (e.g. pride in detail of work, excellent craftsmanship, devotion to the art, the ability to obtain prizes, the readiness to help out rival groups in times of need). She also discovered the attempts on the part of the younger generation of *carnavaliers* to circumvent this exchange relationship by paying established craftsmen to create a *grosse tête* on their behalf. This financial transaction allowed them to enjoy the title of *carnavalier* without bothering to acquire the necessary skills themselves. For the older generation, this 'prostitution' of the craft was seen as a slight on family honour (the title of *carnavalier* is handed down from father to son), and coupled with the stringent rules for the exclusion of females and outsiders from the various associations, it was seen to constitute a threat to the perpetuation of the art and tradition of the carnival.

Finally, Maria's project researched in Las Palmas took a more sociolinguistic direction. The focus on this occasion was on compliments, and arose out of a series of cultural misunderstandings in which the student was involved shortly after she arrived in Spain. In Spanish there are two terms for compliments, with different functions and notions of appropriacy: the first, *piropo*, is almost exclusively sexual and non-reciprocal – the kind which is regularly 'offered' to women by complete strangers in the street; the second, *cumplido*, is a broader category of compliment and almost always requires a response. The fact that many of her informants saw the term *cumplido* as essentially insincere or 'hypocritical' captured her ethnographic imagination and she embarked on the process of categorising the different types of compliment and the way these were carefully managed in terms of appropriacy. Analysing a large amount of verbatim data allowed her to isolate, for example, gender differences in the use of compliments; compliments within relations of unequal power; compliments used to confirm belonging to a group; compliments as highly valued courtship or 'hunting' skills, etc.

These examples of ethnographic projects give some indication of how students typically build on concepts encountered in the course. They also hint at the richness of experience provided by working within an ethnographic framework during the period abroad.

Class Diaries

At the end of the session, as usual, two volunteers were asked to complete a class diary. These diaries had a dual purpose: they fostered the habits of reflection and reflexivity which would be needed for keeping a field diary, and most importantly, they provided an opportunity for students to give their own account of what happened in the session along with any comments and reflections on what they had learned, what worked and what did not, how the class was organised, etc. These comments were extremely valuable contributions to the sessions, providing a barometer and allowing us to make considered modifications or additions as we went along. Making the diaries a regular part of the sessions accustoms students to reflect on their learning and also to be frank in their reactions to aspects of the course: 'Sometimes the vastness of ethnography daunts me, and I feel like I will never be any good at it'; 'I am still worried about the project we have to do at Christmas. It seems rather far away and impossible at the moment'; 'Quite relieved not to have an assignment today, as ethnography has been taking over my life somewhat, even though it's all very interesting.' Where possible, we attempted to take account of the difficulties students experienced; we noted what worked well and why, and this fed into preparation for the following sessions. One example of this was a suggestion about organising group work which came from a class diary in the second week of the course: 'I enjoy the group discussions as I feel that in smaller groups everybody gets the chance to contribute. I did feel, however, that it may be an idea if the groups were mixed around so that we get to know all the other students in the class. For myself, I would feel less shy about voicing my opinions to the whole class if I knew them slightly better.' This resulted in our shuffling student groups for each session, which we felt to be a real improvement. The diaries, then, were another way in which the sessions could be said to 'belong' to the students.

An important aspect of diary writing while on the course was that it helped students tackle expectations and their violation. Just as students will go abroad with many expectations, so students on the ethnography course had to deal with expectations about the course and how it differed from their usual experiences of language modules. Diary writing gave students the opportunity to learn to be reflexive about expectations and to develop curiosity rather than preconceived assumptions which can lead to negativity. The ethnography course aimed to develop skills in diary writing so that field diaries written abroad were not simply outpourings of frustrations or banal generalisations but were interesting, reflexive accounts. These could then be used as part of the data for the students' ethnographic projects.

Diaries about the session on local level politics and exchange appeared to confirm that we were on the right track, both in terms of what the students gained from the session, and the balance of activities provided. We will let the students provide their own conclusion to this description of a session:

> The video helped me understand what occurs in other cultures and their own rituals. The offering of pigs is very similar if not the same as what happens in our own culture when we give gifts. Most people feel an obligation to return a favour or a gift, and when we give we usually, if not always, expect to receive as well.

> Going over what we had written in our assignment about gifts and favours and all the obligations that go with them made it all clearer. Before the actual session it was hard to know exactly what to write and after talking in groups I found there was a lot more I could have added. It is amazing to realise all the rituals that go with what we would normally think of as a simple gesture. The session was useful in the sense that every day we ask a favour of someone or vice versa and we don't usually think of all the interactions that are involved.

Assessment

Since the Introduction to Ethnography course became a module integrated into the undergraduate degree, after the initial experimental period, it was necessary to include formal assessment. Part of this is based on the home ethnography, described in the next chapter, but since 1993 there has been an element of assessment of work during the course itself. The home ethnography counts as 60% and the remainder is allocated to self- and peer-assessment.

It will be evident from this and earlier chapters that the success of the course depends on a high level of commitment from students. They need to participate actively in class sessions and in particular be able to work in groups discussing readings and assignments and preparing plenary presentations. We felt that it was crucial that students remain actively analytical about their classroom contribution, about how and what they were learning, and that the best way of ensuring this was to assess their contribution in some way. It was also important to help them recognise and have acknowledged the difference between their language classes and the ethnography sessions. In the latter, they were negotiating cultural interpretations and there were no 'right' or 'wrong' answers, nor any single correct way to carry out fieldwork assignments. Everyone came to the class with different data, which were not taken in and marked by tutors. Although there was comparison of data, it was not to establish which were better, and being an effective member of the class did not necessarily mean demonstrating understanding. It could mean asking useful questions, being frank about not having understood something or discussing problems about why fieldwork did not run smoothly. Students were often reluctant to engage with such issues in class since they identified them as manifestations of weakness.

Furthermore, the ethnographic skills we hoped students would acquire during the course were not just those of note-taking and indexing, but also those of being a good observer and listener, being receptive and helping others to clarify their ideas, being flexible, showing initiative, demonstrating empathy, reserving judgement about cultural difference and analysing reflexively where one's cultural interpretations may be coming from. The acquisition of such skills and characteristics was clearly a gradual process, not something which could be done in a short burst of activity before an examination. It was therefore important that the assessment should, at least in part, be orientated towards the process, the commitment involved and the ability to take responsibility for one's own learning. We felt that self-assessment would encourage students to assess the extent of their effort and the quality of their learning, their involvement in group work, their contribution to classroom debate. We wanted them to turn the ethnographic eye on themselves, examining critically and reflexively their own behaviour and that of others in their interdependent group.

How did we convince students of the value of this approach? The first step was to negotiate with the class an appropriate set of criteria and an acceptable procedure, rather than attempting to impose these ourselves. In this way students were led to consider what it would take from each of them to make the weekly sessions useful and we could clearly demonstrate that they were to judge each other on criteria they themselves had negotiated. The self-assessment form therefore functions a little like a learner contract.

Criteria chosen by students ranged from the basic quantitative elements which are easy to assess (such as frequency of attendance or completion of assignments and readings), to the qualitative (such as effective group work). In the first class a 10-minute slot was given over to initiating group work. Students discussed in small groups what contributions might be required from each individual to make group work effective, breaking down the component skills, abilities, and contributions which might make for a successful session. Their ideas were then fed back to the class and a decision was made as to which of these should be included as criteria. In terms of the procedure adopted, students also had their say, and perhaps unsurprisingly chose to have staff involved as a 'control' to validate marks in assessment tutorials.

The results of this process of negotiation could be seen in the self- and peer-assessment form with which students declared themselves satisfied. The form was divided into sections covering attendance and preparation, assignments, readings, group work and class discussion, and finally requiring an overall assessment of student contribution. Given the inevitable teething problems which arose when students were first called upon to assess themselves or their peers, we conducted two assessment exercises, each worth 20% of the module marks so that any problems might be ironed out by the second round. The first took place half way into the course (in week 6) and the second at the end. They involved a three-part process:

- Each group member assesses her/his performance against a set of criteria and completes a self-assessment form, giving her/himself an overall mark. This is done individually.
- The peer assessment group (of four students) then meets with the following aims: to compare marks and discuss how they were arrived at, to modify or endorse overall marks. Forms are then handed in to the tutors.
- Finally there is an assessment tutorial with the tutors and peer group present. Tutors further discuss and ratify marks, or encourage moderation of any grossly misjudged marks. Students (and of course tutors) must be prepared to justify their suggested marks at this meeting.

The latter two stages involved the move from private to public assessment. They were by far the most interesting stages and also the stages in which conflict was most likely to arise. The most obvious source of conflict was due to students' unrealistic perception of the value of their own contribution. We were faced with students' inability to judge themselves objectively and with their inability, or refusal, to judge their peers objectively, or even to judge them at all! Also common was an inability to distinguish between effort and quality of output. Some students felt that the effort needed to do all the readings and overcome shyness to carry out the fieldwork assignments should be enough to obtain a high Two/one or First.

In the self-assessment guidelines (Figure 16) space is left in the form between questions for students' comments and notes.

Ethnography self-assessment guidelines

Name:...

Please complete this form and comment in detail in all the spaces provided.

CONTRIBUTION TO THE COURSE: WHY SELF-ASSESSMENT?
The Ethnography Course relies on the commitment and active participation of every member of the class for its success. We value all your ideas and perceptions, they are at the heart of the course. The self-assessment exercise described below reflects the nature of the course, which encourages you to examine critically some 'familiar' aspects of everyday life – including, in this case, your own behaviour as an ethnography student, a member of and contributor to an interdependent group.

You will be asked to complete two self-assessment forms during the course, and will be expected to discuss your own assessment with three other members of the class and have it validated by them.

40% of the total course mark is an assessment of your own preparation and contribution to the effectiveness of the course. Consider how you have contributed to the course sessions. For each of the criteria listed below, comment on how you think you have performed. Note that what we are looking for is self-critical awareness, so do not exaggerate your strengths or your limitations.

When you have written-up your report, arrange to meet with the other three members of your assessment group and discuss in detail your own assessment of your contribution. Then, if necessary, modify your own assessment in the light of the discussion and get it endorsed by the other members of the group.

1 Attendance and preparation
1.1 Attendance record
It is difficult to contribute if you are not actually there. So you need to think about your attendance record. Did you attend always / usually / rarely?

1.2 Assignments: fieldwork
Did you (always / usually / rarely) do the assignments? Assess the quality of your work on the assignments. Did you take notes as suggested? Did you analyse your observations sufficiently and write them up coherently before the class? How much effort did you put into them?

1.3 Assignments: readings
Did you always read the texts in advance of the class? Did you prepare them in such a way that you could comment on them and react to questions in class quickly and meaningfully?

2 Group work and discussions in class
What contribution did you make to the discussions in groups/pairs?

2.1 Contribution to group discussion
Consider the quality of your contribution to the groups and class. To what extent did you contribute information and ideas?

2.2 Receptiveness to others
How receptive were you to the ideas of others? To what extent did you allow others to contribute and listen to what they had to say?

2.3 Effort and initiative
How much effort did you make? Were you just sitting there letting yourself be entertained by the others, or worse, encouraging others to go off at a tangent?
Did you take the initiative when you felt the discussion was going off course?
Did you volunteer to report back from groups in the plenary sessions?

3 Class diaries
How often did you volunteer to do a class diary? How much effort did you make to provide us with useful feedback to improve the course?

4 Overall assessment of your contribution
How much effort have you put into it? How often did you ask questions if something wasn't clear to you? How much did you contribute to effective use of class time by responding quickly rather than waiting for someone else to do / say something? To what extent did you encourage others to contribute? Do you think the course was a better one for the contribution you made?
We are aware that many students invest a great deal of time on the readings and carry out assignments which they find personally challenging. Remember, however, that your overall mark does not only reflect the efforts you have made, but also the quality of your output.

5 Any other comments you would like to add

6 Now give yourself an overall mark according to the following classification:
70–80% excellent in every way (effort made and quality of output)
60–69% very good, well above average
50–59% reasonably good, average
40–49% poor, but a pass
30–39% not good enough, a fail

7 Assessment group meeting
Allow about one hour for your meeting. Start with everybody reading
everybody else's form. You might find it helpful initially to consider
which class (e.g. 60s / 50s) is appropriate for each individual. You
can then refine this in your subsequent discussion. Both your own
and the group's agreed mark should be on the form. Remember, we
are not asking you to be personally critical, but to give careful and
objective assessments of each other's contribution. Consider this an
ethnographic exercise in personal and group reflexivity.

8 Your own suggested mark: ... %
Mark agreed by assessment group: ... %

Signed (1) ....

Signed (2) ....

Signed (3) ....

Signed (4) ....

Final mark agreed with tutors: %

9 Tutor comment:

Figure 16

A further problem was that peer groups sometimes avoided engaging
in debate and found it easier just to endorse marks by signing everyone's
form whatever the mark they had allocated themselves. When marks
were modified, students tended to raise, but not to lower them, the rather
unsurprising result being that assessment groups awarded each other
marks in the same class (usually an upper second) rather than attempting
to differentiate between performances. Although they were set up

informally, the first assessment tutorials were often difficult, even painful events. They required careful preparation on the part of tutors, with discussion of problem cases beforehand. They were the control which prevented students from awarding each other 80% across the board, but it was also crucial that students did not come away with the idea that we were in any case going to impose our own marks, which would invalidate the exercise. There were certain tactics we used to encourage students to re-enter the debate about how their marks were arrived at, and persuade them to approach the exercise with appropriate reflexivity and objectivity. It helped, for example, to remind them of the following: that the self-assessment procedure was in itself a valuable ethnographic exercise in self-observation, that they were not being asked to be person-ally critical of anybody, but to be objective, that in terms of transferable skills, the process was useful (e.g. going for promotion and proving they are worth it, doing jobs which involve evaluation of others, organising team work, etc.).

The second exercise, conducted at the end of the module, ran far more smoothly. Students were more confident about how to approach it. They felt more comfortable about engaging in open discussions of each others' performances, and commented usefully on the difficulties and responsi-bilities of being a student assessor which they had experienced in the first exercise. Tutors seldom intervened, students took control and were less passive. We found it unnecessary to modify any of the suggested marks, peer groups having determined at least their own classifications with what we felt was a high degree of accuracy. They were able to explain how these marks were arrived at through negotiation and demonstrated some maturity in analysing the differences in the performances of indi-viduals between this and the previous exercise. They were also able to make some illuminating statements about the value of self-assessment:

'You've got to know how to judge yourself: it's a skill everyone has to learn.'

'It's good for everyone to think about their strengths and weak-nesses.'

'If people had peers judge them more, there wouldn't be such a stigma about being personal.'

'It is to do with taking responsibility for yourself.'

Particularly gratifying here was the understanding that the ability to self-assess is in itself a skill, one which they will need to exercise contin-uously when doing fieldwork as well as in many other contexts. We were also pleased to find confirmation that this form of assessment helped to increase motivation throughout, and that having one assessment half-way through the course and one at the end allowed self-monitoring in the interim, where deficiencies detected in the first round can be worked upon before the second. Students also seemed to appreciate the exercise as a valuable educational objective in its own right – a part of learning how to learn, and beneficial even when it is problematic.

From the staff perspective, the advantages were that students shared the responsibility of assessment and remained aware throughout of precisely what was required of them. Since the peer-assessment groups were established in the early stages of the course, there was more of a team effort throughout. Students were more aware of each others' contributions to group work and were more democratic about sharing the opportunity to present the findings of the group in plenary sessions. In other words, the exercise helped to bring out the more reticent students and tone-down those who tend to dominate. Overall, therefore, the self and peer assessment exercises encouraged a sense of responsibility which can also affect students' orientation to linguistic and cultural difference while abroad. Instead of only thinking about whether 'they' understand 'you', it is a question of 'you' trying to understand 'them'.

The only disadvantage of this choice of assessment concerned the practicalities of organising such an exercise outside class contact time, although this probably took no more time than marking a batch of essays. It was also a refreshing alternative for staff, more challenging than the impersonal norm of taking in a piece of work and handing it back with a few comments. We got to know our ethnography students better.

Chapter 9
The Student Ethnography Projects

We consider now the most visible outcome of the ethnography course: the projects in their completed form. The main purpose of the chapter is to explain both process and product: the ways in which students are helped to develop their ability to write an ethnographic account, the range of ethnographies which are written and how they are assessed. We present first four brief descriptions of ethnographies – three undertaken in Germany and one in England – to give a detailed impression of what students can in fact produce by the end of the whole process. The process lasts three years: during the introductory course students carry out and write up their first ethnography in their home environment; during the Year Abroad, they collect their data but only begin the writing up; on return to the final year of their university course they write up under the guidance of tutors. The ethnographic projects at Ealing count, as do all Year Abroad projects, towards the final degree classification. All projects, whether ethnographic or not, have a word limit of 5–7000 words but the assessment criteria for ethnographic projects are somewhat different from the others (see below).

In the second part of the chapter we describe the 'home ethnography', the first experience of fieldwork and writing up. This is also an assessed piece of work and the criteria used are the same as for the assessment of the final ethnography. It thus allows students to know from an early stage what is involved in assessment. We then discuss some of the salient characteristics of ethnographies written by students, before describing in some detail the writing process and the role of the tutor. The last section deals with assessment.

Ethnography Projects: Some Examples

1. Studying with a child – an ethnographic study of student single mothers. Daniela G.

The study begins with the simple question 'Who are single mothers?' and proceeds to describe the life of a group of single mothers studying at the Humboldt or Free Universities in Berlin. Daniela starts with some statistical data on single parents in Germany, then describes how she made contact with and gathered her own data from her informants. This is approximately the first quarter of the project. Thereafter she analyses her interviews and observations in terms of three main headings: 'Studying and bringing up children'; 'Daily routine'; and 'Social contacts'. She explains the ways in which the students arrange for the care of their children, how they organise their time very carefully and how they are part of particular kinds of social networks. She does this by quoting frequently from the interview transcripts, using the concepts proposed by the interviewees to describe their lives. For example, she identifies 'die Morgenfrühe' and 'die Schlafenzeiten' (early morning and sleeping times) as crucial concepts with which students organise their and their children's lives. But she also examines the meanings of external concepts which might be used to describe single mothers and their children in order to challenge outsider perceptions. For example, she challenges the conclusion of a study by the Federal Ministry for Youth and Women that single mothers are 'isolated' and 'lonely' by demonstrating from interviews and observation that these women have many social contacts, do not feel lonely and have a network of support to replace the usual concept of 'family'.

2. Female students in Marburg and their external appearance. Rakhee C.

The project begins with an autobiography of the project itself, how the topic arose from Rakhee's own experience of feeling inappropriately dressed during her first week at Marburg University. She mentions briefly that she investigated the topic by interviews and observation. She identifies the issues by describing two groups of female students and their dress, using both her own observations and the vocabulary used by members of one group to describe the other. She explains how, in lectures and seminars, one group dominated by taking seats in the centre of the room, asking questions during the seminar and using an aggressive style of verbal interaction. The other group sat at the edges of the room and spoke to the lecturer quietly after the session had ended.

She then examines each group in turn, by quoting from interviews, to identify attitudes to clothing, using make-up and hair styles and their symbolic meanings. She interviewed members of each group for their accounts of themselves and of the other group, and she also interviewed male students. Since she had begun the project from her own experience, she also interviewed other foreign students, female and male, to explore their interpretations of the symbolism of appearance as well as their individual ways of responding to it in order to be accepted within one of the German groups.

She concludes by analysing her observations of members of each group in public and in the privacy of their own rooms. She argues, drawing upon Goffman to support her analysis, that the question of appearance is symptomatic of projections of images of self, that the dominant group members conformed in public to one image, 'sloppiness' (schlampig) but in private had a self-image of neatness and care.

3. Politeness on public transport in Berlin. Maria A.

Although the title mentions politeness, Maria quickly explains that she found this very difficult to observe and that the project is about interaction in public transport, and in particular about people's use of space and their degrees of contact while on buses, trams, underground or urban overground trains.

She begins with a description of her fieldwork, which consisted mainly of observations but also of interviews. She points out that the history of Berlin is significant for her topic: that she lived in the former East, that she had contact above all with East Berliners, and that East Berliners are the main users of public transport, as West Berliners have their own cars. She also describes how difficult it was to interview people on a topic they found insignificant, when they expected her to be interested in the political events of the last few years.

Nonetheless, she persevered and her analysis of her observations is a detailed account of how people behave in establishing their territory on public transport and in making and avoiding social contact, particularly eye contact. She supports her analysis by frequent use of Goffman and her project is a kind of replication of his work in a different environment.

She concludes by returning to the theme of politeness and the question of whether what she observed can be termed 'politeness'. She also reflects on the methodological difficulties of analysing what is taken for granted and considered 'normal', of making the familiar strange.

4. Living between two cultures: A case study. Katja R.

The study arose out of Katja's interest in British Asians at university. As a German student in Britain, and herself not part of mainstream university life, she was interested in how other students who were bilingual and bicultural managed their student lives. She started by interviewing a number of first year students of South Asian origin but quickly decided to write a case study of one female student. She focused down on the relationship between family obligations, and in particular, pressure to get married young, and the values and assumptions of first year student life.

She soon found that the stereotypes about arranged marriages were over-simplified. Both parents and children acknowledge the symbolic importance of marriage – for the parents as an indication that children have been properly brought up, for the children as an indication of loyalty to the family and the community. However, a close analysis of her informant's comments on marriage suggested that there was room for discussion and negotiation in deciding on her future. A pattern emerged from her informant's language in which 'want' statements and 'prefer' statements from her parents were contrasted. The 'want' statements by her parents were taken as obligatory, the 'prefer' statements as offering an element of negotiation. She concludes by presenting a nuanced view of arranged marriages, as perceived by one student, who was shifting successfully between university and family life.

The 'Home Ethnography'

The ethnographies described in the previous section are those which are written on the basis of fieldwork during residence abroad, and as such represent the cumulative outcome of students' work. However, these are not the only ethnographies they write, as has been mentioned in the account of the ethnography course. During the course, either during the Easter or Christmas vacations, depending on when the course begins and ends, students are asked to write a 'home ethnography'. This is often related to some activity they would undertake during the vacation, or to some local theme in their home area. Some of the titles indicate this:

- 'Brass roots': How and why the brass band tradition maintains an importance in Saddleworth (Yorkshire).
- 'Celtic Daft': what it means to be a Glasgow Celtic football fan.
- 'Right to return': refunding at a customer service desk in a Marks & Spencer's store.
- 'It's a matter of being *furbo*': the Italian idea of queuing.
- 'For one night a year': gift giving in Spain at Epiphany.
- 'Cat and Dog People': an ethnographic study of staff at the RSPCA.
- 'We're the lads': study of a group of friends.
- 'Steam in the Blood': the lives of steam engine owners.
- 'Survival of the fittest': selling double glazing.
- 'Things you can't get at Safeways': Portobello Road Market.
- 'I fry with my little eye' : a study of a fish and chip shop.
- 'All rules are made to be broken': a study of a Serbo-Croat Sunday school in London.

As well as discussion in class and tutorials, students are given written guidance in a step-by-step explanation of what they should do and be thinking about (see Figure 17).

Students are given at this stage the assessment criteria, which we shall discuss later in this chapter, and an explanation of what their tutors and assessors will be looking for in the ethnography when complete. The stress is on ensuring that they introduce into their writing some of the anthropological and sociolinguistic concepts which they have met in the course, demonstrate that they have used ethnographic methods to gather and organise their data, and draw on their knowledge of ethnography in the analysis of their data. They are also given advice about structure. They should ensure that the introduction explains clearly the research question(s) they address and what methods they used. The account should be both descriptive and analytical, and they should include an element of 'reflexivity', discussing their own role in the research process.

The question of what is appropriate style is also discussed. As we shall see below, this is one of the more difficult issues even in the home ethnography, which is written in English. Many are used to writing essays in a style which excludes the first person and, when encouraged to be reflexive and descriptive, may tend to become too colloquial. It is therefore suggested to them that there may be a 'storytelling' style in part of their account, which will be balanced by an academic style in the analysis of their data. As we shall see in the next section and in the section describing the writing process, style and presentation are a significant issue where guidance is crucial.

Introduction to ethnography – vacation assignment
preparing a home ethnography

This assignment gives you an opportunity to put into practice the skills you have learned so far and to apply the concepts you have acquired. We suggest you follow the steps set out below and hope you are going to enjoy doing it.

1. First choose a broad area of interest, e.g.:
Family
Education and socialisation
Gender relations
Social space and non-verbal communication
etc.

2. Identify possible informants in general terms, i.e. who will it be possible to work with fairly easily?

3. Think about a general research problem which interests you, e.g.:
(If you are in a job) what has motivated people to go and do this kind of work and how far did school experience lead them into this?
To what extent does the workplace you are studying create/construct different roles for men and women?
What is it like being a . . . (profession/job) and . . . (add a specific, relevant problem).
How does a local event (e.g. a market) get done, and what does it mean to people who sell/shop there?

N.B. We don't expect anyone to actually pick one of these titles. They are just to give you an idea of the kind of question you may want to ask. Former students have done fieldwork in areas as various as a parish church, an animal shelter, and senior citizens' social clubs.

4. Interview two or three informants and/or the same informant several times
By 'interview' we mean any kind of 'eliciting conversation' in which you have an opportunity not just to participate but to be a researcher and take things further, i.e. test your understanding. This may mean an 'interview' which is specially set up, or it may mean focusing on a particular aspect your informant is talking about, and by showing interest, questioning or prompting to encourage them to talk more about it. If it is a formal ethnographic interview you may be able to tape it. Do remember though how long it takes to do transcriptions.

> 5. Participant observation is a key method of obtaining data, but remember that the focus of the assignment is also on interviewing.
>
> 6. You should start taking notes from the very beginning.

Figure 17

Some Characteristics of Ethnography Projects

One of the main purposes of the ethnography course and the projects is to encourage students to analyse and understand the new environment in which they find themselves and, secondly and, sometimes as a main focus, to come to terms with the difference they experience. It is not surprising then that the examples of final projects described above arise from the immediate environment, from the university where students study or the transport they use to get there, for example. Nor is it unusual that a topic is formulated as a consequence of personal experience, as in the case of Rakhee. Nonetheless, the choice of topic is very wide. Figure 18 gives a few examples.

> *French*
> Le Club de Pétanque à Aubervilliers.
> La Socialisation au Sein d'une Famille Française.
> Le Carnaval de Nice: qui veut devenir Carnavalier ?
>
> *German*
> Alltagsbewältigung der Blinden und ihre Interaktion mit Sehenden.
> Die Kategorisierung ausländischer Studenten durch ihre deutschen Kommilitonen. Ein ethnographischer Bericht.
> 'Ellbogengesellschaft': an ethnographic study of assertiveness in Germany.
>
> *Spanish*
> Prostitutes and Identity in Cadiz.
> Young people in Seville – changing concepts of maleness and femaleness.
> ONCE – an organisation for the blind.

Figure 18

There are other common factors in many projects which are a consequence, of course, of the recommendations and guidance of tutors. Yet these factors can be handled in many different ways and are not a recipe treated as an automatic means to success. We propose here to identify and discuss some of these factors in order to show how the projects are related to the preparatory course and to anticipate some of the criteria by which they are assessed.

Reflexivity

In our analysis of ethnography as a concept in Chapter 5, we pointed out how the experience of ethnography involves epistemological relativity, reflexivity and critical consciousness. Our problem in the Ealing programme was to see how far these dimensions could be introduced into the experience and reflection of linguist ethnographers. We suggested that, for linguists in particular, these aspects of ethnography might be most accessible through their developing awareness of the difference in language used by informants among themselves and their familiar contacts, and the language they might use to outsider ethnographers (Bourdieu, 1977; Cohen, 1983). Ethnographers need to be sensitive to the ways in which their modes of eliciting accounts of cultural practices, and the accounts themselves, may be influenced by their own impact on the situation, by the ways in which they are perceived by those they observe or interview and with whom they interact. This in turn, it is hoped, will lead them to reflect critically upon their own culturally determined pre-suppositions, on what they had taken for granted as natural rather than culturally relative. These are two dimensions of fieldwork and writing an ethnography which we call 'reflexivity'.

Students were therefore encouraged to include in their projects accounts and analyses of the fieldwork process, and they did weave into their texts a reflexive analysis of the process of doing ethnographic research. We have already mentioned how they explain the gradual emergence and formulation of a topic and its significance for them both as researchers and as actors in the social environment they find themselves in. These two are not separable and they include in their reflections the description of the methods they use to gather data. Sometimes this account of methods and their own anxieties or enjoyment of observation and interviewing become the leitmotif of the project. In other cases the project begins with the analysis of the process and then moves to presentation and analysis of data, perhaps returning to a reflexive dimension as part of the conclusion.

In some cases, the analysis of their interaction with others in the field – including their informants – involves the identification of significant effects of their presence on the data collection. They recount their 'mistakes', when people around them notice that fieldwork notes are being written about them, and discuss the, sometimes painful, ethical problems which arise in the relationships they establish with informants. Thus in the best cases, students begin to understand the ways in which their reconstruction of the other's world may differ from the other's experience of that world. On the other hand, there is much less evidence of the second step being taken, towards a relativisation of their own world. It is possible that students consider this to be more suitable for the diaries which some keep and if the ethnography project is to contain reflexive analysis, let alone a critical consciousness of the ways in which ethnographic accounts may be ethnocentric, then an explicit discussion of these issues has to be introduced into the programme.

Data collection and analysis

Students often draw attention to the ways in which they conduct interviews or carry out observations. They document their fieldwork by listing dates of interviews and periods of observation and use these as references in their study. They also discuss the problems of interview transcription and anonymity of informants. In describing their methods of observation, students discuss the degrees and kinds of participation they become involved in. When travelling on public transport in Berlin, Maria not only observes the behaviour of others but conforms herself to the 'unwritten rules' she is in the process of discovering. Having discovered her topic as a result of a feeling of unease about her appearance among students in Marburg, Rakhee changes her own appearance to conform with one of the groups she analyses, and becomes part of their social networks. Daniela, on the other hand, remains an observer of single mothers and had some difficulties in gaining access to them in their specific networks.

Thus in their different ways, students live the dilemma of distance and proximity, which, as we suggested in Chapter 5, is fundamental to ethnography, and which is nonetheless an opportunity to see what those in the situation cannot. As with the issue of reflexivity and relativisation, however, students do not always problematise the experience, by analysing it with the help of appropriate literature, for example. The question remains whether they should be introduced more explicitly to recent debates in anthropology, or whether as linguist ethnographers, it is sufficient that they are aware of different degrees of proximity of their potential as mediators.

They often also undertake document analysis. A project on German perceptions of foreigners, for example, includes an analysis of legal documents defining different kinds of immigration and degrees of German nationality, as well as analysing the categorisations used. This type of data is triangulated with their ethnographic data to provide a wider context within which the detailed cultural interpretations can be judged.

Data presentation takes various forms, some students quoting directly from interviews or observation notes, others describing and para-phrasing. Analysis often includes discussion of specific terms used by informants; for example Rakhee analyses 'schlampig' (sloppy) versus 'gepflegt' (neat, careful), and another student bases her project on the significance of the word 'Leistung' (achievement) in German schools. Thus the analysis is grounded in the data, and concepts evolve as students become more familiar with the environment and the language used within it, refining their research questions as a consequence.

They also draw upon the conceptual literature, either in detail by taking over one person's analytical concepts – Goffman, as we saw in examples above – or by using the concepts they had encountered in the ethnography course. For example, Daniela discusses the 'networks' and 'boundaries' which underpin the social contacts of single mothers.

Writing in a foreign language

The projects are written in the target language and this in itself gives them a particular character. Although marks are not explicitly given for language competence, the use of appropriate register, proof reading, presentation and so on contribute to the overall standard of the project and so the general assessment if it. Students are encouraged to get help from native speakers who may read the drafts for linguistic accuracy and appropriate register.

Writing an ethnographic project in the foreign language raises partic-ular issues. First, when struggling to express their understanding of social phenomena, their refinements of methods for data collection, their personal responses to the demands of fieldwork or their reflexive reassessment of their own culturally determined preconceptions, students might already find themselves pushing at the limits of their command of their *first* language. Some of the issues which arise are not peculiar to ethnography, since there is much debate about requiring language students always to write in the foreign language, whether about literature or area studies. It is, however, the case that students are used to writing most of their course work in a foreign language and the overriding purpose of requiring them to do all projects during the Year Abroad in a foreign language, whether ethnography or not, is to impose greater demands on their language skills and give opportunity for improving linguistic competence.

Those issues which are particular to ethnography include the fact that during the Introduction to Ethnography course, students are socialised into an Anglo-American discourse as the material and theory is largely from that tradition. This means that when they attend courses on anthropology or 'ethnologie' at a university in the foreign country, the methods, approaches or terminology rarely have much in common with their previous experience. They have therefore to transfer the concepts and theory from the ethnography course taught in English into the foreign language. They have to find ways of expressing not only what they say, but how they say it, and what concepts and frameworks they can use to discuss their analysis. As they are involved in this process of writing, the connections between language and culture become particularly clear for many students. Writing in a foreign language gives a greater sense of conceptual 'faithfulness' to the informants and their cultural contexts, and some students feel there is less danger of imposing alien concepts.

Writing in the foreign language also has the advantage of corresponding and interacting with the experience of students themselves, living the demands of their research in the foreign language, with respect to local terms and classifications for example. Yet there are doubtless moments when they would have a feeling of clarity in their first language, while in their foreign language they are seeking to express themselves through a medium they can manipulate with less facility. This sometimes appears in the text as repetition and reformulation of a single point. It is also no doubt a factor in the search for 'fluent' formulation of difficult analytical concepts or methodological terms, which sometimes leads to inaccuracies of syntax or morphology. Problems of orthography, on the other hand, can be overcome by using a spell-checker from a word-processing package for the language in question.

The specific problem of translating terms used during the course can worry students a lot, but most deal with this quite effectively with their tutor's help, either with a glossary at the end, or by using the terms in English (e.g. *going native*, *local level politics*) with a brief explanation in the foreign language within the text. For example, in the introduction to one project there is the following statement:

Ich fand es schwer 'to make strange'. Mein Instinkt zwang mich,
deutsches Verhalten anzunehmen, weil ich angenommen werden
und mich in Deutschland wohl fühlen wollte. Es gab einen Konflikt
zwischen meinem Wunsch mich darin zu vertiefen und meiner Rolle
als teilnehmende Beobachterin.

(I found it difficult 'to make strange'. My instinct forced me to
take on German behaviour, because I wanted to be accepted and
feel at ease in Germany. There was a conflict between my wish to
plunge into it and my role as participant observer.)

Here the student has found the phrase to translate 'participant observer'
but not 'to make strange'. Sometimes, as in the case of Goffman cited
above, translations of work in English exist in the foreign language, and
a student can 'read into' the discourse and quote from the translation.

The problem of register is less easily resolved. Reporting on doing
ethnography can lend itself to an anecdotal style, particularly when there
is strong overlap of subject and object, as when a student in trying to
be more reflexive, constantly brings herself into her observation and
interpretation of the other. Because students have become acquainted
with academic texts largely through extracts, and since those texts tend
to be in English, they have no obvious model on which to draw, unlike
students of anthropology who will have read many ethnographic monographs before they write their own.

To sensitise students to the issues of writing, there is a unit on 'Writing
an Ethnographic Project' during the ethnography course, and there is
opportunity to discuss some of the problems with respect to the home
ethnographies written before students go abroad. The fact that there are
related problems in the home ethnography, written in English, means
that not all can be attributed to writing in a foreign language. Another
way of giving students more practice is by encouraging them to do all
their fieldwork notes and diaries in the foreign language from the start.
This is particularly helpful when there is tutorial support available in
the early stages of 'translating' from the raw data to more abstract theoretical language.

Tutors help with these problems, as we shall see in the next section,
and are themselves aware of the contemporary debates on the significance of the act of writing in ethnographic research (Atkinson, 1990,
1992; Clifford & Marcus, 1986; Marcus & Cushman, 1982). Writing is
itself a cultural production. The ethnographer, in her choice of words,
use of metaphor and decisions about what to highlight and what to play
down, is constructing her 'reality' of the group or scene she has observed.

Ethnographic texts 'do not simply and transparently report an independent order of reality. Rather the texts themselves are implicated in the work of reality – construction' (Atkinson, 1990: 7). This is the case when the studies are of a 'home' group where informants and ethnographer speak the same language. The situation is more complex where data and the ethnographic writing are in different languages, as in most anthropological studies, and is even more complex, as with students on the year abroad, where the study is written in the language of informants which is a second language for students.

It is, for example, possible that the process of writing in the foreign language leads students to impose on the 'reality' they are seeking to interpret metaphors transposed from their first language or simplifications resulting from an imperfect grasp of the foreign language. As pointed out in Chapter 5, anthropologists have become aware of the need to be critically self-conscious about these risks (Asad & Dixon, 1985) It is thus evident that there are specific issues of writing created by the particular circumstances of the course and the requirement to write in the foreign language which are complex and need to be taken into account both by students themselves as researchers and by tutors, particularly in assessment.

Valuing the Process

The final 'product' is in most cases a text of some 7000 words, and in exceptional cases longer, written in a fluent and largely accurate register appropriate to academic writing. Projects are divided by chapters, and follow the usual academic conventions. They are personal reports with a strong sense of reflexivity, but they are also academic reports based on original data collected in the field and requiring particular linguistic and cultural competences. However, the process of writing is frequently not an easy one and tutorial work is essential. In this section we shall describe the evolution of one project from a first draft written at the end of the Year Abroad to the finished report, which is bound and submitted for formal assessment.

The student, Sophie, was a student of Spanish and French and spent the first part of her Year Abroad in Spain before going to Nice where she was to do her ethnographic project, briefly discussed in Chapter 8. At first she was uncertain as to her area of research, but her stay coincided with the spectacular Carnaval, which seemed to her to be an important part of local life. She became interested in what went on behind the scenes: what went into the creation of the Carnaval, who was

responsible for making the floats and orchestrating the event. Her fieldwork led her to some key informants, M. Provigna, the president of
an association called 'Les Artisans' and locally known as 'king' of the
'carnavaliers', and Annie Sidero, who has written about the Carnaval's
history. Annie Sidero belongs to a family which has for generations
produced 'carnavaliers', but cannot be a 'carnavalière' in her own right
since the title is handed down from father to son. She has nonetheless
organised carnivals as far afield as Bradford and Blackpool and is a
campaigner for the right of women to join the exclusive ranks of the
'carnavaliers'.

Sophie's main research question was soon narrowed down to an exploration of hierarchy, boundaries and exclusion in the world of the
'carnavaliers'.

The first involvement of Sophie's tutor, Shirley, was when Sophie sent
a collection of documents from her fieldwork, including:

- locally published documents about Annie Sidero;
- transcripts of interviews/ethnographic conversations with her four
  main informants;
- an index of recurring themes;
- articles from a publication *Le Monde en Carnaval*;
- an index of recurring themes in the interviews with 27 headings;
- information about the structure, organisation, history of the
  carnival;
- descriptions and notes from her own observations;
- a field diary.

The challenge of writing is often daunting for students. 'To tell you
the truth,' Sophie wrote, 'I don't really know where to start on my
research question of inclusion/exclusion.' The difficulty can partly be
accounted for by her producing what Burgess (1984) calls 'substantive'
fieldnotes, which are largely a continuous and descriptive record, rather
than 'analytic' fieldnotes which draw out concepts based on interpretation of the data. It is also partly a question of the contrast between the
excitement of fieldwork and the discipline of writing up. In tutorials she
would talk easily about doing ethnography rather than writing: 'I mean,
it's good fun, you know, going out there and seeing loads of people and
interviewing, but it is hard, really hard, writing up.'

Her excitement which was so palpable during the tutorial was not
transmitted in the draft. She gave a lengthy and intoxicating oral
account of the opening night of the carnival which was supplemented
by photos. She described the early buzz of excitement, the increasingly

unruly activities and the final ritual burning of floats. She also recounted her growing curiosity about what went on behind the scenes. However, her written account did not linger over the spectacle. Sounds, sights, the atmosphere and even the smells of the carnival were all worth recording, but she omitted them. Shirley pointed out that as a reader she would like to be 'grabbed' by the carnival just as Sophie herself was. Instead her draft began without impact, 'I decided to do a study of . . .', and all the drama was lost. They discussed how she was overwhelmed by the environment, which she felt unable to capture on the page, and the difference between that and something more familiar, like an ethnography of the office where she worked. The comparison helped her to see what was lacking in her writing.

Once she got started, Sophie began to enjoy it: 'Well, I've started! I'm really enjoying it, but organising and finding the right data to put in is a bit mind-blowing . . .' It is typical that students do not recognise the quality of some of their data. Collecting it has often entailed substantial effort, but they then begin to take it for granted. In the preparatory course much emphasis is placed on becoming steeped in one's data from the early stages, entering into a constant dialogue with it and indexing it so that it is accessible for interpretation and readily retrievable. Yet students often do not recognise the potential of their data. In Sophie's first draft, for example, some significant points were only mentioned in passing, and in the first tutorial Shirley was able to elicit far more information than was in the draft. There was a balance to be struck between relating the data to the anthropological concepts she had learnt about in the preparatory course and the thick description crucial to an ethnographic account. Discussion in tutorials helped with the former but then Sophie became so involved with the conceptual analysis that she began to write a fairly superficial account because she felt that the detail was banal: 'You get so immersed in it, you know so much about it, you think, oh, everyone else must do too.'

So at this stage, her analysis was not adequately grounded in an account of the data and there was little evidence for her claims. She was reminded of an early assignment in the preparatory course where the emphasis was on 'making strange' and on providing a highly focused, fine-grained description of what seemed too self-evident to be worth comment, and she realised that she had become so absorbed in the relationship of concepts to data that she had dismissed the most obvious and was not providing the reader with a sufficiently detailed description. Initially, she was equally dismissive of her field diary, notes on 'how people were and how they were as informants and stuff, and how the interviews went. Just silly things that I thought I'd write down'. However she gradually realised 'they were actually quite handy', providing an *aide-mémoire*, some new trains of thought and particularly some valuable reflexive comments on her informants' response to her as a young female researcher interested in the gender politics of the world of the 'carnavaliers'. As a consequence, she was able to introduce a sensitive reflexive dimension into her report, contrasting the ways in which Annie Sidero and her male informants had responded to the same questions and accounting analytically for the taciturn response of some of the 'carnavaliers'.

The general organisation of the report was also a problem. The first draft had been written without a sufficiently detailed plan, and she had not properly formulated her main research questions, as became evident in the discussion with Shirley: '... the boundaries they've built around themselves, the carnavaliers, and it's preventing the main philosophy of the carnival, and its passion, it's their life. My main theme is inclusion/exclusion. It's just trying to put in other sub-headings which are the most connected, like hierarchy and honour, things like that, family, but I mean there's so much, I've just so much ...' Sophie's index was a help but Shirley encouraged her to produce a 'scatter sheet' – also used by staff in writing up their own work as we saw in Chapter 6. This is a kind of mental map, on one sheet of paper, with people, events, concepts major themes, key words, etc. jotted down at random, from which connections can be established between the various items.

In the analytical sections of her report, Sophie related her material well to some of the anthropological concepts encountered in the preparatory course. These included family, gender, boundaries, hierarchies and local level politics. Some of her data required her to become acquainted with new concepts. She noticed the significance of status for the 'carnavaliers': 'It's their pride that strikes you most when you meet them.' So Shirley provided her with some of the literature on honour and shame, which helped her to consolidate her analysis and see how it was related to other work.

Some material was presented through diagrams and charts. Students do not always spot the appropriate place for this. For example, the organisation of bodies responsible for the carnival is complex, and in discussion of how this should be presented Sophie discovered it was both a good way to present material to the reader and a way of organising her own thoughts (see Figure 19).

> Représentation schématique de l'hiérarchie des corps du carnaval
>
> NICE
>
> LA VILLE DE NICE
>
> LE COMITÉ DES FÊTES
> (This committee chooses the theme of the carnival and is responsible for the overall running of the carnival)
>
> LES QUATRE ASSOCIATIONS DE CARNAVALIERS
>
> LES ARTISANS • LES AS • L'UNION • L'AMICALE
>
> LE PRÉSIDENT
>
> LE CHARISTE
> (Who organises the construction of the floats)
>
> LE GROUPISTE
> (An established maker of the 'grosses-têtes'.)
>
> LE SOLITAIRE
> (A young carnavalier making his first 'grosse-tête')

Figure 19

Her diagrams included a flow chart of the hierarchy of organising bodies, a list of her main informants and their functions in the carnival, and a breakdown of the different tasks and roles people have in preparing for the carnival according to hierarchy and gender. This latter diagram helped her to establish how rigid the separation of tasks actually was; for example, how the peripheral work is undertaken by those who can never become carnavaliers, including foreigners and women. She then realised that the tasks allocated to women were largely the traditional ones they also undertake in the family environment, such as sewing, following instructions for painting and generally playing supportive roles.

On the other hand, Sophie's use of verbatim data demonstrated a common problem among students, namely that they think the quotations 'speak for themselves'. Shirley helped her with developing analysis of quotations, looking more closely at the language used, which was particularly important since there was a common discourse among male informants which needed to be made visible. She needed to give more attention to key words, to how informants spoke about issues, to the names and categories they used to describe their world. For example, as we have seen, Sophie had gained a strong impression of the pride of her informants in their work and status as 'carnavaliers'. She reported this as fact, but without detailed analysis of the discourse; where 'fierté' and honour are mentioned, there is little evidence to substantiate the claim that they are proud to hold the exclusive title of 'carnavalier'.

Finally, there is the question of style, tone and voice in an ethnographic report. We discussed earlier the issues arising from writing in a foreign language, but there are also other characteristics of the genre which are new to students. Writing an ethnographic report gives students the opportunity to produce a distinctive and original piece of work, which is both personal and academic. In many cases, students produce a piece which is too informal throughout. The style of the account, combined with inadequate analysis of data can mean they end up sounding like an informant rather than an ethnographer.

As we saw earlier, Sophie had a variety of sources: her own observation notes and informant interviews, historical and background information and anthropological literature. The report would be a combination of voices: her personal voice, that of her informants, and that of the academic researcher. Unlike many students, she found it difficult to write herself into the report, perhaps due to her training in writing essays where the first person is strictly avoided. So Sophie and Shirley discussed the report as a piece of writing with a plot, with moments of surprise and suspense, and Sophie decided that in part her report would be a narrative account of her own 'voyage of discovery', starting with the broad picture, the excitement of the carnival as spectacle, then the formulation of her 'storyline': what's behind the carnival, what goes into making it, who are the people at work behind the scenes.

Her analytic conclusion was grounded in the detailed data she had collected and was also informed by her reading about the carnival and more general anthropological notions of exclusion:

L'exclusion contredit la définition fondamentale du carnaval

Antoine (a retired carnavalier) lui-même a déclaré à propos du carnaval que "ça fait un ensemble".

Cependant, actuellement le carnaval ne démontre pas un ensemble, mais est constitué de petits groupes qui sont jaloux les uns des autres, et qui excluent rigoureusement certaines personnes. Antoine ne semblait pas conscient de ces divisions et de la contradiction évidente entre sa définition du carnaval et la véritable situation; peut-être, il ne voulait pas y faire face.

Annie, par contre, est résolue de réaliser sa propre définition d'un carnaval comme "un facteur d'intégration culturelle et de lutte contre l'exclusion", malgré le sectarisme des carnavaliers qui règne dans le carnaval de Nice aujourd'hui. Annie est sûre que la situation changera; "il faudra bien qu'un jour il change; c'est en train de changer, quand même en trois ans".

En revanche, M. Bozzano n'est pas si optimiste: "Ça c'est difficile. C'est pour le demain. C'est changer la mentalité complète du carnaval."

Translation

Exclusion runs counter to the fundamental definition of the Carnival
Speaking of the carnival, Antoine himself declared that "It's a harmonious whole." Today's Carnival does not, however, reveal a whole, but is made up of small groups who are envious of each other and who work hard to exclude certain people. Antoine did not seem aware of these divisions and of the glaring contradiction between his definition of the carnival and the real situation; perhaps he did not want to confront the issue.

Annie, on the other hand, is determined to bring into being her own conception of the carnival as "a force for cultural integration and part of the struggle against exclusion" in spite of the reigning spirit of sectarianism the Carnavaliers bring to the Nice Carnival today. Annie is sure that the situation will change: "It will have to change one day; there has been a process of change going on in spite of everything over the past three years."

M. Bozzano, on the other hand, is not so optimistic: "That will be difficult. It's something for the future. It would mean changing the entire mentality of the Carnival."

Sophie's conclusion was a neat and ironic one but she still had a great deal of work to do to show *how* the detailed data analysis led her there. The process of writing up is thus a complex one where tutorial help is crucial. Each situation is of course different, but this account of how Sophie and Shirley worked together perhaps gives an impression of the nature of the process and the relationship between student and tutor at this stage.

Assessment Procedures

Ethnographies are not the only kind of project students may do during the Year Abroad. Those who have not followed the Introduction to Ethnography course carry out Area Studies projects. However, all projects are dealt with according to the same procedures, even though the assessment criteria are different. They are awarded a provisional mark based on the text, by one or two internal examiners and one external examiner from another university. The mark is then confirmed or amended after a 20-minute oral examination, conducted in the foreign language, at which the external and at least one internal are present.

External examiners are briefed by the ethnography team the first time ethnography projects are submitted to them. They are generally less accustomed to certain features, for example the reliance on first-hand data and student interpretations of them, or the often unfamiliar bibliographies, which are usually related to methods or concepts, rather than being country specific as in Area Studies projects, or the issue of generalisability of cultural patterns on the basis of the study of a small group. Furthermore, examiners are not always familiar with the object of study, and the substance, if not all the theory of cultural interpretation, may well be more familiar as it relates to cultural patterns that they do know. This leads to very lively debate and discussion, and provides students with a valuable opportunity to translate what they have learnt for an 'outsider' who is usually a native or near-native speaker and is regarded as an expert on the culture and society of that country.

In the oral examination itself, students are also given a chance to develop or clarify ideas that perhaps were not satisfactorily expressed in the written text. This often results in marks being slightly raised after an oral examination, when the external examiner has verified the value of the project. Examiners have commented favourably on the originality of students' research and conclusions, on their engagement with their topic, on their initiative in developing a topic and on the use of first-hand data. We mentioned above the significance of reflexive analysis by students of their own effect on the situation in which they are working, and the ways in which they critically reflect on their own cultural knowledge. This does not always appear explicitly in their project text, but it often emerges clearly in the oral examination as students are questioned on how they decided to interpret their data in particular ways.

Examiners also raise problems peculiar to ethnographic projects, with respect for example to what can be considered evidence and how generalisable the findings may be. This is another reason why it is important that students include an explicit description of the circumstances of the research, with a reflexive account of how data were obtained and analysed.

The formal criteria for assessment are familiar to students from their Home Ethnography (see Figure 20). In order to explain what can be achieved in practice, we shall describe one successful ethnography which was awarded a first-class mark and which we have referred to, in passing, already.

Grace's study was entitled 'Die Kategorisierung ausländischer Studenten durch ihre deutschen Kommilitonen. Ein ethnographischer Bericht'. She begins with an introductory explanation of the structure of the 'report', which has two initial chapters describing 'the development of the research problem' and the report on the fieldwork, methods and sources of data collection. The development of the research problem arose from her own initial response to the expectations of her

---

Assessment criteria

- The ability to pose interesting and innovative questions that lead to an illumination of the material.
- Evidence of theoretical understanding of reading to underpin the particular study.
- The ability to use appropriate data collection methods both systematically and creatively.
- A proper recognition of some of the methodological problems involved in the collection of ethnographic data.
- A proper recognition of ethical issues related to informants.
- The ability to select, order and describe research material in a coherent and persuasive way.
- An ability to draw interesting, analytical conclusions from it which demonstrate underlying patterns and cause.
- Sensitivity to language use in its social and cultural contexts and an understanding of the construction of concepts and meanings out of the language used by participants in social settings.
- Initiative, commitment and reflexivity in developing an ethnographic project.
- The amount of effort put in to overcome difficulties, collect data systematically, etc.

Figure 20

German student peers with respect to what is appropriate behaviour, and secondly from her noticing how foreign students tended to meet with each other and have little contact with their German peers. She points out that although, at first glance, the report appears to be about foreign students, it is in fact about German students and how they respond to foreign students.

After these two methodological chapters, there is a 'background' chapter to explain how and why foreign students come to Germany in general and to the University of Marburg in particular, where Grace was enrolled herself as a student. The next chapter is based on document analysis and interviews with those in charge of the office for foreign students. It analyses the categorisation of students to be found in the law and in the declarations of officials and politicians.

The next two chapters are introduced as an analysis of the categorisations used in the student culture with respect to foreign students, for which the legal categorisations serve as a backdrop, but which do not coincide with the legal and official categories. Both chapters are focused on the ways in which foreign students can adapt and be accepted by their German peers, thus revealing the ways in which German students expect others to present themselves. The first of these chapters considers the factors which are unchangeable, such as physical appearance, country of origin and length of residence. The second analyses the factors where foreign students can change, such as development of linguistic competence and the adoption of German value systems with regard to 'order' and 'proficiency' for example, or social skills and sexual behaviour.

The final chapter summarises the hypothesis which guided the work and the findings. It also includes a critique of the research reflecting on its limitations, on the effects the doing of the ethnography had on Grace's understanding of her own situation in Germany as a student, and on what she felt she learnt about German value systems in general. The report finishes with endnotes which give the sources of statements in the text, including the dates when interviews took place, and an appendix which lists all the sources of data: interviews with German and foreign students, observations in the refectory, cafeteria, lectures, student parties and so on, again with dates, and a bibliography of work on foreign students in Germany.

One of the major strengths of Grace's work is in her understanding of methodological issues. For example, she explains the ways in which she found and interviewed informants, making distinctions between those who were already known to her and those who were new. She describes the advantages and disadvantages of each, and how the move from acquaintance or friend to interviewer could affect the subsequent relationship. She also analyses her own expectations of what would happen in interviews, which topics might be sensitive and difficult to discuss, and then explains how these expectations were not always fulfilled and the effects on the course taken by the interview. She concludes her discussion of the interview process with foreign students as follows:

> Durch die Interviews mit den ausländischen Studenten lernte ich vor allem, wie entscheidend meine Rolle als Interviewerin war. Meine Erwartungen, Vorurteile und Ängste konnten die Interviews beein-flussen, und meine Interpretation von ihnen. Obwohl ich die Meinungen der Interviewpartner erforschte, erforschte ich gleicher-weise meine eigene Rolle und mit jedem Interview verbesserte ich meine Methoden und entwickelte meine Rolle.
>
> (Through the interviews with the foreign students I learnt above all how decisive my role as interviewer was. My expectations, prejudices and anxieties could influence the interviews and my interpretations of them. Although I was researching the opinions of my interview partners, I was simultaneously researching my own role, and I improved my methods and developed my role with each interview.)

It is clear from this and similar passages in the report that the ethnog-raphy meets the criteria concerned with ethical issues and reflexivity. The careful documentation of data collection and citation from inter-views and documents, together with the discussion of the difficulties of interviewing and observing are further strengths in respect of method-ology criteria.

The data analysis chapters can be divided into those which are based on 'public' data, – the statistics on foreign students, the legal documents and interviews with representatives of the office for foreign students – and 'private' data from interviews and observations in the university. The former are presented in a way which draws upon anthropological concepts of boundaries and social groups. The latter are analysed in terms of over-arching categories which Grace has extracted from the descriptive and narrative language of the interviews. She uses quota-tions to support the categories grounded in the data. For example, she argues that one crucial mode of adaptation is in 'alltägliche Sitten' (daily customs) and refers to an extract from an interview:

> Um gesellschaftlichen Kontakt zu haben, muß der Ausländer bestimmte soziale Fähigkeiten lernen, z.B. Rino aus Indonesien sagte:

"Am Anfang fühlte ich mich nicht wohl dabei, in Kneipen zu gehen, weil ich nicht wußte, wie man sich verhalten mußte. Es gibt überall kulturelle Regeln, die man lernen muß. Aber jetzt weiß ich genau, was ich machen muß, wenn ich in Kneipen gehe, auf Feten, zum Tanzen oder mit Frauen umgehen soll."

(In order to have social contact, the foreigner must learn certain social skills, for example Rino from Indonesia said: "At the beginning I didn't feel at ease going to pubs, because I did not know how to behave. There are cultural rules you have to learn everywhere. But now I know exactly what I have to do when I go to pubs, to parties, to dances or how to behave with women.")

She also uses appropriate literature, for example to support her identification of the significance of sexual behaviour as a crucial factor in adaptation, as also appears in the quotation from Rino.

The sub-headings for these chapters give an indication that Grace has ordered her material according to the analytical categories she has identified, not yielding to the temptation of letting descriptive material dominate. From her initial questions about why foreign and German students seem to remain separate, she has developed an analysis which demonstrates nuances in the particular situation she was observing and links with general social issues of how Germany is responding to an influx of foreigners in recent years. Thus criteria such as 'ability to draw interesting, analytical conclusions from (research material) which demonstrate underlying patterns and cause' are well met by Grace's account. As was pointed out by one of the assessors, 'Grace raises many interesting questions and is looking for new ways of understanding what everyone is conscious of.' It is also worth remembering at this point that students write in the foreign language and that the external examiner commented on her fluency and accuracy saying that 'the project itself is positively stylish in its narrative confidence'.

It is important to have some relatively objective way of assessing cultural learning and the ethnography represents the best way that we have found of doing this. It is possible to assess how much cultural knowledge has been learnt in more traditional ways, through essays or tests, if by that we mean positive facts about the school system, trends in popular music or aspects of a society's history or myths, for example. But, when cultural learning concerns the everyday and the values and beliefs of a particular group and also involves an awareness of the student's own cultural being, then an ethnographic study provides the intellectual and emotional space to display such learning.

But in this chapter, we have also tried to stress the importance of the process of writing an ethnographic project as well as the final outcome. As we have suggested, for many students the process of being there, collecting data and analysing it was just as important as the writing up and, in any event, cannot be separated off from it. In the next chapter we look more closely at the process of learning while abroad and use students' evaluations to examine the whole programme from the ethnography course through to the final year of the modern languages degree course after the ethnographic studies have been completed.

Chapter 10
'The Year Abroad': An Ethnographic Experience

Student Interviews

The preceding chapters have focused on the teaching and learning process during the ethnography course. The core of the Ealing project is, of course, the period of fieldwork during the Year Abroad. For the students, as we shall see, the integration of their fieldwork into the whole process of preparation and of writing up and being assessed on their return, was a crucial experience and one quite different from that which is offered on more traditional modern languages programmes. This was indeed one of the main aims of the Ealing project as curriculum development, and the research element of the project included a focus on the evaluation of the integration process. For this reason, students in the first cohort were interviewed on their return, during their first term back in Ealing.

Evaluation was also carried out informally through class diaries of each session of the ethnography course and through the field diaries which students were strongly encouraged to keep and which they were free to submit or not as part of their project. In this way, ongoing evaluation of the ethnography project as a whole can be maintained but the in-depth interviews reported here can only represent the experience of doing ethnography for the original group. An additional factor to bear in mind is that this group of students was closely monitored. They were as they called themselves 'the guinea pigs'. So their representations of the experience of being student ethnographers may well have been affected by the Hawthorne effect (in which the very process of being researched on can make the experience more positive for the group studied).

The focus of the interviews was very much on their experience while in Spain or Germany, doing their fieldwork. All the students had spent several months in two countries, since they studied two languages, but

210

their ethnographic studies had been carried out in the first country they visited, in the first half of their Year Abroad, from September to January or February. The project in the second half of the year was less substantial and intended to be of the kind usually required in Area Studies courses – a long essay about an aspect of the society in which they were living, usually library-based. Although the interviews concentrated on their first placement, some students carried over their ethnographic skills into their writing of the second project and this suggested that 'doing ethnography' was compelling, even when more traditional and less ambitious projects were all that was required.

The experience of doing an ethnographic study was still a vivid one for them after being back in England for several months, and despite the intervening stay in a second country. The interviews dealt above all with the fieldwork, but also attempted to stimulate discussion on the Introduction to Ethnography course and the writing-up and follow-up phase. They found, on the whole, the former difficult to discuss separately from their fieldwork; it had become an integrated experience and in that respect already demonstrated the success of the Ealing project overall. The follow-up phase, including tutorials and writing their ethnography projects, was being completed at the time of the interviews and was therefore very much in their minds.

In the first year of the project, nine students volunteered to participate and it is their experience which is reported here. They were all attached to a university rather than in a work placement or acting as language assistants in schools, although one of the group, Antonia, had arranged to be an 'au pair' for a family in Seville and studied her five-year-old charge Quino as part of her ethnography (see Chapter 2).The students spent about five months in two out of the three target countries, France, Germany and Spain, and undertook their ethnographic projects in either Germany or Spain.

In succeeding years, the numbers grew quickly as the reputation of the 'ethnographers' became established in the institution, so that a class usually contains about 20 students. They all go abroad as students, but developing language learners as ethnographers could work equally well with those going to a work placement or as language assistants.

During their semester in Germany or Spain, they were visited on one occasion by one of their ethnography lecturers. This was part of the existing practice, and other students also received one visit from a lecturer. This allowed students to discuss their work, to assess their progress with the lecturer and, in some cases, encouraged them to review and organise their field notes for the discussion. Tutorials were held with a group in a particular location – in Seville, in Granada, in Marburg, in Berlin – and with individuals. Lecturers took notes during these visits, which are used here, to give an impression of student accounts of their experience mid-way through their fieldwork.

In the Field

The following is taken from notes made by Ana during her visit to the students in Seville, in November, some two months after their arrival. They focus on the conversations she had with Gary. Two weeks before the visit, when Gary had been in Seville for only six weeks, he wrote to Ana saying that 'I'm now having *big* doubts about the whole thing. I'm seeing too many things – fault of being taught how to make strange? Changing ideas for the project every hour, i.e. food, gambling, shouting. You name it, I've thought of it!'. But during the visit Ana and Gary were able to clarify things together:

> Gary is making fairly good progress – living with a Spanish man, Rafael, who has put him in contact with a lot of people e.g the ex-mayor of Seville. Gary commented: 'I've been casting my net wide to get a feel for what I want to look at, which has made me do a lot more, talk a lot more and go to loads of places I would never have gone to before.'
>
> When I arrived he had already started narrowing down. Now his project is on Sevillano identity, looking at how Sevillanos differentiate themselves from others who are considered to be less 'andaluz'. He has narrowed it down to analysing what the barrio he lives in is all about. His key informants are: R., his landlord, who has been involved with the local 'hermandad' organising for the 'Feria'; A, the housekeeper who calls herself Sevillana but is from a pueblo near Seville and JL who is also involved in the Feria but on a more popular level than Rafael. JL is from a 'barriada' – a nearer suburb of Seville and is also involved in singing and 'romerias' (procession).
>
> Gary is exploring, for example, the role played by the two main virgins in Seville in the construction of identity. (There are hundreds for almost every barrio but the people he has met are 'followers' of the two main ones e.g. on everyone's key rings etc.). Most of Gary's notes are 'headnotes' – he hasn't started indexing yet but we worked out a rough plan with analytical categories which he is working on now. He commented: 'I've become really weird with all this ethnography. I'm living it 24 hours a day. So I couldn't stop if I wanted to.'

His main problem has arisen over the issue of informal interviewing. He had not told anyone what the topic of his ethnography
was going to be when he went out one night with JL to a popular
flamenco bar. Gary started to question him about his barriada,
how he felt about being Sevillano. Gary was bombarding him with
questions and JL called him 'cabezón' (stubborn, pigheaded) for
pretending to be a bit dumb. Because of this difficulty with JL, we
discussed the next day the pros and cons of telling JL about the
project. We decided that Gary would say that he had just had a bril-
liant idea to do his project on what makes Sevillanos so special as
a result of talking to JL. Gary did not want to say he had been
studying him all along as they had become good friends over the
last two months. Gary needed to change his approach a little from
'playing stupid'. I suggested that he stopped asking 'why' or 'what
does that mean' questions and instead just tried phatic communication or repeating back the others' words. He found this much more
productive.

More generally, the group of students in Seville had really become
a group. They help each other, even collect notes for each other and
give moral support by going to each other's sites. For example, Gary
goes to church with Antonia and, as well as classes on the anthropology of Seville, he joins her in the anthropology of religion classes.
Also, certain general things overlap in their ethnographies such as
'performance' as an aspect of Sevillano identity. Gary also drew
parallels with his home ethnography on his group of friends in
a Yorkshire village, specifically to do with issues of inclusion
and exclusion.

Gary said that, like all the others, on the one hand, he felt at home
now, he had a life in Seville and he did not want to go to his next
placement and was going back for the Feria as he felt he could not
possibly miss it now. On the other hand, he said that ethnography,
by virtue of looking always for patterns below the surface, had made
him see things in a far less romantic way. So he had to deal, initially,
with a certain disillusionment and negativity, before getting to appreciate it again. For example, the group are still quite critical of some
aspects of Sevillano life, which they say is because they understand
it better. In particular, they are critical of what they call the 'theatre'
side of Spanish life: 'Everything is for show'. It will be interesting
to see if they can develop this idea into a more relative, analytic
view – that in a sense everyone is a 'social actor'. I talked a little
about Goffman in this respect.

Ana's comments demonstrate the importance of the lecturer's visit in the early stages of doing an ethnographic project. For Gary, the mix of general moral support, confidence boosting that what he was doing was not 'weird', specific help with methods and some conceptual nudges to remind him and the others to stand back a little from the data to be more analytical, all helped to steer him at a crucial moment in his developing project.

On their return to England, at the beginning of the fourth year of their course and after a semester in another country, students had further tutorials to discuss their writing up of their projects, and seminars in which they presented their work to others in the group. It was at this point that the interviews took place.

Preparation and 'The Real Thing'

In their evaluation of the ethnography course, students were unanimous in finding the course both rather unnerving at first but later exciting, quite different from their other courses, valuable as preparation and, more broadly, educational in making them 'continually question and re-examine things that I took for granted'. One student summed it up this way: 'The course tackled fundamentally significant issues. It has given method, structure, confidence and legitimacy to the study of areas which have always interested me.' However, although students found the ethnography course interesting and worthwhile in itself, bringing them to reflect on themselves and the cultural practices in their own society, it was all preparation for 'the real thing'. This in fact fell into two parts, the fieldwork and writing up, for although students were encouraged to begin to write their ethnography project while in Spain or Germany, they in fact did so on their return to England. Those who had made a start found that it did not work:

> **Grace:** And the thing was I just couldn't write in Germany. I tried to write in Germany, I just couldn't. Because I was living with a lot of people I'd interviewed and it felt like I was living it every day and I just couldn't get a clear perspective on it at all. And it was only when I left Germany that I could concentrate and actually sit down and write it.

The choice of a topic was linked in different ways to the ethnography course. Students were encouraged to choose at the end of the ethnography course while they were still in Ealing, in part to ensure they had an initial focus and also so that lecturers could help them before they left. In some cases this did actually become the basis for their project.

In Gary's case, as we mentioned above, it was a development of his 'Home ethnography', done, in his case, during the Easter vacation.

Gary: We decided two months before we went out. Actually we did the Easter ethnography.
Interviewer: Yes I remember reading, I found that really interesting.
Gary: I think I chose it because of the Easter one because that was about identity as well. And it just seemed an obvious thing to do, I don't know why.

In more frequent cases however there was a complete change:

Toni: . . . what I was going to do didn't work so I changed. I went to church and it occurred to me when I was there (. . .) I was going to do it on women, like my French one. I thought it would be a good idea, especially since my French one had an ethnographic bit but it just didn't work out. I didn't know what was going to be there when I arrived.

Anna: I wasn't getting anywhere. But also a lot of people found that when we got there . . . it was all very well choosing a title here but when we got to Spain there was a thing that struck us much more than what we'd already thought of. You know things we saw in the street, that'd be a great project to do, you know, it was so obvious but you'd never think of them here.

In other cases, as we saw in the analysis of projects in chapter nine, a topic arose out of students' early experience of the country, in the first weeks of their stay. One student felt she was treated as a foreigner, yet differently from some other foreigners, and the question of German perceptions of foreigners became her theme. Another started from an existing interest in dance:

Sandra: Yeah so then what I started to do, there was this bar in particular. There was a bar in particular in Granada that they just exclusively played the Sevillanas. And so I decided, you know, I started to go there because I love the dance myself, I mean I've been to Andalusia before, and it's a really fun dance you get a lot of pleasure doing it. So I started to go and I just started to observe it.

Data Collection

Much of the ethnography course had focused on data collection and analysis. Students had already had experience of participant observation, of interviewing, of reviewing and indexing their field notes, partly from weekly assignments and partly from their 'home ethnography'. In the field, they engaged in different kinds of interviewing, sometimes audio-recording conversations and interviews and sometimes in informal contexts where they made written notes afterwards. Grace reported how she ensured her interviewing was on a systematic basis, by comparing official documentation with the opportunities in her immediate environment:

> **Grace:** Oh yes, so then I started interviewing people, on my floor basically, 'cause that was my only real contact with foreigners, and through them I met other people. And I tried to take a fairly broad section of what was (indistinct) I had figures from the President of the University's office, it was something about a breakdown of what nationalities there were (indistinct).
> **Interviewer:** That's very resourceful.
> **Grace:** I tried to try and get a cross-section because, well because otherwise I was in danger of just talking to . . . I knew a lot of Indonesians and things like that. So I sort of, like, a mixture of Chinese, Iranian, Palestinian, Persian. And then I did interviews with Europeans and Americans as well. But mainly stuck to the ones who weren't European.

Gary, developing his home ethnography, took an opposing approach, deciding not to make his topic explicit at first, as we have seen earlier. People assumed he was writing a project about 'Expo1990', while in fact he was studying concepts of local identities in Seville. He did this largely through participant observation, and very informal interviewing of people around him, trying to clarify their ways of talking about themselves as people of Seville:

> **Interviewer:** So by Christmas you'd got your main informants sorted out in your mind?
> **Gary:** Yeah.
> **Interviewer:** Did you ever interview them in a more formal way?
> **Gary:** What do you mean by formal?
> **Interviewer:** Well . . . 'Can I come along and talk to you about . . .'
> **Gary:** No, no. (Indistinct) . . . in bars. And then the other people I knew I didn't, I mean obviously if they started talking about it, I did try and get things out of them. I didn't go out of my way to interview everybody.

Students also described different levels of participation and observation. Initially, it was not always evident to them, despite earlier experience, how their observation could help with their topic, for example with the project on German perceptions of foreigners.:

> **Grace:** Observation was a huge problem, I just couldn't understand how to get anything out of observation. And, you know, 'cause I used to sit downstairs in the University cafeteria which is where all the foreigners would group together and it was a place where you could make connections between who sits with Germans and who doesn't.

She nonetheless persevered, attending various lectures and seminars as well as the cafeteria before turning to interviewing, which proved productive.

Sandra, working on the theme of the Sevillanas, was more of a participant and found this gave her plenty of material:

> **Sandra:** They knew that (what the topic was), because I would talk ... and every time I went out and I met different people I would always get talking about Sevillanas. Any excuse I had. And they love talking about them. It's a very passionate subject in Andalusia. And so then if I was with a friend I would dance with them. The thing is there's so much pressure to dance it, from what I've found through my participant observation, was that you'd be watching a roomful of people dancing Sevillanas and yet you'd be watching two couples and one couple would attract you so much and yet the other wouldn't. And I thought well wait a minute you know they're doing exactly the same dance.

At this point in Sandra's account, there is evidence of how students become interested in semantic analysis. They focus on the language of their informants and on specific keywords. Sandra identified the keyword 'gracia' (grace) and explains how she noticed this in the way people talked about the dance:

> **Sandra:** So then this element of being graceful or 'having grace' came into it. So they were saying, 'Well that's what differentiates them you know, they have to have grace.' So I was thinking, I've got to look at this dance, and I spent hours I mean I couldn't even tell you how many hours. I mean throughout the whole six months I don't know maybe twenty, thirty hours a week just watching the dance and trying to distinguish the elements of what having 'grace' meant.

A similar situation is described by another student:

> **Christiane:** ... the thing is that I had an informant and I was using him quite a lot and I was saying, 'Well you know there are certain

words that I don't understand, I don't understand what it actually means so can you explain it to me?' And he would do it like that, used to do it like that.

They also, in some cases, kept diaries, which served a double purpose of allowing them to give vent to their doubts and emotional stresses, and also to serve as a collection of observations:

> **Grace:** Well I kept a diary like we were supposed to, every day, and that really helped enormously. Even if I didn't do anything the whole day, I'd take the diary, because there were things that came up in the diary that you pick out afterwards, and you know they're such a help, this little instance you don't realise.
> **Interviewer:** And stuff as well that you might forget later?
> **Grace:** Oh totally. I put down all my thoughts about the whole thing you know. Any of the grievances I had or anything like that.
> **Interviewer:** Are we going to see this or is this . . .
> **Grace:** I think Hanns (tutor) saw it. I've still got it somewhere. And that really helped, 'cause later you make connections and think, 'Oh that happened to me earlier'.

In another example, the diary merges into field notes and an alternative to using a tape-recorder for interviews:

> **Chris:** I used it for some of that, questioning the whole point of why I was doing it. Just thoughts that came into my mind however disconnected I just put it down. 'What's the point of doing this?' Followed round by . . . – I don't know who it was – a male prostitute followed me – 'What's the point?' I used to stick in my diary – 'interesting'. I was enjoying it but 'What the hell am I doing?' That kind of thing. Also, trying – making comments of a reflective nature – myself – and about the nature of each of the informants and the source – where I got the information from, as to why it may or may not be a meaningful piece of data – either given or been received and interpreted and what might have influenced what I actually put in the main part as data. Did not use tape recorder, I could not have, really couldn't have handled the volume of stuff coming over. I would have to be spending hours listening to the tape and trying to decipher.

In fact, during their stay they said they were totally immersed in their project and 'couldn't stop taking notes'. At the same time, there were other students from Ealing who were not doing ethnography projects and who perhaps felt that the ethnographers formed a clique, always talking about 'identities' and 'boundaries' and so on. The ethnographers compared themselves with their colleagues and felt that they had become involved in the society around them more quickly, had a more sensitive awareness of, for example, forms of politeness in Spain, and sometimes felt embarrassed by their colleagues who made less effort to adopt appropriate ways of behaving. They also felt greater ownership of their projects and saw them as very different from the factual account they were used to writing:

> **Grace:** At college you get loads of facts. Most of it isn't your own, but this is all your own. None of this is anyone else's.

The Writing Process

One of the issues which students felt insecure about at the point when their tutors visited, was the style in which they should write their projects. They needed at this relatively early stage to discuss writing-up in general, but the question of 'reflexivity', which had been introduced in the course, was still worrying them. Most of their academic writing up to that point required an impersonal style, but as we saw in the analysis of finished projects earlier, they were encouraged to analyse their relationship with informants in the field, and the possible impact of their own presence on the data they were collecting.

On the other hand, there is little evidence either in the projects themselves, or in the interviews cited here, of a reflexive reassessment of their own pre-suppositions about the environment they found themselves in and also their own environment in England. It would be surprising if the experience of analysing the values and meanings of people in another cultural environment did not have this effect. What was perhaps lacking in our work with students was an explicit incentive to see reflection on self and the relationship of their own cultural values to those of the people they were studying as a legitimate aspect of foreign language work. It is only recently that this aspect of language learning has become an explicit objective stated in curriculum documents at secondary school level, and it is even less evident in higher education. Traditionally, the attention of language teachers and their learners has been focused exclusively on the foreign, leaving reflection on the self at best to tacit learning. Only in the case of translation exercises is there explicit comparison and contrast, and the purpose is to search for equivalences, implying an underlying uniformity, rather than to face difference and the challenge of 'denaturalisation' of the all-too-familiar .

Students were also concerned, during their tutors' visits, about the assessment of their projects, which they knew would be part of their final degree classification. On the other hand, they knew that it counted for only 5% of the total, a peculiarity of the institution but symptomatic of the low priority given to work from the Year Abroad in many other universities. In fact, their commitment to the project led to a higher than average grade across the group.

The writing process itself came at a later stage, although the degree of integration with fieldwork varied. From one point of view, the process was constant and not really separable, even if the writing was delayed until the following summer:

> **Toni:** I'm handing it in on Friday. It seems to have just dragged on for ever now 'cause it's been over a year since we went, and we've been doing it since then. And really apart from the time that I was in France, and even then I was thinking about it, and the other girl I was with, Kate, was going through it as well, we kept noticing how much it influenced us then. So we were never free of it for the whole year, even though we weren't actually working on the project in France, and all through the summer writing it all up, yeah, sorting it all out, and now typing it up, because it's so long.

Even when a certain distance has been achieved and with it a perspective that allows the writer to reflect on how they are going to organise the work, the experience of writing varied. Whereas Grace said she 'hated it', because 'I had the ideas but maybe the categories weren't clear', others found it less difficult. Anna was the kind of writer who mulls things over and then sits down to write.

> **Anna:** I'd already worked it out in my head in which categories I wanted them all to go, I'd already worked out. So when I worked it out, when I wrote it up it wasn't too difficult, just getting the data together I think and working out what a tradition is and which parts belong to an institution maybe, and just working out what the actual, like, the headings would be. How this information had to be sorted.

Sandra reported two stages in her writing-up on the Sevillanas. She had come to some conclusions while still in Spain, but began to question them as she gained more time and distance – and then she reviewed the whole dissertation in a concentrated period after returning to England:

> **Sandra:** Because I mean I went to Spain (again) this summer but I went to the north and I remember I was talking to people about my

conclusions then, but I mean, I started to question them. And I was thinking well you know wait a minute, it can't be as empty. But I didn't pursue it any further until afterwards. I came back and I started reading over it and I handed it in here. And they (the tutors) were saying you know I was always talking about this empty performance and that's when you know I took it home and in a week I mean I just basically lived it, like maybe two weeks ago, completely got into it. And you know I started to see these things and I also started to see different aspects. Religion came into it as well. Image came into it.

We suggested when analysing the ethnographies, that writing in a foreign language is an unusual aspect of these projects, and students were clearly aware of this issue. They felt that accuracy was not their main problem, but rather their awareness of semantic fields and connotations.

They had often made a particular effort to study the semantics of their topic and this doubtless heightened their feelings of inadequacy, and yet also increased their sensitivity to the language. Grace speaks for herself and others when comparing with English. It is a moot question whether, if writing in English, they might have encountered simply a different kind of problem:

> **Grace:** I think the main problem is being able to express, you know, in the correct way. You're never sure when you're writing it in German if you're actually saying what you wanted to say in English. Because obviously they're so, like, something in English may mean something different in German and not in a huge way but in a small way. You know, different connotations or words or something you know, or things like that.

The effect of writing in a foreign language, after acquiring the discourse of ethnography in English, was evident in the finished projects, and there was the constant danger of simplification and transposition of modes of interpretation embodied in the writing itself. The students themselves were aware of repetitions and grasping at terms in their writing; 'trying to translate things like "going native" and "participant observation"', as one student put it. It was felt to be a particular problem by those who had begun to learn the language at the start of their university course:

> **Toni:** Yes it is hard because my Spanish isn't that brilliant, even though as I say it did get better when I was in Spain, I think. But it's hard enough to express some concepts of ethnography in English let alone do it in a language that's not even my second language

because I was *ab-initio*, like Christiane. So I don't know. A lot of the time I couldn't express exactly how I wanted to or put it in any depth or any subtleties, nothing. And it's all very repetitive probably for that reason. That's the only way that I could do it and get across everything that I want to as best I can, so it wasn't all bad.

Other difficulties included the wish to put into the project the whole experience, the feelings – 'there are lots of feelings that are not there' – and the personal development involved:

Toni: It is very difficult and more than anything else it's frustrating because you can't really, or I haven't been able to and I know other people are frustrated with theirs. There isn't any way that you can condense into a project of that size everything that you went through to get to the state where you can actually write about the project. You'd have to be having a sabbatical and writing novels to be able to do it and we're not, so it is frustrating because there's so much more that you want to say or so many more parts of the net that you want to explore but you really can't. And even having cut it down as much as we have, they're still too long.

Living the Ethnographic Life

Some students thus regretted that they could not describe 'everything that you went through', and others needed their field diaries to express some of that feeling and reflect upon it. The Year Abroad is for many people a moment of significance in their lives as linguists. It is a period of major change. Doubtless part of this is general maturation, but linguists certainly consider that there is at least an acceleration of that process, and probably much more, because of the demands and stresses involved.

One of the hypotheses of the project was that there would be some specific advantages in using ethnographic methods. Although there are many purposes for the Year Abroad, the major ones seen from the universities' point of view are the increase in students' understanding of a society where their target language is spoken, and an improvement in their mastery of the language itself. It is nonetheless possible for students to spend a substantial period in another country and have little contact with native speakers or with the institutions and practices around them. This is particularly the case when students live in university hostels with other foreign students, and take courses designed specifically for foreign students. We hoped that ethnography would at least bring students into closer contact with their environment.

In practice they felt that doing ethnography was the dominant factor in their stay, in contrast to those doing Area Studies projects:

Grace: Their project (referring to other Ealing students) was something that they could just go home after lectures and do for an hour or two, you know, and that's it and finish and that's it, switch off. They would be researching it in books or whatever as well as pamphlets and whatever. But it was something that you had to do all the time, ethnography is something you had to do all the time, so I felt it made my time there more productive for me.

For some it became such a dominant factor, that they began to feel annoyed:

Christiane: And I was really angry and thought, 'Heck I'm not doing ethnography. I'm just going to have a social life.' But ethnography doesn't leave, I mean doesn't go, it's there to stay. And I found myself saying well you know I left the ethnography I said, well that's it you know. 'Stuff this whole project I'm going down to the pub', I'd been invited to the pub. And we were sitting in this pub and I was talking to these German friends and I started looking because they were people I was living with and my ethnography was about them. I started looking at the way they were sitting and why they suddenly, in that particular set-up, chose to speak to certain people about certain things. You know I was thinking, 'Oh, Christiane this is getting a bit crazy. Here you are at eleven o'clock at night in a pub trying to relax and you're doing ethnography, it can't go on.'

Others echoed the notion of 'getting a bit crazy' with phrases such as 'why can't I just enjoy this' (Gary) and 'I kept seeing all the way through the things that related to my project . . . I would probably, you know, have done my head in, in the end' (Toni).

One effect for those who went to Spain, was to remove quite quickly the illusions they had. They reported this to their tutor when she visited them and again when reflecting on their stay in the following year:

Sandra: I went to Granada with a very romantic idea of Sevillanas, very romantic idea. You know, I believed this whole image of Spain, you know, sun . . . I mean even though I go there every summer I still have this very touristic image of Spain because that's all I do, I go to the sun, I go to the beach, sunny weather, go out. And so I went to Granada, decided to do Sevillanas and went in with a very romantic view of it. I absolutely love Sevillanas you know, I love dancing so, you know. But then when I started to do this ethnography I started to see. I didn't actually at the beginning realise. It wasn't obvious, the social and moral values in the dance aren't obvious so I didn't actually figure this out till maybe two weeks ago. So I just had this like really big transition from having such a romantic idea of it to a completely depressed view about it.

It is particularly interesting to see how Sandra first had an indefinite sense of disillusionment and only later was able to analyse the dance in terms of its values. This then gave her a deeper satisfaction through her increased understanding. This is a parallel process to that which sometimes took place in the classroom during the course. We saw how students resisted the analysis of gift-giving as exchange and 'poisonous' but then, at least in part, accepted that at a more analytical level there was another way of looking at gifts. The ethnographer quickly gains a quite different view of a country she might be familiar with in another role.

With respect to increased knowledge of the country and people, some students attributed this directly to the ethnography project:

> **Grace:** It really was basically about the Germans, how they view everything, their perception. Even though it was through the foreigners talking about the way Germans saw them. But I think I have a really much better understanding of how the Germans tick now than I did.
> **Interviewer:** In what way?
> **Grace:** Just things like why, what motivates their kind of behaviour, things like that. I mean one of the major chapters in our project was about German law and how rigid it is and people just do tend to stick to the law you know.

So, here we have evidence of how some stereotypes can persist, although with a qualification in the phrasing 'just do tend to'. One of the effects of doing ethnography was to reduce this way of observing. Already during visits from tutors, it was noticed that students were being 'more cautious about hasty generalisations' and the 'usual clichés'. In contrast to Grace's statement, Christiane takes one such generalisation, that German students study a lot, and qualifies it as a consequence of her observations:

> **Christiane:** It doesn't mean that the whole nation does the same thing, that's one of the things you learn too. I also know that. OK, I was with German people, German students and they were

particularly nice in that particular set-up. But I can't say that all German people are very nice people as a result of that. It was in that set-up, it was with these people. But I can understand also better about the way they see life. There was one thing, about the German students: they study a lot. Well I mean it is a bit of a myth actually. It is true to say that some people do study a lot but some others do not study that much. But it is depending on what they're doing, what stage of their studies. All sorts of factors come into it.

The point was reinforced by Sandra who made an explicit link with the demands of ethnography:

> **Sandra:** Well I think, you know, the conclusions that you come up with (in) ethnography, you can't just come up with them if you've just seen it once. So you know you need to be culturally aware, you have to spend a hell of a long time actually looking at it. And every time you look at a certain situation you observe different things and then they lead you on to other things.
> **Interviewer:** So it would make you more wary now of jumping quickly . . .
> **Sandra:** Oh yeah I don't take things at first glance at all.

This kind of circumspection about the extent of their knowledge was pursued by Toni, who suggests there are distinct limitations to the understanding and to the sense in which one might feel at ease in a foreign country. She argues that if one has not been brought up in a certain culture there are some things, 'tiny, stupid things', which remain beyond one's grasp and that the difference creates a tension. It is of course precisely such tiny things which the ethnographers were studying in specific aspects of their environment. This tension leads to an awareness of being an insider to a certain point, but with a critical perspective which, elsewhere, we have called 'critical cultural awareness' (Byram, 1997a):

> **Toni:** And you've already had an upbringing somewhere else that's played a part in creating the person that you are, you can't lose that, there's nobody who's a neutral person. So I suppose that's one thing that really did become apparent, you know, you felt as I said before, they let you into their group or they let you become involved, but only up to a point. But it's far enough for you to be teetering on the edge between feeling really bad about what you say about them and actually realising that you'll never be one of them so why should it matter what you say.

Interviewer: But in a way what you've been saying is you become more critical than they would be of themselves. Do you think that's true or not?

Toni: Yes. Probably due to two things, the fact that you did start as an observer and you are purposely looking at them with specific questions in mind. And the other reason being what we've just said: that you weren't brought up that way.

So the critical perspective has been heightened by the task of formulating and investigating questions in the ethnography, and Toni at least has gained a complex insight into the nature of social groups, intergroup relationships and the process of socialisation.

Language Acquisition

The issue of having close contact with people around them, through interviews and observations and sometimes from participating and friendships, is also related to the question of language acquisition. We did not set out to measure language acquisition as others have done (Coleman, 1996; Dyson, 1988) but we did ask students for their views. One, Anna, felt that she had not made noticeable progress because she had been quite proficient already, having lived a year in Spain on a previous occasion. Grace said she felt she had not made as much progress as in her understanding of 'Germans and German culture': 'I know it's a learning process but for me it was more a learning process about Germans and German culture than about German language.' Others felt that doing ethnography had obliged them to make contacts despite their reticence:

Toni: The first thing is I think my language improved (indistinct) . . . because it made me approach situations differently. It made me more bold where perhaps I wouldn't have been before. Regardless of my ability in the language I'd just, like, go for it, and so that helped ultimately.

Christiane: Well it did help because it forced me, as I say, to go and talk to people, which I wouldn't have done. I would have quite . . . I think I would have quite happily sat down at my desk and done my law work, taken my books. I would have quite happily done that because I felt so cut off when I arrived in Germany, that that's basically what I would have done.

Christiane also compared this favourably with attending university language classes in Germany, which were either too difficult when intended for native speakers or too crowded with little opportunity to speak, when provided for foreigners.

The students and their tutors had already remarked at the time of the visit that the project forced them out into the community and 'gave us something to talk about', particularly improving their listening skills through speaking with local people. In retrospect they contrasted this with an Area Studies project which they had seen their colleagues engaged in:

> **Gary:** Getting back to the language thing, I hadn't thought about this, but first of all there were three other students there and thinking back now, they never used to sit ... The only Spanish person living there was the landlord but I used to sit with him for hours and used to talk to him about Sevillian identity. So yeah it did. It did improve it.

> **Sandra:** Yeah. And you have to speak to people, whereas if you're doing Area Studies you don't have to speak to anybody at all really, I mean you can just go into a library and do that.

Finally, we return to the issue of doing semantic analysis as part of the ethnography project and the attraction this has particularly for linguists. One student said her sensitivity to words in the foreign language had been enhanced:

> **Christiane:** Yes. I've always done that anyway with French and English because I'm interested in words, I like words. I like the use of words. I like playing with words. And before ethnography I suppose I didn't know that the same word would have, to certain people, slightly different meanings. I mean it's so slight at times it's very difficult to see. Because I would tend to use the dictionary's interpretation or meaning of certain words and OK that's very interesting but what is even more interesting is how people see that word, rather than what the dictionary says.

Here we see the interests of the linguist and the ethnographer clearly coinciding.

Summing Up

We said earlier that the Year Abroad is often experienced as a cause of change and maturation. Not surprisingly, the ethnographers shared this and attributed much of it to doing ethnography:

Christiane: Because I realise now that I am changing, my views are constantly changing and it's very unsettling, especially when changes are really sort of really big changes. And it changes you as a person and you don't know quite who you are anymore and what you think anymore and where you're going. It's like being in this dark room and not finding the door. You know that it's there and you're going to find it you know, but it's that time when you do ethnography which is very . . . And it's the learning about yourself in terms of a person, it was a bit frightening at times.

This fear of the effect on oneself is compounded by the anxiety felt at constantly observing others and looking for explanations of them which prevents a more familiar relationship. Several students spoke about this in some detail, talking of their tendency to 'start to look at lots of things in different ways, including people, and people around you . . . sometimes, you know, it is better to live in ignorance' (Toni). A similar concern is expressed by Sandra:

Sandra: . . . because you learn a lot through experiences in life and this ethnography is a very big experience, for me anyway. And it's good because you don't take things just as cut and dried, you start looking at a situation. But then as I say when you look at situations you might not like the conclusions that you come out with. You know, they might be negative conclusions. And then you think, 'Oh God' and then you start asking questions about yourself, questions about people that you know. And then if you always, like, come up with an answer at the end that you might not like, you feel really . . . 'Is there anything good out of it?'

She feels, too, that there is sometimes a need to discuss this, perhaps with support from tutors, and we are again reminded of the ways in which, already in the classroom, students had found some issues unsettling. Perhaps some of this is the effect of having the opportunity to talk about the Year as a whole, as well as about doing ethnography. This is certainly an important facet of the integration of the Year into the whole course, and one which is often neglected.

Finally, two students had interesting remarks about their career plans. Grace said she would 'like to do something a bit more socially orientated' and Sandra thought she might take an MA in Social Anthropology rather than in interpreting, as had been her earlier intention. Although we did not set out to make linguists into ethnographers, 'living the ethnographic life' was clearly a major experience for these young people.

Chapter 11
Conclusions and New Perspectives

It has been our purpose in this book to argue for a new understanding of language learning, one which starts from the fact that linguistic learning has to be integrated with cultural learning in order to respect the nature of intercultural communication. We have not only presented an argument but demonstrated an approach on the basis of a case study. The argument is also being made elsewhere (Kramsch, 1998) and the conclusion that language teaching should aim to develop in learners an intercultural competence, rather than an imitation of a native speaker competence, is being increasingly accepted, for example in the 'Common European Framework of Reference' of the Council of Europe (Council of Europe, 1998). What we hope to have demonstrated in this book is how, in one set of circumstances, language learners can become intercultural speakers through ethnographic practice.

In this final chapter, we shall review the issues and the approach we have represented from two perspectives: the significance of the Ealing project for individual learners involved in it, and the ways in which the 'language learners as ethnographers' approach can influence learning and teaching in other circumstances and situations.

Ethnographers as Intercultural Speakers

Two juxtaposed quotations from earlier chapters demonstrate one dimension of our approach to language teaching/learning and its significance for language learners. In Chapter 3 we quoted Pocock:

Social anthropology is concerned with the whole of life, and not just something you do until six o'clock. The study of social anthropology encourages you to have a new kind of consciousness of life; it is a way of looking at the world, and in that sense it is a way of living. (1975: 1)

This was closely echoed in Chapter 10 by Grace:

(. . .) it was something you had to do all the time, ethnography is something you had to do all the time, so I felt it made my time there more productive for me.

The fact of 'doing ethnography' had created for Grace, and others, a mode of engagement with her new environment, a means of understanding and relating to it, which she felt other linguists from Ealing did not have. This mode of engagement involves the students in a heightened sense of awareness as they participate in the routine acts of their life abroad. It requires a constant questioning of the way things are done and an active approach to find their significance.

Nonetheless, it has been a central tenet of our approach that our ethnographers were not attempting to become the social anthropologists whom Pocock is describing. They remain linguists and language learners with a new and charged sense of communication and interaction, as another quotation from Chapter 10, from Christiane, shows:

I like words. I like the use of words. I like playing with words. And before ethnography, I suppose I didn't know that the same word would have to certain people slightly different meanings.

She goes on to contrast 'the dictionary's interpretation' with 'how people see that word'. The false transparency of a bilingual dictionary, with its apparent one-to-one relationships between language and meanings, is replaced by the discovery of complex relationships. Those relationships are also evident in how students talk about their writing, in the self-conscious use of language, in the ways in which they struggle with a foreign language both because they feel less secure in their linguistic competence, and because they are aware of the heavy charge, the embeddedness of language in the environment and the culture which people 'do'. Their understanding of language and of themselves as linguists has been radically affected by their ethnographic life.

At the end of Chapter 2, we suggested four broad categories of learning which our approach would facilitate:

• local social and cultural knowledge;
• processes of interrogation and relativisation;
• observation, social interaction and analytic skills;
• personal development.

We have discussed in Chapters 9 and 10 how students – 'language learners as ethnographers' – developed in these different ways, as seen from their own accounts and as evident in their projects. No doubt they did so to differing levels and degrees of intensity, and as with all educational process, we cannot know the longer-term effects (but see below for a case study of one student).

We have also suggested that their development as linguists can be understood in terms of the concept of 'the intercultural speaker'. This is above all someone who can see and analyse relationships between cultural practices associated with one language, often their first language, and the language and cultural practices of 'others'. They do so as a learner, as someone who is still conscious of constantly acquiring new linguistic and cultural insights. That learning process is however not only focused on the other language and cultural practices but also on what they have hitherto taken for granted and left unquestioned in their own (Todorov, 1988).

'Les savoirs'

The characteristics of the intercultural speaker can be defined as five 'savoirs' or competences additional to those which are more linguistic (Byram, 1997a). Briefly they are:

- *Attitudes*: curiosity and openness, readiness to suspend disbelief about other cultures and belief about one's own (savoir être).

The indications of the ways in which the ethnographic life led students not only to be open to the environment and cultural practices they met but also to reconsider their own taken-for-granted world are to be found particularly in their reflections analysed in Chapter 10. This sense that you cannot 'take things cut and dried' is encapsulated in Sandra's refusal to jump to conclusions:

> **Sandra:** Well I think, you know, the conclusions that you come up with (in) ethnography, you can't just come up with them if you've just seen it once. So you know you need to be culturally aware, you have to spend a hell of a long time actually looking at it. And every time you look at a certain situation you observe different things and then they lead you on to other things.
> **Interviewer:** So it would make you more wary now of jumping quickly . . .
> **Sandra:** Oh yeah I don't take things at first glance at all.

Similarly, in the writing-up of the project, as one student commented, the writer's world and that of the group being studied mesh together:

When you are doing ethnography, it's you and the place, it's you and the people. You can't *not* write yourself into it. You are part of it.

- *Knowledge*: of social groups and their products and practices in one's own and in one's interlocutor's country, and of the general processes of societal and individual interaction (savoirs).

The knowledge which they acquired was specifically local, about the social and cultural practices and underlying beliefs which they met in their chosen topic, and more generally in the local world in which they interacted with their informants and others. For example, the study of the French pétanque club in Aubervilliers led to knowledge about social relationships between the younger and older players. In another case, it is again Sandra's careful account of the stages of her growing under-standing which reveal the 'insider' knowledge she acquired. She had started by looking at Flamenco and then moved on to the Sevillanas dance because it was less 'staged' and more part of everyday life:

> Las Sevillanas are staged as well but they're danced in class, they're danced in bars. If there's a fiesta, they're danced out in the streets. So I thought that was very interesting and the fact that why this dance in particular was danced. Sevillanas is a dance, a Flamenco, but you can't call it Flamenco because it's separated from the others because its practised in everyday life. Whereas Flamenco nowadays you just see it staged . . .
> . . . by going out to bars and discos, I would always bring up the subject of the Sevillanas and people kept on saying to me, they had to have 'grace' or in Spanish, 'gracia'. And you know I was thinking, 'what the hell is this 'gracia'?' . . .
> What it is I found that to have 'grace' you have to be accepted by the people in your culture, and the way you're accepted in the dance . . . is that you have to represent 'gracia'. Now having 'gracia' is to show that you are able to use stylistic movements in the dance, also you have to have a certain talent to dance and you have to have self-esteem . . . There's two different roles for men and women in the dance, it represents a collective identity . . . they're portraying their own social and moral values in the dance . . . so 'grace' isn't natural at all.

- *Skills of interpreting and relating*: ability to interpret a document or event from another culture, to explain it and relate it to documents from one's own (savoir comprendre).

It was above all in their projects that students demonstrated their ability to interpret one set of events, one set of practices, in ways which made them evident to their readers. They drew on the concepts and theory of social anthropology to do so, and their task was all the more complex because they were establishing relationships between the language in which they had first met these, English, and the language in which they had experienced and investigated their topic and were producing a written report, Spanish, German or French. Chris talked about how he interrogated his own interpretations and tried to be reflexive about them:

> . . . trying to make comments of a reflective nature – myself – and about the nature of each of the informants and the source, where I got the information from – as to why it may or may not be a meaningful piece of data.

He did his second project in France after spending five months in Seville. He chose to do a topic on why there was no longer any bullfighting in Toulouse. He found himself comparing the bullfighting he had seen in Spain with how this event had been experienced in Toulouse:

> [the people of Toulouse] go slightly more wild because they are so isolated within the community they have adopted in Toulouse – between two natural areas of bullfighting. They adopted the Spanish style pure and simple. The only period in fact when there was any bullfighting activity was when they wanted to be different, they wanted to exaggerate something. They wanted to be gatekeepers, I didn't say it in those terms, but that's basically how I perceived it. They wanted to be in charge of some wild, exciting, exotic, external, therefore, cultural phenomena. Because they were close to, but not really quite part of genuine ones. It was an exploration of identity and belonging and all that.

Here he is using one phenomenon to understand another and the concept of gatekeeper and identity to place it within a theoretical frame.

- *Skills of discovery and interaction*: ability to acquire new knowledge of a culture and cultural practices and the ability to operate knowledge, attitudes and skills under the constraints of real-time communication and interaction (savoir apprendre/faire).

This is the activity of fieldwork *par excellence*, what we described above as 'observation, social interaction and analytic skills'. This became so much a part of students' experience that they could not escape it even 'after six o'clock'.

Rachel studied the blind students at Marburg university and explains how this brought her into constant interaction with others as she used her ethnographic skills to observe and analyse:

> I think the greatest thing was that I really did get to know the people I was writing about ... I think I got to know a lot more German people that way than I would have done doing another project – because you're more involved. I mean you have to speak and you have to listen. I mean it's not a matter of going to the library – you know get some books out and just sit in the library, you know you have to meet people and talk to people and that's what I liked about it really ... you get more enjoyment, more satisfaction yourself in doing it because you know it's your own work, you know you've done it yourself and you really do know what you're talking about ... I had to listen a lot because I couldn't record so I was really relying on my notes, which at the beginning I found quite difficult but later I sort of was able to take notes and if I wrote them up quickly afterwards I usually got most of the information.

Grace, when thinking back on her study of overseas students, valued the knowledge she had gained from interactions, from 'living the experience':

> ... before, if it wasn't in a book, I'd be jumping you know, I'd be really nervous, you know. Why can't I get something really solid about this out of a book ... I think this way is more integrated, isn't it, because you have to live the experience to be able to write it, you have to participate in it.

- *Critical cultural awareness/political education*: an ability to evaluate critically and on the basis of explicit criteria perspectives, practices and products in one's own and other cultures and countries (savoir s'engager).

In our earlier definition of the intercultural speaker (Byram, 1997a), this element was described in terms of language teaching/learning mainly in the classroom, and was seen as part of the educative responsibilities of the teacher which go beyond mere instruction. In the Ealing project, teachers/lecturers were instrumental in providing the framework, developing students' ethnographic skills and ethnographic imagination, but it was above all during fieldwork and in their constant reflections, often to be found in their journals rather than in their projects as such, that students became self-conscious about their own perspectives, practices and products. It was, as Christiane said, 'very unsettling', and 'a bit frightening at times'.

Toni, again on the subject of bullfighting, was able to take a more critically evaluative view of an activity which she didn't like:

> I'm not going to barge into their culture, and say no you can't do it because it's linked up with too many other things or it must be. My logic tells me from having done the religion part that it must be. It doesn't alter the fact that I don't like it, it just means that I can look at it in a more objective way and I can argue my position more objectively as well as by saying you know they say it's art. And I say, well yes it is the art but there's no need to put vaseline in their eyes and cotton wool up their noses, knowing you have to kill them in the end. You can have the art without it.

This is not to say that the students discussed here were 'complete' intercultural speakers as a consequence of their ethnographic learning, for this would be a self-contradiction. They remained acutely aware of the unfinished nature of their learning. As linguists, they were particularly aware of this with respect to their linguistic and sociolinguistic competences. As ethnographers, they knew that their 'savoirs' remained partial, had to be constantly questioned, even if they had to come to some conclusions in their written-up projects as they neared the deadline for submission.

What, in a classroom environment, we have called 'critical cultural awareness', a teacher-led reflection on the ethical viewpoint in comparative analysis of cultures, becomes in fieldwork engagement with the minutiae of local interactions and the processes which are both observed and, as participant, experienced. For Sophie, the politics of the *carnavaliers* are in the processes of power and position – and the marginalisation of women. The evolution for Antonia of a critical cultural awareness of the relationships between religious practices and eating and drinking is in the gradual problematising of the discourse.

Individual Development in the Year Abroad

As we have noted from the beginning, the Year Abroad is a tradition for language learners which, as an obligatory phase of higher education studies, is peculiar to Britain. Conceived as part of the language learning process, it inevitably also has other effects on the individuals involved. For some, it coincides with a first separation from home and family. For others, it also involves living as an isolated foreigner in a new community.

The effects in personal maturation, as opposed to the development of linguistic and intercultural competence, are inevitably idiosyncratic and part of the personal biography (Alred, 1996). Students may change their career aspirations, like Grace and Sandra in the Ealing project. They may change their physical appearance like a young woman interviewed in an earlier project which was a stimulus for the development of the Ealing project:

> I've completely changed, appearance, physical appearance. I've grown my hair. I used to have really short permed hair, very very curly, very very short. And I've grown in the idea of becoming chic and French-like. I've changed my style of dressing, becoming more conscious of what I'm wearing, rather than just putting something on in the morning. But that's all obviously an influence of being in France. Because they do have this idea, you know, they are conscious of what they are wearing and how they look. So I mean I have changed physically an awful lot and people didn't recognise me when I came back. (Byram & Alred, 1993: 56)

For some the experience has an effect on their social identities, particularly their national identity, as these accounts from two informants from the same research show:

> I have never really thought of being English as something that was important to me anyway. But going over there, I realised the great differences that exist between countries. So I suppose, at the beginning especially, I felt very much English. You are the representative of your country. But then I felt less English in the way I really settled into their culture and got very used to it and in fact I prefer it. So in that way I don't feel English at all. So I do and I don't.
>
> I would love to be French, but you can't. I can never be French because you have to be born French. I could be a European. I couldn't be French though. There's no way you can become French. You could live in France. You could speak French but you'll never be French unless you're actually born French. (Byram & Alred, 1993: 54)

There may also be longer-term effects which have not yet been investigated.[1] Evans also argues that the Year Abroad is crucial to the formation of the identity of 'linguist' analogous perhaps to a rite of passage:

> A degree in Modern Languages is a sandwich course and the meat is the year abroad. It is scarcely an exaggeration to say that no other

degree, no other subject, offers this opportunity (. . .) Only students in vocational subjects like Law, Medicine or engineering have such an intensely formative experience built into their programme of studies and of these only Medicine in its later stages offers anything like the same human challenge. (Evans, 1988: 42)

It is interesting to see how in the decade or so since Evans was writing, the opportunities have been opened up to other students through European Union programmes, in particular ERASMUS and SOCRATES, and this is an area for extension of our approach as we shall see later.

Evans argued too, as we have, that the crucial dimension is that of identity: 'The experience is so formative that it involves basic issues of identity', and he found a similar range of attraction and rejection of new identities: from 'I think I'm English (. . .) I prefer to stay in England' to 'Spanish is me. I am more me speaking Spanish than English. I felt wrong speaking English' (Evans, 1988: 48).

It is possible therefore to argue that such effects of the Year Abroad are independent of the approach taken to linguistic and cultural learning. On the other hand, our ethnographic approach clearly involves the whole person, and this has been a leitmotif of our work encapsulated in the quotations from Pocock and from the student Grace at the beginning of this chapter. Language learners as ethnographers are inevitably engaged with the otherness of their new environment not just as an opportunity to improve linguistic competence and their ability to produce appropriate utterances, but as whole social beings who are developing, defining and being defined in terms of their interactions with other social beings. As ethnographers and intercultural speakers, they negotiate a particular relationship with those around them, a relationship traditionally described as participant observation, although this fails to capture the complexity of the reflexive effect on the linguist-ethnographer. Once more this is best articulated by Christiane in Chapter 10:

And it changes you as a person and you don't know who you are anymore and what you think any more and where you're going. It's like being in this dark room and not finding the door. You know that it's there and you're going to find it (. . .) and it's the learning about yourself in terms of a person. It was a bit frightening at times.

So the Ealing project to develop language learners as ethnographers is not just a methodology and a set of techniques for preparing language students to profit from the opportunity for language learning during a period of 'immersion'. Such a metaphor does not reflect the complexity of language-and-culture, teaching-and-learning, neither in residence abroad nor in the processes of the classroom. The project is concerned with the affective, the emotional, with the acting out of new identities, and this means that we need to reconsider the ways in which we conceptualise what is traditionally called 'language learning'.

From Language Learning to Intercultural Interaction

The label 'language learning' is very convenient because it reflects the focus of the activity of teachers and learners, their concern with the linguistic code which is the most evident problem they have to solve if they are to succeed. The concern with language is reinforced by the use of language as an indicator of identity – 'I am X because I speak X'; 'You are an X citizen and should speak X' – and this is a position taken by those who govern nation-states. These were issues addressed in one of the units during the ethnography course (Unit 13) and in Chapter 4 of this book. Similarly, much professional academic effort in the modern period of language teaching, since the Reform Movement in the 1880s, has centred on the description of linguistic codes, and how these are internalised by infants, children and adults, as first, second or other languages.

The language teaching profession has become increasingly sensitive to labels, distinguishing language teaching from language learning, or distinguishing the study of a language as an object for analysis from learning and acquiring the competence required to communicate. The major contribution of 'the communicative approach' has been not to introduce yet another teaching method but to change the purpose of language learning: from language as a key to high culture to language as a basis for everyday communication. At the same time, the communicative approach coincided with the flourishing of mass secondary education in Europe and mass higher education in North America, and seemed to offer the means of making language learning available, and necessary, not just for a social elite, but for everyone.

'Communication' thus seemed, and perhaps still seems, to be the key word to encapsulate the aims of language teachers. It is certainly a dominant word in governmental and similar statements about the purposes of language teaching in many education systems. Unfortunately, as we pointed out in Chapter 2, 'communicative competence' has been interpreted too narrowly by language teaching professionals (Byram, 1988), and it is for that reason that we need, reluctantly in some respects, to introduce another label, namely 'intercultural competence', to emphasise a re-conceptualisation of language learning.

The description of learning we have provided in previous chapters has in fact put little emphasis on learners' internalisation of a linguistic code, but this is not to say that it is unimportant, either for the learners or for the teachers. Our decision to teach the ethnography course in English rather than Spanish, German or French, was an acknowledgement of the linguistic difficulties students would have with a new discipline in their foreign language, although they did have some readings in these languages. Students themselves became very aware of the complexity of internalising a linguistic code, that it is not the relatively simple matter they had encountered in the classroom up to that point. They talked about the issues in their ethnographic reports, about the advantages and disadvantages of having been taught the Introduction to Ethnography Course in English, the problems they had to face when finding no literal and easy translations of some of the concepts they had been working with, and what all this taught them about the nature of language and its relationship to the cultural realities and practices they had observed.

While aware of these issues, however, our emphasis has been deliberately on other dimensions of learning to interact with speakers of another language in their own environment. We have done so to redress the balance, not to ignore the acquisition of linguistic competence. We have also followed this emphasis because of the nature of the learners being described and the learning conditions they were experiencing.

These factors, of course, determined our specific approach, but at this point we want to argue that a general view of 'language learning' in terms of 'intercultural interaction' can be developed from the particular case of the Ealing project, a view which has evolved from our view of language learners as ethnographers, and as intercultural speakers not merely as 'competent communicators'.

The most important point is that learners are not simply, and not centrally, acquiring skills. The process in which they are involved engages them as people, requires them to reflect upon and analyse how they interact with others. The process is thus both cognitive and affective, but the affective is not merely a reduction of anxiety or the creation of appropriate attitudes and motivation in order to facilitate the internalisation of a linguistic code, as has been suggested by much of the research on the affective dimension of language learning (e.g. Gardner & MacIntyre, 1993; Dörnyei, 1998) – important as this may be. It is, rather, an engagement with a new social identity which is integral with the acquisition of methods and concepts for reflection and analysis.

Ethnography provides the means, and the mind-set, to develop those dimensions of intercultural interaction which have hitherto been ignored, those 'savoirs' (*être, comprendre, apprendre, s'engager*) which are crucial to being a successful intercultural speaker, not merely an unsuccessful imitator of a native speaker.

An ethnographic approach thus requires learners to engage in academic study, in intellectual engagement with new concepts and new ways of analysing social phenomena, and in higher education this is entirely appropriate. It ensures that 'language learning' has an educational purpose, a development of the whole person, and this in turn ensures a proper justification for 'language learning' in higher education. As well as, and not instead of, the study of the high culture written in another language, learners in higher education are introduced to the study of intercultural interaction, which largely takes the form of verbal and non-verbal communication. This has two dimensions: conceptual analysis and methodological issues of data collection. What makes the ethnographic approach, as a basis for such study, different from literary studies or area studies is the emphasis on both cognitive classroom-based analysis and experiential learning in fieldwork, both in the home country environment during the ethnography course, and in the other country during the period of residence.

There are also implications of this view of 'language learning' for 'language teaching'. We have described in earlier chapters how those teaching the ethnography course, and advising on and assessing the students' ethnographic projects, had to reconsider their focus and professional identities. We have described not just 'language learners as ethnographers' but also 'language lecturers as ethnographers', who engaged in similar learning processes to those of their students. In some respects, this was more difficult, since lecturers have established themselves as 'language people' (Evans, 1988) whereas student learners are still involved in a process of professional identity formation.

Since we hope that readers of this book will include higher education language people, with specialist interests in literary studies, area studies or other fields, we do not underestimate the implications of our view of 'language learning' for 'language teaching'. It is for this reason that we offered in Chapters 2, 3 and 4 an overview of the issues which we have engaged with ourselves, of the journey we have made, and in later chapters an account of the ethnographic learning by staff as well as students.

Language Learners as Ethnographers: A Generalisable Approach?

The generalisation of our view of intercultural interaction and of the language learner as ethnographer and intercultural speaker takes several directions:

- towards different kinds of learners in other sectors of both compulsory and post-compulsory education, including life-long education;
- towards learners in higher education other than language people;
- towards other kinds of language people, in particular translators and interpreters;
- towards learning limited to the classroom and learners' immediate environment, as opposed to residence abroad and long-term fieldwork.

The question of generalisation has to be seen in two ways. First, we are confident that our description of what is involved in intercultural interaction is relevant to all learners. Whatever their age, occupation or degree of identification as language people, they can only be successful to the extent that they become intercultural speakers. It is worth repeating at this point that the concept of intercultural speaker encompasses a wide range of levels of proficiency and effectiveness. It is not an all-or-nothing concept, although it may be that there is a minimum level of intercultural competence needed for successful interaction with interlocutors of another cultural identity, particularly in some affective dimensions of relativisation. If the notion of intercultural interaction is relevant to all learners, so, we would argue, the model of the intercultural speaker must be generalised, and it is for this reason that we traced the evolution of the theory in Chapter 2.

In fact, the history of language teaching and learning has been subject to increasing refinements of purposes as research and understanding of the nature of language in use has developed. One of the innovations of the Reform Movement and its successors in the early part of the twentieth century was to recognise and introduce into language teaching the significance of spoken language. The communicative approach added the emphasis on the use and functions of language in social interaction, and the introduction of sociolinguistic and discourse competences to complement linguistic competence. The notion of interculturality adds a further dimension: the recognition of social identities involved in any interaction, and the significance of understanding the constantly changing worlds and lives of 'the other', always important but particularly so when the interaction takes learners into other languages and societies. Since the aims and purposes of language learning in many contemporary contexts are very clearly to enable learners to interact personally with 'the other', there can then be no doubt that the notion of interculturality must be generalisable.

The second dimension of generalisation concerns the ethnographic approach to the development of intercultural competence. We have argued in the first part of this chapter that the Ealing project demonstrates how the ethnographic approach develops and enhances the characteristics of the intercultural speaker. It does so because it involves learners in a type of interaction with people of another language and society which makes them conscious of and reflexive about cross-cultural relationships by engaging them directly with the local and the specific. They develop both linguistic and intercultural competences in the experience of fieldwork interaction as both verbal and non-verbal, as embedded in a 'context of situation' (Firth, 1968).

The question is therefore whether the ethnographic approach can be extended to other learners in other situations, to the groups identified at the beginning of this section. Perhaps the most crucial issue is whether learners have opportunity for investigative fieldwork, but we also need to ask whether the concepts and methods introduced during the Introduction to Ethnography Course can be accessible to other types of learner, particularly those who are younger.

In the European context, the opportunity for direct personal interaction with people of another language and society is quickly becoming available for many learners. In European Union countries, there are a number of schemes to encourage mobility of learners in various education sectors. In the wider Europe, such mobility is much less frequent although there is doubtless a strong potential if practical and financial difficulties can be overcome. In other contexts, for example North America or Japan, the notion of study abroad is also well established both for language people and other students. Where fieldwork opportunities and the possibility of participant observation are not available, however, one option is ethnographic interviewing (Spradley, 1979), the exploration, over a number of encounters, of people's perceptions, narrations and conceptualisations of their experience. This could be carried out at a distance through telematic channels such as video-conferencing, especially as the quality of the technology improves. The affective engagement with others in such intercultural experience will doubtless be different from that in the field but may also be valuable and valid.

The adaptation of fieldwork for younger learners has been the subject of some experimentation (Snow & Byram, 1997) and involved presenting learners with investigative skills; but there is a need for further systematic work. On the other hand, the extension of fieldwork and an ethnographic approach should not in principle present significant difficulties in courses for interpreters and translators, for whom the role of the intercultural speaker as mediator is central.

Similarly, adult learners in higher, further or lifelong education who are not language people but for example engineering students, or local politicians involved in town-twinning, will in principle also find the ethnographic approach accessible. An Introduction to Ethnography Course for engineers or politicians who are to spend some time in another country is easy to envisage and their fieldwork investigations would doubtless reflect their particular experience of local cultural practices in an engineering company or a town council. This is not to underestimate the difficulty of persuading those in charge of preparing such people that an ethnography course is necessary, but the extension of our approach is conceptually feasible and relatively manageable.

The major difficulty in generalisation is to learning situations where learners cannot break out of the walls of the classroom, where neither fieldwork nor telematics are available. The difficulties of presenting learners with intercultural experience, with opportunities to engage with others, to investigate and analyse and to establish relationships, are evident and not underestimated. They are perhaps also the reason why many teachers, themselves often with no intercultural experience, focus exclusively on linguistic competence, with perhaps some attention to sociolinguistic and discourse competences, but certainly no attempt to develop intercultural competence. This therefore remains an imponderable, but insofar as the social and cultural conditions of the contemporary world are the source of new experiences of interculturality and the re-conceptualisation of the learner as ethnographer and intercultural speaker, it is also possible that classrooms too will change in as yet unforeseen ways which will facilitate the acquisition of intercultural competence.

Finally, there is the issue of generalisability for the Ealing students themselves. What have they been able to take from the experience and integrate into their lives over the years since they left Ealing?

We conclude the book with the views of one student, Chris Day, and his reflections, looking back eight years. Since leaving university, Chris has taken a post-graduate teaching certificate and now teaches Spanish in Devon, at Exeter College of Further Education. He remembers clearly the excitement of taking the ethnography course and the 'shock' it gave him:

> I started seeing things which I used to see all the time but never
> interpreted ...which was presumably one of the main aims ...
> looking for meaning and patterns and clues ... getting into the
> grammar of meaning rather than the grammar of language ...

The experience of doing the project is still vivid: 'I had some unusual
evenings out chatting with certain male transvestite prostitutes'; as is
writing it up: 'I was reasonably satisfied with a 14,000 word block-busting
Spanish project – that was an achievement in itself'. From the experience of the course, collecting the data and writing up, he identifies three
areas which have had a profound and long-lasting effect on the way he
sees the world. The first was concerned with empathy, with the skills
of interpreting and relating, mentioned above:

> It had never occurred to me before the project to look at things from
> other people's point of view. That's one thing I overcame through
> this ethnography project, not to use your own vision, your own
> terms to describe things as a first resort. It was a huge step not only
> to see and speak to people but communicate with them in their own
> terms which was an excellent thing and one of the long-lasting effects.

The second area concerned attitudes more generally:

> Another general effect it has had – the preparation and the whole
> ethnography terminology – is the effect of enabling me and I suppose
> all of us to handle ambivalence, ambiguity which is an important
> language learning skill – a deep structure, a deep grammar leading
> beyond just language.

The third area, connected to both of the first two, relates to a general,
perceptual level – the way one looks at the world:

> I don't still hang around with prostitutes in bars chatting! But I can
> probably spot different things going on around – I think it's a broader
> more perceptive level – very few things would shock or surprise me
> now. I wouldn't let myself be surprised. So that's been a long-lasting
> effect on me.

He recognises that ethnography 'can't change the kind of person you
are if you're never going to be a curious, open, empathetic kind of person,
I don't think it can make you one' but 'it can develop things which are
in you'. So, if a student is receptive to change and ready to develop, the
experience of doing ethnography can have a long-term influence.

Reflecting on himself as a former language learner and now a language
teacher, he sees ethnography as making the links between language

learning skills, interpreting otherness and taking on a new social identity. He makes connections between the 'urgent need' to communicate
in the foreign language and the whole process of writing an ethnographic
project:

> I'm better at learning language from people – I listen more to the
> message in what people are doing – the effect on my Spanish
> learning. The absolute urgent need to take in, understand, interpret
> and re-present something which is difficult to get your head around.

So every act of communication is, in a sense, a miniature ethnography
project in which it is necessary to:

> find something out and subsequently make sense of it to myself and
> then present my findings.

The process of doing this, Chris argues, affects one's social identity so
that one may be able to pass oneself off as Spanish:

> I've always held in the back of my mind what a marvellous thing
> to pass myself off as a speaker of another language. I suppose I
> must have learnt from the ethnography thing, as well, a more neutral
> way of being so that I can, to an extent, be taken for a Spanish
> person through things that I've absorbed – posture, body language.
> Heightened awareness from the ethnography would have con-
> tributed to that. (Ethnography) sparked off a huge curiosity – an
> interpenetration of the culture and me – such that I behave, feel
> and act to it like members of that group – like Spanish people but
> not fully . . .

He takes things further in linking his partial membership of the group
with his development of cultural knowledge. The relationship between
this new knowledge and changing identity he attributes to an ethnographic approach which he contrasts with a 'tourist, info, consumer'
approach:

> Getting into Spanish culture identifying with it – building up a
> complex and detailed picture of it – that I wouldn't have done if I
> had had a tourist, info, consumer kind of approach as opposed to
> the ethnographic, bifocal approach. I see that through a thick version
> of what I think it means. I think the ethno project did achieve that
> – to take in things from the inside. There's a word in Spanish – I
> can't think of the word in English, maybe that's part of it – 'asumir'
> – to assume one's responsibilities, it feels like it grows out from
> within you – it becomes part of you rather than responsibility being

placed upon you. It doesn't necessarily start outside you – do you know what I mean?

Since many students of modern languages in higher education are likely to become teachers, the long-term effects of ethnography on Chris as a language teacher are relevant here. He contrasts the idea of teaching language skills that can then be used on others with a more reflective approach to language learning and teaching:

> A customs officer once said to me 'Oh I've learnt some Spanish. I really enjoy *using it on other people*'. He obviously hadn't done any ethno!

Instead Chris tries to:

> put over the idea that it's possible to look at the world in a very different way and I do it at a linguistic level – with simple phrases at beginners' level. I try to give a feel for how a Spanish attitude to life or things is represented in simple things in the language. I also ask bilinguals if it is possible to think without using a language. The bilingual kids say 'yes'. They're used to having an idea in Language A and having it slightly different, untranslatable, in language B and realising that they're got an idea that they can't quite express in either language. It's possible to think something in Language A which can't be formed in Language B because you haven't got the tools. But because the idea exists in Language A, it's just that Language B is inadequate not the nature of ideas. I don't say this to 16 year olds because they would just look at me. But you just have to 'word' it – something as simple as 'me gusta' – 'It pleases me' – suggests that Spanish people look at things as they come to them as opposed to the English 'I like it'. 'You're lucky' as opposed to 'Luck touches you' which maybe suggests a more receptive attitude to life. I try by adopting odd points of view, asking slightly awkward questions about interpretations of why people speak in a certain way – why certain language is used – that it's possible to see things in quite a different way but they are OK people.

In small but frequent ways, Chris uses the ethnographic experience to introduce to language students the idea that language and cultural practices are 'wired in together' (Agar, 1994). But he remains a language learner as well as a language teacher:

> My life is largely made up of language learning and language teaching and accumulated cultural knowledge and awareness.

So, Chris is still a 'language learner as ethnographer'. The original course undertaken eight years ago 'took me places where I wanted to go' and he is still crossing borders and boundaries. The challenge of being an intercultural speaker is always present for Chris and any other language learner who wants to take it up. What is important is setting off on the journey and remaining a traveller in the new places and spaces of an intercultural world.

Note

1. A new project to carry out a follow-up study with a cohort of students 10 years after their Year Abroad began in March 1999.

Bibliography

Agar, M. (1980) *The Professional Stranger.* New York: Academic Press.
Agar, M. (1986a) *Speaking of Ethnography.* Beverly Hills, CA: Sage.
Agar, M. (1986b) *Independents Declared: Dilemmas of Independent Trucking.* Washington, DC: Smithsonian Institute.
Agar, M. (1991) The biculture in bilingual. *Language in Society* 20, 167–81.
Agar, M. (1994) *Language Shock.* New York: William Morrow.
Alix, C. and Bertrand, G. (eds) (1994) *Pour une pédagogie des échanges.* Special Issue of *Le Français dans le Monde.* February–March 1994. Paris: EDICEF.
Alred, G. (1996) Being abroad – becoming a linguist: a discussion of the psychosocial effects of the Year Abroad. Paper presented at the Research seminar on The Year Abroad, University of Lancaster, UK, January 1996.
Althusser, L. (1971) Ideology and ideological state apparatuses. In L. Althusser *Lenin and Philosophy* (pp. 121–73). New York: Monthly Review.
Andersen, H. and Risager, K. (1979) Fremmedsprogsundervisningens socialiserende funktion. *Forskning in Fremmedsprogspaedagogik.* Copenhagen: Statens humanistiske Forskningsraad.
Anderson, B. (1983) *Imagined Communities: Reflections on the Origins and Spread of Nationalism.* London: Verso.
Asad, T. (1973) *Anthropology and the Colonial Encounter.* London: Ithaca Press.
Asad, T. (1980) Anthropology and the analysis of ideology. *Man* 14, 60–77.
Asad, T. and Dixon, J. (1985) Translating Europe's others. In F. Barker (ed.) *Europe and its Others* (pp. 170–7). Colchester: University of Essex.
Atkinson, P. (1990) *The Ethnographic Imagination: Textual Constructions of Reality.* London: Routledge.
Atkinson, P. (1992) *Understanding Ethnographic Texts.* London: Sage.
Atkinson, M. and Heritage, J. (1984) *Structures of Social Action: Studies in Conversation Analysis.* Cambridge: Cambridge University Press.
Bailey, F. (ed.) (1971) *Gifts and Poisons: The Politics of Reputation.* Oxford: Basil Blackwell.
Bakhtin, M. (1981) *The Dialogic Imagination.* Austin: University of Texas Press.
Barley, N. (1990) *Native Land.* London: Penguin.
Barro, A. and Grimm, H. (1993) Integrating language learning and cultural learning: An ethnographic approach to the year abroad. In J. Coleman and A. Rouxville (eds) *Integrating New Approaches: The Teaching of French in Higher Education* (pp. 147–64). London: CILT.
Barro, A. and Jordan, S. (1995) The effect of ethnographic training on the year abroad. In G. Parker and A. Rouxville (eds) (pp. 76–90).

Barro, A., Jordan, S. and Roberts, C. (1998) Cultural practice in everyday life: The language learner as ethnographer. In M. Byram and M. Fleming (eds) (pp. 76–97).

Barth, F. (ed.) (1969) *Ethnic Groups and Boundaries: The Social Organisation of Cultural Difference.* Boston: Little, Brown.

Bartlett, F. (1932) *Remembering.* Cambridge: Cambridge University Press.

Barton, D. (1994) *Literacy: An Introduction to the Ecology of the Written Word.* Oxford: Blackwell.

Basnett, S. (ed.) (1997) *Studying British Cultures: An Introduction.* London: Routledge.

Bauman, R. and Sherzer, J. (eds) (1974) *Explorations in the Ethnography of Speaking.* Cambridge: Cambridge University Press.

Baumgratz, G. (1985) Transnational and cross-cultural communication as negotiation of meaning: Objectives, sociological and psychological implications and methodological problems. In Goethe-Institut/Ralf Eppender (ed.) *Comprehension as Negotiation of Meaning.* Munich: Goethe Institut.

Baumgratz-Gangl, G. (1990) *Persönlichkeitsentwicklung und Fremdsprachenerwerb.* Paderborn: Schöningh.

Baumgratz-Gangl, G. (1993) *Cross-cultural Competence in a Changing World.* Special edition of *European Journal of Education* 28(3).

Beale, C. (1990) 'It's all in the asking': A perspective on problems of cross-cultural communication between native speakers of French and native speakers of Australian English in the workplace. *Australian Review of Applied Linguistics* 8 (7).

Beattie, J. (1962) 'Tis the season to be jolly – Why?' *New Society,* 27 December.

Beaujour, M. (1981) Some paradoxes of description. *Yale French Studies* 61, 27–59.

Beeman, W. (1986) *Language, Status and Power.* Bloomington: Indiana University Press.

Bennett, M. (1986) Towards ethnorelativism: A developmental model of inter-cultural sensitivity. In M. Paige (ed.) *Cross-Cultural Orientation. New Conceptualizations and Applications* (pp. 33–64). Lanham, MD: University Press of America.

Berger, P. and Berger, B. (1972) *Sociology: A Biographical Approach.* New York: Basic Books.

Berger, P.L. and Luckmann, T. (1966) *The Social Construction of Reality.* Harmondsworth: Penguin.

Besnier, N. (1990) Language and affect. *Annual review of Anthropology* 19, 419–51.

Bhabha, H. (ed.) (1990) *Nation and Narration.* London: Routledge.

Billig, M. (1995) *Banal Nationalism.* London: Sage.

Bourdieu, P. (1977) *Outline of a Theory of Practice.* Cambridge: Cambridge University Press.

Bourdieu, P. (1991) *Language and Symbolic Power.* Edited and introduced by J.B. Thompson, transl. by G. Raymond and M. Adamson. Cambridge, MA: Polity Press.

Briggs, C. (1986) *Learning How to Ask.* Cambridge: Cambridge University Press.

Brislin, R. (1993) A culture-general assimilator: Preparation for various types of sojourns. In M. Paige (ed.) *Education for the Intercultural Experience* (pp. 281–99). Yarmouth, ME: Intercultural Press.

Brislin, R. (1994) *Intercultural Communication Training: An Introduction.* Thousand Oaks: Sage.

Brøgger, F. (1993) *Culture, Language, Text: Cultural Studies within the Study of English as a Foreign Language.* Oslo: Scandinavian University Press.

Brown, P. and Levinson, S. (1987) *Politeness: Some Universals in Language Usage.* Cambridge: Cambridge University Press.

Burgess, R. (1984) *In the Field: An Introduction to Field Research.* London: Allen & Unwin.

Buttjes, D. (1991) Mediating languages and cultures: The social and intercultural dimension restored. In D. Buttjes and M. Byram (eds) (pp. 3–16).

Buttjes, D. and Byram, M . (eds) (1991) *Mediating Languages and Cultures: Towards an Intercultural Theory of Foreign Language Learning.* Clevedon: Multilingual Matters.

Buttjes, M and Kane, L. (1978) Theorie und Zielsetzung der Landeskunde im Fremdsprachenstudium. *Anglistik und Englischunterricht* 4, May, 51–61.

Byram, M. (1988) 'Post-communicative' language teaching. *British Journal of Language Teaching* 26 (1), 3–6.

Byram, M. (1994) Cultural learning and mobility: The educational challenge for foreign language teaching. In *Fremdsprachen and Hochschule* 41, 5–22.

Byram, M. (ed.) (1994) *Culture and Language Learning in Higher Education.* Clevedon: Multilingual Matters.

Byram, M. (1995) Acquiring intercultural competence: A review of learning theories. In L. Sercu (ed.) *Intercultural Competence: A New Challenge for Language Teachers and Trainers in Europe. Vol. 1: The Secondary School* (pp. 89–99). Language and Cultural Contact 12. Aalborg: Aalborg University Press.

Byram, M. (1997a) *Teaching and Assessing Intercultural Communicative Competence.* Clevedon: Multilingual Matters.

Byram, M. (1997b) Cultural studies and foreign language teaching. In S. Basnett (ed.) (pp. 53–64).

Byram, M. (ed.) (1997c) *Face to Face. Learning Language-and-Culture through Visits and Exchanges.* London: CILT.

Byram, M. and Alred, G. (1993) *'Paid to be English'. A Book for English Assistants and their Advisers in France.* Durham: University of Durham School of Education.

Byram, M., Esartes-Sarries, V. and Taylor, S. (1992) *Cultural Studies and Language Learning: A Research Report.* Clevedon: Multilingual Matters.

Byram, M. and Fleming, M. (eds) (1998) *Language Learning in Intercultural Perspective: Approaches Through Drama and Ethnography.* Cambridge: Cambridge University Press.

Byram, M., Morgan, C. and colleagues (1994) *Teaching-and-Learning Language-and-Culture.* Clevedon: Multilingual Matters.

Byram, M. and Zarate, G. (1994) *Definitions, Objectives and Assessment of Sociocultural Competence.* Strasbourg: Council of Europe.

Canale, M. and Swain, M. (1980) Theoretical bases of communicative approaches to second language teaching and testing. *Applied Linguistics* 1, 1–47.

Candlin, C. (1981) *The Communicative Teaching of English: Principles and an Exercise Typology.* London: Longman.

Candlin, C. (1987) Beyond description to explanation in cross-cultural discourse. In L. Smith (ed.) *Discourse across Cultures: Strategies in World Englishes* (pp. 22–35). New York: Prentice Hall.

Carter, R. and Long, M. (1991) *Teaching Literature.* London: Longman.

Cheater, A. (1986) *Social Anthropology: An Alternative Introduction*. London: Oxford University Press.

Churchland, P. (1995) *The Engine of Reason: The Seat of the Soul*. Cambridge, MA: MIT Press.

Cicourel, A. (1992) The interpenetration of communicative contexts. In A. Duranti and C. Goodwin (eds) (pp. 291–310).

Clark, H. (1996) Communities, commonalities and communication. In Gumperz and Levinson (eds) (pp. 324–55).

Clifford, J. (1992) Traveling cultures. In L. Grossburg, C. Nelson and P. Treichler (eds) (pp. 96–112). *Cultural Studies*. New York: Routledge.

Clifford, J. and Marcus, G. (eds) (1986) *Writing Culture: The Poetics and Politics of Ethnography*. Berkeley: University of California Press.

Clyne, M. (1995) *Inter-cultural Communication at Work: Cultural Values in Discourse*. Cambridge: Cambridge University Press.

Coates, J. (1993) *Women, Man and Language: A Sociological Account of Gender Differences*. 2nd edn. London: Longman.

Coates, J. (1996) *Women Talk: Conversation Between Women Friends*. Oxford: Blackwell.

Cohen, A. (ed.) (1983) *Belonging*. Manchester: Manchester University Press.

Coleman, J. (1995) The current state of knowledge concerning student residence abroad. In G. Parker and A. Rouxville (eds) (pp. 17–42).

Coleman, J. (1996) *Studying Languages: The Proficiency, Background, Attitudes and Motivation of Students of Foreign Languages in the United Kingdom and Europe*. London: CILT.

Cope, B. and Kalantzis, M. (1993) *The Powers of Literacy: A Genre Approach to Teaching Writing*. London: Falmer Press.

Cope, B. and Kalantzis, M. (eds) (2000) *Multiliteracies: Literacy Learning and the Design of Social Futures*. London: Routledge.

Cowan, J. (1991) 'Going out for coffee?' Contesting the grounds of gendered pleasure in everyday sociability. In Loizos and Papataxiarchis (eds) (pp. 180–202).

Council of Europe (1998) *A Common European Framework of Reference*. Strasbourg: Council of Europe.

Crapanzano, V. (1986) Hermes' dilemmas: The masking of subversion in ethno-graphic description. In J. Clifford and G. Marcus (eds) (pp. 51–76).

Dark, S., Digard, M., Nicholas, R., Simpson, A., Smith, P. and Byram, M. (1997) The study visit and cultural learning. In M. Byram (ed.) (pp. 36–60).

Davis, J. (1992) *Exchange*. Oxford: Oxford University Press.

Delamont, S. (1995) *Appetites and Identities: An Introduction to the Social Anthropology of Western Europe*. London: Routledge.

Delors, J. (1996) *Learning: the Treasure Within*. Report to UNESCO of the International Commission on Education for the Twenty-First Century. Paris: UNESCO.

Dörnyei, Z. (1998) Motivation in second and foreign language learning. *Language Teaching* 31, 117–35.

Douglas, M. (1966) *Purity and Danger*. London: Routledge & Kegan Paul.

Doyé, P. (1992) Fremdsprachenunterricht als Beitrag zu tertiärer Sozialisation. In Buttjes *et al.* (eds) *Neue Brennpunkte des Englischunterrichts* (pp. 280–95). Frankfurt a.M.: Peter Lang.

Drew, P. and Heritage, J. (1992) *Talk at Work: Interaction in Institutional Settings.* Cambridge: Cambridge University Press.

Dubin, F. (1989) Situating literacy within communicative competence. *Applied Linguistics* 10 (2), 171–181.

Duranti, A. (1997) *Linguistic Anthropology.* Cambridge: Cambridge University Press.

Duranti, A. and Goodwin, C. (eds) (1992) *Rethinking Context: Language as an Interactive Phenomenon.* Cambridge: Cambridge University Press.

Dyson, D. (1988) The year abroad: The effect on linguistic competence of the year abroad by students studying French, German and Spanish at degree level. Oxford: Oxford University Language Learning Centre.

Edwards, J. (1985) *Language, Society and Identity.* Oxford: Blackwell.

Egan-Robertson, A. and Bloome, D. (eds) (1998) *Students as Researchers of Culture and Language in their own Communities.* NJ: Hampton Press.

Ellen, R. (ed.) (1984) *Ethnographic Research: A Guide to General Conduct.* London: Academic Press.

Ellis, R. (1994) *Second Language Acquisition.* Oxford: Oxford University Press.

Evans, C. (1988) *Language People: The Experience of Teaching and Learning Modern Languages in British Universities.* Milton Keynes: Open University Press.

Evans-Pritchard, E. (1937) *Witchcraft, Oracles and Magic among the Azande.* Oxford: Oxford University Press.

Fairclough, N. (1989) *Language and Power.* London: Longman.

Fairclough, N. (1992) *Discourse and Social Change.* Cambridge: Polity Press.

Fairclough, N. (1996) A reply to Henry Widdowson's 'Discourse analysis: a critical view'. *Language and Literature* 5 (1), 1–7.

Fardon, R. (ed.) 1990 *Localising Strategies: Regional Traditions in Ethnographic Writing.* Edinburgh: Scottish Academic Press.

Featherstone, M. (1992) *Cultural Theory and Cultural Change.* London: Sage.

Fernandez, J. (ed.) (1991) *Beyond Metaphor: The Theory of Tropes in Anthropology.* California: University of Stanford Press.

Firth, J.R. (1968) A synopsis of linguistic theory. In F.R. Palmer (ed.) *Selected Papers of J.R. Firth 1952–59.* (pp. 168–205). London: Longman.

Fishman, P. (1983) 'Interaction: The work women do'. In B. Thorne, C. Kramarae and N. Henley (eds) *Language, Gender and Society* (pp. 89–101). London: Newbury House.

Fishman, J. (1991) *Reversing Language Shift.* Clevedon: Multilingual Matters.

Fiske, H. (1989) *Understanding Popular Culture.* Boston: Unwin Hyman.

Forsythe, D. (1989) German identity and the problem of history. In E. Tonkin *et al.* (eds) *History of Ethnicity* (pp. 137–156). London: Routledge (ASA 27).

Foucault, M. (1972) *The Archeology of Knowledge and the Discourse on Language.* New York: Pantheon.

Frake, C. (1964) How to ask for a drink in Subanun. *American Anthropologist* 66 (6), 127–32.

Frankenburg, R. (1968) British community studies: Problems of synthesis. In M. Bauton (ed.) *The Social Anthropology of Complex Societies* (pp. 123–54). London: Tavistock.

Freed, B. (1995) *Second Language Acquisition in a Study Abroad Context.* Amsterdam: Benjamins.

Furnham, A. and Bochner, S. (1986) *Culture Shock: Psychological Reactions to Unfamiliar Environments.* London: Routledge.

Gardner, R. (1985) *Social Psychology and Second Language Learning.* London: Arnold.

Gardner, R. and MacIntyre, P. (1993) A student's contributions to second-language learning. Part II: Affective variables. *Language Teaching* 26, 1–11.

Gass, S. and Varonis, E. (1985) Variation in native speaker speech modification to non-native speakers. *Studies in Second Language Acquisition.* 7, 37–58.

Gee, J. (1992) *The Social Mind: Language, Ideology and Social Practice.* New York: Bergin and Garvey.

Gee, J. (1996) *Social Linguistics and Literacies: Ideology in Discourses.* 2nd edn. London: Taylor & Francis.

Gee, J. (1999) *An Introduction to Discourse Analysis: Theory and Method.* London: Routledge.

Geertz, C. (1973) *The Interpretation of Cultures.* New York: Basic Books.

Giles, H. and Byrne, J. (1982) An intergroup approach to second language acquisition. *Journal of Multilingual and Multicultural Development* 3, 17–40.

Gilmore, D. (1987) Honour, honesty and shame. In D. Gilmore (ed.) *Honour and Shame and the Unity of the Mediterranean.* Washington, DC: American Anthropological Association.

Gilroy, P. (1987) *There Ain't No Black in the Union Jack.* London: Hutchinson.

Glaser, B. and Strauss, A. (1967) *Discovering Grounded Theory: Strategies for Qualitative Research.* New York: Aldine.

Goffman, E. (1959) *The Presentation of Self in Everyday Life.* New York: Doubleday Anchor.

Goffman, E. (1963) *Behaviour in Public Places: Notes on the Social Organisation of Gatherings.* New York: Free Press.

Goffman, E. (1972) *Relations in Public Life.* Harmondsworth: Penguin.

Goodenough, W. (1964) Cultural anthropology and linguistics. In D. Hymes (ed.) *Language in Culture and Society: A Reader in Linguistics and Anthropology* (pp. 36–9). New York: Harper & Row.

Grillo, R. (1989) Anthropology, language, politics. In R. Grillo (ed.) *Social Anthropology and the Politics of Language* (pp. 1–24). London: Routledge.

Grillo, R., Pratt, J. and Street, B. (1987) Anthropology, linguistics and language. In J. Lyons, R. Coates, M. Deuchar, G. Gazdar (eds) *New Horizons in Linguistics* 2 (pp. 268–95). London: Penguin Books.

Grossberg, L., Nelson, C. and Treichler, P. (eds) (1992) *Cultural Studies.* New York: Routledge.

Gudykunst, W. (1989) Cultural variability in ethnolinguistic identity. In S. Ting-Toomey and F. Korzenny (eds) *Language, Communication and Culture* (pp. 222–43). Newbury Park, CA: Sage.

Gudykunst, W. and M. Hammer (1983) Basic training design: Approaches to intercultural training. In D. Landis and R. Brislin (eds) *Handbook of Intercultural Training* Vol 1. *Issues in Theory and Design* (pp. 118–54). New York: Pergamon Press.

Gullestad, M. (1984) *Kitchen-Table Society.* Oslo: Universitetsforlaget.

Gumperz, J. (1968) The speech community. In *The International Encyclopedia of the Social Sciences* (pp. 381 – 6). London: Macmillan.

Gumperz, J. (1982a) *Discourse Strategies.* Cambridge: Cambridge University Press.

Gumperz, J. (ed.) (1982b) *Language and Social Identity.* Cambridge: Cambridge University Press.

Gumperz, J. (1992a) Contextualisation and understanding. In A. Duranti and C. Goodwin (eds) *Rethinking Context: Language as an Interactive Phenomenon* (pp. 229–52). Cambridge: Cambridge University Press.

Gumperz, J. (1992b) Contextualisation revisited. In P. Auer and A. di Luzio (eds) *The Contextualisation of Language* (pp. 39–54). Amsterdam: John Benjamins.

Gumperz, J. (1996) The linguistic and cultural relativity of inference. In J. Gumperz and S. Levinson (eds) (pp. 359–73).

Gumperz, J. and Hymes, D. (eds) (1972) *Directions in Sociolinguistics: The Ethnography of Communication*. New York: Oxford University Press.

Gumperz, J. and Levinson, S. (1996a) Introduction: Linguistic relativity re-examined. In J. Gumperz and S. Levinson (eds) (pp. 1–18).

Gumperz, J. and Levinson, S. (eds) (1996b) *Rethinking Linguistic Relativity*. Cambridge: Cambridge University Press.

Habermas, J. (1987) *The Theory of Communicative Action*. Trans. T. McCarthy. Boston: Beacon Press.

Hall, E. (1959) *The Silent Language*. New York: Anchor Books/Doubleday.

Hall, S. (1990) Cultural identity and diaspora. In J. Rutherford (ed.) *Identity, Community, Culture, Difference* (pp. 222–37). London: Lawrence & Wishart.

Hall, S. (1992) The question of cultural identity. In S. Hall, D. Held and T. McGrew (eds) *Modernity and its Futures* (pp. 274–316). Cambridge: Polity Press.

Hallam, L. and Street, B. (eds) (1999) *Cultural Encounters: Communicating Otherness*. London: Routledge.

Hammersley, M. (1992) *What's Wrong with Ethnography?* London: Routledge.

Hammersley, M. and Atkinson, P. (1983) *Ethnography: Principles in Practice*. London: Tavistock.

Hannerz, U. (1992) *Cultural Complexity: Studies in the Social Organisation of Meaning*. New York: Columbia University Press.

Hatch, E. (1983) Simplified input and second language acquisition. In R. Anderson (ed.) *Pidginisation and Creolisation in Second Language Acquisition* (pp. 64–86). Rowley, MA: Newbury House.

Heath, S. B. (1983) *Ways with Words*. Cambridge: Cambridge University Press.

Heller, M. (1992) The politics of code-switching and language choice. *Journal of Multilingual and Multicultural Development* 13 (1&2), 123–42.

Heller, M. (1994) *Crosswords: Language, Education and Ethnicity in French Ontario*. Berlin: Mouton de Gruyter.

Henriques, J. et al. (1984) *Changing the Subject: Psychology, Social Regulation and Subjectivity*. London: Methuen.

Herzfeld, M. (1992) *The Social Production of Indifference: Exploring the Symbolic Roots of Western Democracy*. New York: Berg.

Hewitt, R. (1986) *White Talk, Black Talk*. Cambridge: Cambridge University Press.

Hobsbawm, E. (1992) Ethnicity and nationalism in Europe today. *Anthropology Today*. 8, 1, 4–8.

Hofstede, G. (1984) *Culture's Consequences: International Differences in Work-Related Values*. Beverly Hills, CA: Sage.

Hofstede, G. (1994) *Cultures and Organisations: Software of the Mind*. London: HarperCollins.

Hoggart, R. (1957) *The Uses of Literacy*. London: Chatto.

Holec, H. (1981) *Autonomy and Foreign Language Learning*. Pergamon for the Council of Europe.

Holland, D. and Quinn, N. (eds) (1987) *Cultural Models in Language and Thought.* Cambridge: Cambridge University Press.

Hymes, D. (1966a) Introduction: Toward ethnographies of communication. *American Anthropologist* 66(6), 12–25.

Hymes, D. (1966b) Two types of linguistic relativity. In W. Bright (ed.) *Sociolinguistics* (pp. 114–67). The Hague: Mouton.

Hymes, D. (1972) On communicative competence. In J. Pride and J. Holmes (eds) *Sociolinguistics* (pp. 269–93). Harmondsworth: Penguin

Hymes, D. (1974) *Foundations in Sociolinguistics: An Ethnographic Approach.* Philadelphia: University of Pennsylvania Press.

Hymes, D. (1996) *Ethnography, Linguistics, Narrative Inequality: Toward an Understanding of Voice.* London: Taylor & Francis.

Jurasek, R. (1996) Using ethnography to bridge the gap between study abroad and the on-campus language and culture curriculum. In C. Kramsch (ed.) *Redefining the Boundaries of Language Study* (pp. 221–49). Boston: Heinle and Heinle.

Kane, L. (1991) The acquisition of cultural competence. In D. Buttjes and M. Byram (eds) (pp. 239–47).

Kasper, G. (1994) Wessen Pragmatik? Für eine Neubestimmung fremdsprachlicher Handlungskompetenz. *Zeitschrift für Fremdsprachenforschung* 6 (1), 69–94.

Keller, G. (1991) Stereotypes in intercultural communication: Effects of German–British student exchanges. In D. Buttjes and M. Byram (eds) (pp. 120–35).

Kim, Y. and Gudykunst, W. (eds) (1988) *Theory in Intercultural Communication.* Newbury Park, CA: Sage.

Kim, Y. (1998) *Communication and Cross-cultural Adaption: An Integrative Theory.* Clevedon: Multilingual Matters.

Klein, W. (1984) *Second Language Acquisition.* Cambridge: Cambridge University Press.

Kohlberg, L., Levine, C. and Hewer, A. (1983) *Moral Stages: A Current Formulation and a Response to Critics.* Basel: Karger.

Kolb, D. (1984) *Experiential Learning.* Englewood Cliffs: Prentice-Hall.

Kramer, J. (1990) *Cultural and Intercultural Studies.* Frankfurt a. Main: Peter Lang.

Kramer, J. (1997) *British Cultural Studies.* Munich: Wilhelm Fink Verlag.

Kramsch, C. (1993) *Context and Culture in Language Teaching.* Oxford: Oxford University Press.

Kramsch, C. (1995) Rhetorical modes of understanding. In T. Miller (ed.) *Functional Approaches to Written Texts: Classroom Applications* (pp. 61–78) TESOL, France, 2/2.

Kramsch, C. (1996) The cultural component of language teaching *Language, Culture and Curriculum* 8 (2), 83–92.

Kramsch, C. (1998) The privilege of the intercultural speaker. In M. Byram and M. Fleming (eds) (pp. 16–31).

Kramsch, C. and McGonnell-Ginet, S. (eds) (1992) *Text and Context: Cross-disciplinary Perspectives on Language Study.* Lexington, MA: D.C. Heath.

Kress, G. (1985) *Linguistic Processes in Socio-cultural Practice.* Oxford: Oxford University Press.

Kroeber, A. and Kluckhohn, C. (1952) *Culture: A Critical Review of Concepts and Definitions.* Cambridge, MA: Harvard University Press.

Kuper, A. 1983 *Anthropology and Anthropologists.* 2nd edn. London: Routledge.

Lacoste, M. (1993) Le 'travail' du malade dans la consultation hospitalière. In J. Cosnier, M. Grosjean and M. Lacoste (eds) *Soins et Communication: Approche interactioniste des relations de soins.* (pp. 85–98). Lyons: University of Lyons Press.

Lacoste, M. and Levy, E. (1994) A là recherche de l'information-voyageurs. ms. Paris: University of Paris-Nord.

Lakoff, G. (1987) *Women, Fire and Dangerous Things: What Categories Reveal about the Mind.* Chicago: University of Chicago Press.

Lakoff, G. and Johnson, M. (1980) *Metaphors We Live By.* Chicago: University of Chicago Press.

Lantolf, J. (ed.) (1999) *Sociocultural Theory and Second Language Learning.* Oxford: Oxford University Press.

Lantolf, L. and Pavlenko, A. (1995) Sociocultural theory and second language acquisition. *Annual Review of Applied Linguistics* 15, 108–24.

Lave, J. and Wenger, E. (1991) *Situated Language Learning: Legitimate, Peripheral Participation.* Cambridge: Cambridge University Press.

Le Wita, B. (1988) *Ni Vue Ni Connue: Approche Ethnographique de la Culture Bourgeoise.* Paris: Fondation de la Maison des Sciences de l'Homme.

Le Wita, B. (1994) *French Bourgeois Culture.* Cambridge: Cambridge University Press. (Trans. of 1988).

Legutke, M. and Thomas, H. (1991) *Process and Experience in the Language Classroom.* London: Longman.

Leinhardt, G. (1964) *Social Anthropology.* Oxford: Oxford University Press.

Levinson, S. (1996) Relativity in spatial conception and description. In S. Levinson and J. Gumperz (eds) (pp. 177–202).

Lincoln, B. (1986) Introduction. In *Discourse and the Construction of Society: Comparative Studies of Myth, Ritual and Classification* (pp. 3–12). New York: Oxford University Press.

Little, D. (1994) *Strategic Competence Considered in Relation to Strategic Control of the Language Learning Process.* Strasbourg: Council of Europe.

Loizos, I. and Papataxiarchis, E. (eds) 1991 *Contested Identities: Gender and Kinship in Modern Greece.* Princeton: Princeton University Press.

Long, M. (1983) Native speaker/ non-native speaker conversation and the negotiation of meaning. *Applied Linguistics* 4, 126–41.

Lucy, J. (1992) *Language, Diversity and Thought.* Cambridge: Cambridge University Press.

Lutz, C. and Abu-Loghod, L. (1990) *Language and the Politics of Emotion.* Cambridge: Cambridge University Press.

Malinowski, B. (1922) *Argonauts of the Western Pacific.* London: Routledge.

Malinowski, B. (1923) The problem of meaning in primitive languages. In C.K. Ogden and I.A. Richards (eds) *The Meaning of Meaning* (pp. 296–336). New York: Harcourt, Brace & World Inc.

Manes, J. (1983) Compliments: A mirror of cultural values. In Wolfson and Judd (eds) (pp. 96–102).

Marcus, G. and Cushman, D. (1982) Ethnographies as texts. *Annual Review of Anthropology* 11, 25–69.

Mauss, M. (1954) *The Gift: Form and Function of Exchange in Archaic Societies.* London: Cohen & West.

McCarthy, M. and Carter, R. (1994) *Language as Discourse: Perspectives for Language Teaching.* London: Longman.

McDermott, P. and Gospodinoff, K. (1979) Social contexts for ethnic borders and school failure. In A. Wolfgang (ed.) *Nonverbal Behaviour* (pp. 175–96). New York: Academic Press.

Meara, P. (1994) What should language graduates be able to do? *Language Learning Journal* 9, 36–40.

Melde, W. (1987) *Zur Integration von Landeskunde und Kommunikation im Fremdsprachenunterricht*. Tübingen: Gunter Narr Verlag.

Meyer, M. (1991) Developing transcultural competence: case studies of advanced foreign language learners. In D. Buttjes and M. Byram (eds) (pp. 136–58).

Miller, D. (1989) Appropriating the state on the council estate. *Man* NS 23/2, 353–72.

Milroy, L. (1980) *Language and Social Networks*. 2nd edn. Oxford: Blackwell.

Mitchell, C. (1984) Case studies. In Ellen (ed.) (pp. 237–39).

Moerman, M. (1988) *Talking Culture: Ethnography and Conversation Analysis*. Philadelphia: University of Pennsylvania Press.

Mohan, B. (1986) *Language and Content*. Reading, MA: Addison-Wesley.

Montgomery, M. (1993) Institutions and discourse. *British Studies Now*, July 1993, 2–3.

Murphy, E. (1988) The cultural dimension in foreign language teaching: Four models. *Language, Culture and Curriculum* 1, 147–63.

O'Brien, U. (1994) Ethnic identity, gender and life cycle in Northern Catalonia. In V. Goddard, J. Llobers and C. Short (eds) *The Anthropology of Europe: Identities and Boundaries in Conflict* (pp. 191–208). Oxford, Providence: Berg.

Ochs, E. (1997) Linguistic resources for socializing humanity. In S. Levinson and J. Gumperz (eds) (pp. 407–37).

Ochs, E. and Schieffelin, B. (1979) *Developmental Pragmatics*. New York: Academic Press.

Parker, G. and Rouxville, A. (eds) (1995) *The Year Abroad: Preparation. Monitoring, Evaluation*. London AFLS/CILT.

Paulston, C. (1992) *Sociolinguistic Perspectives on Bilingual Education*. Clevedon: Multilingual Matters.

Pennycook, A. (1994) *The Cultural Politics of English as an International Language*. London: Longman.

Piaget, J. and Weil, A. (1951) The development in children of the idea of the homeland and of relations with other countries. *Institute of Social Science Bulletin* 3, 561–78.

Pocock, D. (1975) *Teach Yourself: Understanding Social Anthropology*. London: Hodder & Stoughton.

Prabhu, N. (1987) *Second Language Pedagogy*. Oxford: Oxford University Press.

Raeburn, R. (1978) Motorway. Unpublished student paper. University of Sussex.

Rampton, B. (1995) *Crossing: Language and Ethnicity among Adolescents*. London: Longman.

Richards, J. (1986) *Approaches and Methods in Language Teaching*. Cambridge: Cambridge University Press.

Richards, J. and Schmidt, R. (eds) (1983) *Language and Communication*. London: Longman.

Richterich, R. and Chancerel, J. (1978) *Identifying the Needs of Adults Learning a Foreign Language*. Strasbourg: Council of Europe.

Rivers, W. (1983) *Communicating Naturally in a Second Language: Theory and Practice in Language Teaching*. Cambridge: Cambridge University Press.

Roberts, C. (1993) Cultural studies and student exchange: Living the ethnographic life. *Language, Culture and Curriculum* 6 (1) , 11–17.

Roberts, C. (1995) Language and cultural learning: An ethnographic approach. In A. Jensen *et al.* (eds) *Intercultural Competence. Vol 2: The Adult Learner* (pp. 53–69). Aalborg: Aalborg University Press.

Roberts, C. (1997) The year abroad as an ethnographic experience. In M. Byram (ed.) (pp. 62–76).

Sacks, H. (1992) *Lectures on Conversation*. G. Jefferson (ed.). MA: Blackwell.

Sacks, H., Schegloff, E. and Jefferson, G. (1974) A simplest systematics for the organisation of turn taking. *Language* 50, 696–735.

Sahlins, M. (1990) Food as symbolic code. In J. Alexander and S. Seidman (eds) *Culture and Society* (pp. 94–101). Cambridge: Cambridge University Press.

Sanjek, R. (ed.) (1992) *Field Notes*. Ithaca: Cornell University Press.

Sapir, E. (1949) The status of linguistics as a science. In D. Mandelbaum (ed.) *The Selected Writings of Edward Sapir in Language, Culture and Personality* (pp. 160–66). Berkeley: University of California Press. (Reprinted from *Language* 1929, 5, 207–14).

Saville-Troike, M. (1982) *The Ethnography of Communication*. Oxford: Blackwell.

Schank, R. and Ableson, R. (1977) *Scripts, Plans, Goals and Understanding*. Hillsdale, NJ: Erlbaum.

Schieffelin, B. and Ochs, E. (1986) *Language Socialisation across Cultures*. New York: Cambridge University Press.

Schumann, J. (1978) *The Pidginisation Process: A Model for Second Language Acquisition*. Rowley, Newbury House.

Schutz, A. (1964) The stranger: An essay in social psychology. In A. Schutz (ed.) *Collected Papers*. Vol. 2. The Hague: Martin Nijhoff.

Scollon, R. and Scollon, S. (1995) Somatic communication: How useful is orality for the characterization of speech events and cultures? In U. Quasthoff (ed.) *Aspects of Oral Communication* (pp. 19–30) Berlin: Walter de Gruyter.

Seelye, H. (1984) *Teaching Culture: Strategies for Foreign Language Educators*. IL: National Textbook Company.

Seelye, H. (1988) *Teaching Culture: Strategies for Intercultural Communication*. IL: National Textbook Company.

Sercu, L. (ed.) (1995) *Intercultural Competence: A New Challenge for Language Teachers and Trainers in Europe. Volume 1*. Aalborg: Aalborg University Press.

Sheerin, S. (1989) *Self-access*. Oxford: Oxford University Press.

Sheridan, D., Street, B. and Bloome, D. (2000) *Writing Ourselves – Mass Observation and Literacy Practices*. NJ: Hampshire Press.

Singer, A. and Street, B. (eds) (1972) *Zande Themes*. Oxford: Blackwell.

Singer, E. (n.d.) Money on the table. Unpublished student project. Ann Arbor: Michigan State University.

Singerman, A. (ed.) (1996) *Acquiring Cross-Cultural Competence: Four Stages for American Students of French*. Lincolnwood, IL: National Textbook Company.

Skehan, P. (1999) *A Cognitive Approach to Language Learning*. Oxford: Oxford University Press.

Slobin, D. (1996) From 'thought' and 'language' to 'thinking for speaking'. In J. Gumperz and S. Levinson (eds) (pp. 70–96).

Snow, D. and Byram, M. (1997) *Crossing Frontiers. The School Study Visit Abroad.* London: Centre for Information on Language Teaching and Research.

Spradley, J. (1979) *The Ethnographic Interview.* New York: Holt, Rinehart & Winston.

Spradley, J. (1980) *Participant Observation.* New York: Holt, Rinehart & Winston.

Spradley, J. and McCurdy, D. (1988) *The Cultural Experience: Ethnography in Complex Societies.* 2nd edn. IL: Waveland Press.

Standards for Foreign Language Learning: Preparing for the 21st Century (1996) Yonkers, NY: National Standards in Foreign Language Education Project.

Stern, H. (1983) *Fundamental Concepts of Language Teaching.* Oxford: Oxford University Press.

Stern, H. (1992) *Issues and Options in Language Teaching.* Oxford: Oxford University Press.

Stocking, G. (ed.) (1983) *Observors Observed: Essays on Ethnographic Fieldwork.* Madison, WI: University of Wisconsin Press.

Street, B. (1984) *Literacy in Theory and Practice.* Cambridge: Cambridge University Press.

Street, B. (1993) Culture is a verb. In D. Graddol, L. Thompson and M. Byram (eds) *Language and Culture* (pp. 23–43). Clevedon: Multilingual Matters/British Association of Applied Linguistics.

Tambiah, S. (1968) The magical power of words. *Man* NS 3 (2), 175–208.

Tannen, D. (1984) *Conversational Style.* Norwood, NJ: Ablex.

Tannen, D. (1990) *You Just Don't Understand: Women and Men in Conversation.* New York: William Morrow and Co.

Tannen, D. (ed.) 1993 *Gender and Conversational Interaction.* New York: Oxford University Press.

Thompson, E. (1968) *The Making of the English Working Class.* London: Gollancz.

Thompson, J. (1991) Introduction. In P. Bourdieu (pp. 1–31).

Thornton, R. (1983) Narrative ethnography in Africa, 1850–1920, *Man* 18, 3, 502–20.

Thornton, R. (1988) Culture: A contemporary definition. In E. Boonzaeir and J. Sharp (eds) *Keywords.* Cape Town: David Philip.

Ting-Toomey, S. (1988) Intercultural conflict styles: A face negotiation theory. *International and Intercultural Communication Annual* 12, 213–35.

Todorov, T. (1988) Knowledge in social anthropology: Distance and universality. *Anthropology Today* 4 (2), 2–5.

Towell, R. and Hawkins, R. (1994) *Approaches to Second Language Acquisition.* Clevedon: Multilingual Matters.

Trim, J. (1983) Yes but what do you mean by 'communication'. In C. Brumfit (ed.) *Learning and Teaching Languages for Communication: Applied Linguistic Perspectives* (pp. 70–81). London: Centre for Information of Language Teaching.

Valdes, J. (ed.) (1986) *Culture Bound: Bridging the Culture Gap in Language Teaching.* Cambridge: Cambridge University Press.

van Ek, J. (1975) *The Threshold Level.* Strasbourg: Council of Europe.

van Ek, J. (1986) *Objectives for Foreign Language Learning.* Strasbourg: Council of Europe.

van Ek, J. and Trim, J. (1991) *Threshold Level 1990.* Strasbourg: Council of Europe.

Villegas, A.M. (1991) *Culturally Responsive Teaching.* Princeton: ETS.

Wallace, C. (1992) Critical literacy: Awareness in the EFL classroom. In N. Fairclough (ed.) *Critical Language Awareness* (pp. 59–92). London: Longman.

Wallman, S. (ed.) (1979) *Ethnicity at Work*. London: Macmillan.
Warner, M. (1994) *Managing Monsters: Six Myths of Our Time*. London: Vintage.
Wenden, A. and Rubin, J. (1987) *Learner Strategies in Language Learning*. London: Prentice-Hall International.
Werner, O. and Schoepfler, G. (1989) *Systematic Fieldwork*. Vols 1 and 2. CA: Sage.
Whorf, B. (1956) *Language, Thought and Reality: Selected Writings of Benjamin Lee Whorf*. (ed. J. B. Carroll). Cambridge, MA: MIT Press.
Widdowson, H. (1978) *Teaching Language as Communication*. Oxford: Oxford University Press.
Widdowson, H. (1988) Aspects of the relationship between culture and language. *Triangle 7: Culture and Language Learning*. Paris: Didier.
Widdowson, H. (1990) *Aspects of Language Teaching*. Oxford: Oxford University Press.
Widdowson, H. (1995 Discourse Analysis: A critical view. *Language and Literature* 4 (3), 157–72,
Wilkins, D. (1976) *Notional Syllabuses*. London: Oxford University Press.
Williams, R. (1958) *Culture and Society 1780–1950*. London: Chatto & Windus.
Williams, R. (1976) *Keywords*. London: Fontana.
Williams, R. (1981) *Culture*. London: Fontana.
Willis, F. *et al.* (1977) *Residence Abroad and the Student of Modern Languages*. Bradford: University of Bradford Modern Languages Centre.
Willis, P. (1977) *Learning to Labour: How Working Class Kids Get Working Class Jobs*. New York: Columbia University Press.
Wolfson, N. and Judd, E. (eds) (1983) *Sociolinguistics and Language Acquisition*. London: Newbury House.
Woolard, K. (1989) *Double Talk: Bilingualism and the Politics of Ethnicity in Catalonia*. Stanford: Stanford University Press.
Zaharlick, A. and Green, J. (1991) Ethnographic research. In J. Flood *et al.* (eds) *Handbook of Research on Teaching the English Language Arts* (pp. 205–25). New York: Macmillan.
Zarate, G. (1986) *Enseigner une Culture Étrangère*. Paris: Hachette.
Zarate, G. (1991) The observation diary: An ethnographic approach to teacher education. In D. Buttjes and M. Byram (eds) (pp. 248–60).
Zarate, G. (1993) *Représentations de l'étranger et didactique des langues*. Paris: Hachette.

Index